Hindu Approaches to Spiritual Care

by the same author

Personhood, Illness, and Death in America's Multifaith Neighborhoods
A Practical Guide
Lucinda Mosher
ISBN 978 1 78592 784 3
eISBN 978 1 78450 717 6

of related interest

Spirituality in Hospice Care
How Staff and Volunteers Can Support the Dying and Their Families
Edited by Andrew Goodhead and Nigel Hartley
Foreword by the Rt Revd Dr. Barry Morgan
ISBN 978 1 78592 102 5
eISBN 978 1 78450 368 0

Treating Body and Soul
A Clinician's Guide to Supporting the Physical, Mental and Spiritual Needs of Their Patients
Edited by Peter Wells
ISBN 978 1 78592 148 3
eISBN 978 1 78450 417 5

Values in Health and Social Care
An Introductory Workbook
Ray Samuriwo, Ben Hannigan, Stephen Pattison and Andrew Todd
ISBN 978 1 78592 063 9
eISBN 978 1 78450 320 8

Multifaith Care for Sick and Dying Children and Their Families
A Multi-disciplinary Guide
Paul Nash, Madeleine Parkes and Zamir Hussain
ISBN 978 1 84905 606 9
eISBN 978 1 78450 072 6

HINDU APPROACHES TO SPIRITUAL CARE

Chaplaincy in Theory and Practice

Edited by Vineet Chander
and Lucinda Mosher

Jessica Kingsley *Publishers*
London and Philadelphia

See pp. 7-8 for permissions

First published in 2020
by Jessica Kingsley Publishers
73 Collier Street
London N1 9BE, UK
and
400 Market Street, Suite 400
Philadelphia, PA 19106, USA

www.jkp.com

Copyright © Jessica Kingsley Publishers 2020

All rights reserved. No part of this publication may be reproduced in any material form (including photocopying, storing in any medium by electronic means or transmitting) without the written permission of the copyright owner except in accordance with the provisions of the law or under terms of a licence issued in the UK by the Copyright Licensing Agency Ltd. www.cla.co.uk or in overseas territories by the relevant reproduction rights organisation, for details see www.ifrro.org. Applications for the copyright owner's written permission to reproduce any part of this publication should be addressed to the publisher.

Warning: The doing of an unauthorised act in relation to a copyright work may result in both a civil claim for damages and criminal prosecution.

Library of Congress Cataloging in Publication Data
A CIP catalog record for this book is available from the Library of Congress

British Library Cataloguing in Publication Data
A CIP catalogue record for this book is available from the British Library

ISBN 978 1 78592 605 1
eISBN 978 1 78592 606 8

Printed and bound in the United States

SFI label applies to the text stock

To all of my teachers, beginning with my parents; and especially to Radhanath Swami, my mentor and ever well-wishing friend. Thank you for being my exemplar of care and compassion.

VC

To the many followers of Sanatana Dharma–students, colleagues, interviewees, friends–who, over the years, have been my companions on the path toward interfaith understanding. Without you, this project would never have been.

LM

Acknowledgments

Gratitude is extended to the following for permission to excerpt their publications:

Arsha Vidya Research and Publication Trust
From Swami Dayananda Saraswati, *Bhagavadgita*, Volume 2 (2011). © Swami Dayananda Saraswati, Arsha Vidya. Used with permission.

The Bhaktivedanta Book Trust International, Inc.
From A.C. Bhaktivedanta Swami Prabhudapa, trans., *Srimad Bhagavatam* (1987).

From A.C. Bhaktivedanta Swami, *The Krishna Book* (1970).

Texts courtesy of The Bhaktivedanta Book Trust International, Inc. www.Krishna.com. Used with permission.

Los Angeles Review of Books
From "Pick a side, we're at war" by Jeffery D. Long (September 4, 2014).

Nilgiri Press
From *The Upanishads*, translated by Eknath Easwaran, founder of the Blue Mountain Center of Meditation, copyright 1987, 2007; reprinted by permission of Nilgiri Press, P.O. Box 256, Tomales, CA 94971. www.bmcm.org.

Ramakrishna Math, Chennai
From Swami Saradananda, *Sri Ramakrishna: The Great Master*, Vol. II, trans. Swami Jagadananda (Mylapore, India: Sri Ramakrishna Math, 1952).

Ramakrishna-Vivekananda Center of New York
From *The Upanishads Volume 1*, Translated into English with commentary by Swami Nikhilananda. Published by Ramakrishna-Vivekananda Center of New York © 1949, 1952, 1956, and 1959 by Swami Nikhilananda. Used with permission.

From *The Gospel of Sri Ramakrishna* (Abridged Edition), Swami Nikhilananda (translator). Published by Ramakrishna-Vivekananda Center of New York © 1942, 1948, 1958 by Swami Nikhilananda.

From *Vivekandanda: The Yogas and Other Works,* published by Ramakrishna-Vivekananda Center of New York. © 1953 by Swami Nikhilananda, Trustee of the Estate of Swami Vivekananda.

Taylor and Francis
From Vineet Chander, "A Room with a View: accommodating Hindu religious practice on a college campus," in *The Journal of College and Character* (May 2013).

Gratitudes

A complex edited volume comes together successfully only with help from many people. We co-editors therefore extend hearty thanks to Natalie Watson, former senior commissioning editor at Jessica Kingsley Publishers, for her help in shaping our proposal; to Maddy Budd and many others at JKP who have been instrumental in bringing it from idea to reality; to our wonderful contributors, who met deadlines graciously; to interviewees whose wisdom and experience informs several chapters; to publishers and individuals to quote portions of their material; and to the Dharma Association of North America for celebrating this publication at its 2019 annual meeting.

We are grateful to our respective mentors and others who, over the years, were instrumental in our formation as scholars who could conceive and execute an enterprise such as *Hindu Spiritual Care*—chief among them, Vineet's colleagues and friends at the Office of Religious Life at Princeton University and Lucinda's at Hartford Seminary. Likewise, our gratitude extends to our many students, from whom we have learned much.

We would be remiss if we did not also acknowledge our debts to the communities that nourish our spirits and inform the approach we take to our work—particularly, the Bhakti Center (New York City); Govardhan Ecovillage (Maharashtra, India); Virginia Theological Seminary; and St Mary's Episcopal Church (Green Cove Springs, Florida). And, of course, we wish to convey our deep and abundant appreciation of our families, and especially our spouses—Ami Chander and Barrie Mosher—whose consistent support while this volume was under construction was valuable beyond measure.

—*Sri Krishna Janmashtami 2019*

Contents

Introduction 15

Part One: Foundations of Care

The Necessity of a Hindu-American Chaplaincy 27
Rita D. Sherma

Theoretical Foundations for Hindu Chaplaincy in
Advaita Vedanta 31
Varun Khanna

An Advaita Vedanta Theology of Spiritual Care:
Reverence, Diversity, and Detachment 39
Anantanand Rambachan

A Theology of Spiritual Care from a Bhakti Tradition 49
Shaunaka Rishi Das

Body, Mind, and Breath: Yoga as a Framework for Integrative
Spiritual Care 61
Christopher Key Chapple

The Yoga Sūtras of Patañjali in the
Context of College Chaplaincy. 71
Vineet Chander

The Bhagavad-Gita's Theological Anthropology as a
Foundation for Hindu Pastoral Care 83
Viraj Patel

Rama in the Forest: A Hindu Chaplaincy Framework
for Grief Resolution from the Valmiki Ramayana. 93
Ramakrishnan Parameshwaran

Does God Really Care?:
A Hindu Response to the Problem of Suffering   105
Gopal K. Gupta

How Does the Goddess Help Us Handle Pain and Suffering?:
A Shakta Theological Foundation for Hindu Chaplaincy . . .   115
Rachel Fell McDermott

Lessons from the Upanishads for the Spiritual Caregiver . . .   123
Madhu Vedak Sharma

Part Two: Care in Context

Becoming Board-Certified:
A Trail-Blazing Chaplain's Reflection   133
Swami Sarvaananda

The Hospital Chaplain at Work: A Hindu Perspective   141
Shamā Mehtā

Connecting to the Energy of Grace: End-of-Life Care   149
Joseph Ghanashyam Caruso

Hindu Chaplaincy as Karma Yoga in the Tradition of
Sri Ramakrishna and Swami Vivekananda
An Interview with Swami Tyagananda   157
Jeffery D. Long

A Hindu Chaplain at a Jesuit Catholic University   167
Brahmachari V. Sharan

Space for Spiritual Care   177
Asha Shipman

Spirituality in the University: Community and Diversity. . . .   185
Tahil Sharma

Military Service and Spiritual Care by and for Hindus   193
Vineet Chander and Lucinda Mosher

Tough Love: Prisons, Hinduism, and Spiritual Care   201
Ramdas Lamb

Hinduism and Coaching in the Corporate Realm   213
Rasanath Das

Part Three: Care at Crossroads

Nurturing Knowledge: The Importance of
Hindu Academics as Spiritual Caregivers 223
Murali Balaji

Vocational Counseling: A Hindu Approach 231
Pulin Sanghvi

Hindu Spiritual Care of LGBTQ People. 239
Raja Gopal Bhattar

The Food-Centric Chaplain 245
Vaishali Gupta Chandrashekar

Spiritually Counseling a Couple Prior to a
Wedding: A Hindu Approach 253
Amrutur V. Srinivasan

Hindu Approaches to Climate Trauma 261
Gopal D. Patel

Dealing with Trauma: Re-interpreting Hindu
Narratives as Lessons for Healing 269
Shrestha Singh

Bibliography 279

Contributors 287

Subject Index 293

Author Index 301

Introduction

In recent years, chaplaincy (professional spiritual caregiving in hospitals, prisons, the military, universities, schools, fire or police departments, airports, and even large corporations) has become decidedly more multifaith. In the US, Canada, and the UK, a growing number of Hindus are pursuing this calling—or wish to. Meanwhile, particularly in hospital settings, chaplains of various religions must tend on occasion to Hindus. While there are several excellent chaplaincy textbooks and handbooks on the market, few of them give specific attention to Hindu matters. While there are handbooks on Jewish and Buddhist spiritual caregiving, there is as yet no parallel resource for or about Hindus. With this volume, we seek to fill that lacuna.

Before we proceed, it might be beneficial to more clearly define concepts like chaplaincy and pastoral or spiritual care themselves. Surprisingly, perhaps, this proves a rather challenging task. Despite efforts by accrediting and endorsing bodies such as the Association of Professional Chaplains (APC) to offer definitions and standards of practice, the field lacks definitional clarity. Clinicians and academicians do not agree universally on the meaning of terms such as *chaplaincy* or *pastoral care;* some even resist standardization, insisting that they are fluid and ought to be defined (and practiced) differently based on context.[1] What is clear is that the term *chaplain* is ancient, having originated in the early Christian milieu as the designation of a clergyperson with a special ministerial assignment. Emmanuel Lartey suggests that the concept of pastoral care as a discrete field seems to have originated in 1967, when it was used to refer to "helping acts done by representative Christian persons, directed towards the healing, sustaining, guiding, and reconciling of troubled

---

[1] W.W.C. Ashley (2014) "Counseling and Interventions." In S. Roberts (ed.) *Professional Spiritual and Pastoral Care: A Practical Clergy and Chaplain's Handbook.* Woodstock, VT: SkyLight Paths Publishing, p.123.

persons, whose troubles arise in the context of ultimate meanings and concerns."² It is this sense that *chaplain* most often implies as it is used presently in the US. This sense is echoed in Buddhist chaplain Jennifer Block's definition of chaplaincy as "a modern-day discipline and profession at the intersection between [a faith tradition]…and suffering."³

For better or worse, the Christian-rooted model of pastoral care remains chaplaincy's foundational paradigm. At the same time, as institutions hosting chaplains have begun to move away from privileging Protestant Christianity and toward a recognition of a multiplicity of faiths, pastoral care's definition has become broader and more inclusive. Willard Ashley suggests that *pastoral care* today may refer to any work that is "concerned with the support and nurturance of persons and interpersonal relationships, including everyday expressions of care and concern" and that aims to return individuals "back into their community with renewed hope, increased wisdom, and spiritual strength."⁴ Similarly, Daniel Schipani has pointed to a "significant shift… away from a monoculture approach" and a "'monopoly' of Christian pastoral care" to a "more inclusive, 'multifaith' approach" that speaks to the experiences of "spiritual caregivers from various religious and non-religious…traditions and perspectives."⁵ Indeed, some would go as far as to argue that terms such as *pastoral care* and *chaplain* be wholly replaced by more inclusive language, such as *spiritual care* and *spiritual care professional*. While we respect and sympathize with those who advocate for this shift, we also see value in retaining—yet also intentionally re-defining—the originally Christian terminology. Hence, throughout this book, we speak of Hindu chaplaincy and use *pastoral care* and *spiritual care* largely interchangeably.

Even if the old terminology obtains, the way chaplains see themselves and the work they do certainly is changing. Where old definitions of *chaplain* described a representative of a faith community's established norms, the new approach describes pastoral care in terms of "attitude and presence." In fact, *presence* has become something of a key characteristic

---

2   E.Y. Lartey (2003) *In Living Color: An Intercultural Approach to Pastoral Care and Counseling*, 2nd edition. Philadelphia: Jessica Kingsley Publishers, p.21.
3   J. Block (2012) "Toward a Definition of Buddhist Chaplaincy." In C.A.Giles and Willa B. Miller (eds) *The Arts of Contemplative Care: Pioneering Voices in Buddhist Chaplaincy and Pastoral Work*. Boston, MA: Wisdom Publications, p.3.
4   Ashley, p.124.
5   D.S. Schipani (2013) *Multifaith Views in Spiritual Care*. Kitchchener, Ontario: Pandora Press, pp.1–2.

of more broadly defined pastoral care. For example, Buddhist scholar Judith Simmer-Brown instructs chaplains "to be simply present" and "to not turn away from [the] suffering," but rather to "generate the heart of compassion" in the midst of it. The chaplain, she says, must "return again and again to the immediacy of whatever is happening," equipped with "clarity of mind, gentleness of heart, and a listening ear."[6]

Indeed, the work of Buddhist chaplains in the west has significantly contributed to, and expanded, the definition of pastoral care. Sensei Pat Enkyo O'Hara describes it as "the way of compassionate care [that] is as natural as your spontaneous gesture while at ease."[7] Such spontaneous compassion awakens when the chaplain accesses a "rather ordinary quality that can be quite challenging to acquire—true presence" and "originates from a heart/mind that is clear and responsive..."[8] The chaplain's efficacy is thus inextricably tied to his or her own meditation and contemplative practice. In fact, some suggest that this concept of *contemplative care*— "the art of providing spiritual, emotional, and pastoral support in a way that is informed by a personal, consistent contemplative or meditation practice"—is distinct from the more generic *spiritual care*.[9]

We must acknowledge that chaplaincy largely remains, as Rabbi Rena Blumenthal notes, "a job invented and in many ways still defined by liberal Protestant tradition" and that the default assumption persists that a Hindu chaplain and his or her traditional Christian counterpart would simply "do the same work, but with a different set of texts and rituals."[10] Yet, at the same time, we can acknowledge that the role of the chaplain continues to develop. In the context of the "rapidly evolving, multicultural, multi faith context of the twenty-first-century [university or college] campus" in particular, notes former Harvard University chaplain Lucy Forster-Smith, the role of the chaplain changes in meaning from community to community, and even within communities "falls outside of clear categories" and into "a liminal space [that] can serve as a source of strength."[11] The college chaplain functions "at the intersection of tradition

---

6   J. Simmer-Brown, "Foreword," in *The Arts of Contemplative Care*, p.xiii–xvi, at p.xiii–xiv.
7   P.E. O'Hara (2012) "Preface," in *The Arts of Contemplative Care*.
8   O'Hara, p.xiv.
9   C.A. Giles (2012) "Editor's Preface," in *The Arts of Contemplative Care*, p.xvii.
10 R.S. Blumenthal (2013) "'Not So Religious': Jewish Chaplaincy in the Twenty-First Century." In L. Forster-Smith (ed.) *College and University Chaplaincy in the 21st Century*. Woodstock, VT: SkyLight Paths Publishing, p.99.
11 L. Forster-Smith (2013) "Introduction," in *College and University Chaplaincy in the 21st Century*, pp.xvii–xviii.

and innovation, secularity and the sacred, and in some ways, hope and despair."[12]

We come to this project as a Hindu and a Christian—a university chaplain and a scholar of multi-religious concerns with expertise in chaplaincy education. We have no choice but to situate ourselves and our work in these existent definitions—fluid as they are. We are acutely aware of the history of pastoral care as a profession. At the same time, we believe it is critical to go beyond merely "plugging in" to historical models. We believe that chaplains must inquire into the role played by their own tradition and faith in forming their approach to caregiving in theory and practice.[13] With Daniel Schipani, we insist that they must ask two related but discrete questions. First, what are the theological "sources or 'foundations'…scriptures, philosophies, and teachings…" within their tradition that "inform, illumine, and orient" their approach to spiritual care?[14] Second, what are the related competencies, skills, and attitudes by which this approach "actually 'works' in practice" and defines "professional excellence"?[15] Put more simply, for purposes of this book: what difference does one's own Hindu belief and practice make to *why* and *how* one serves as a professional spiritual caregiver?

In asking why, chaplains begin to form a personal theology of spiritual care. The fact is that the caregiver's theology does matter in pastoral care situations; in this respect, says Schipani, chaplains are called to be both "reflective practitioners" and "pastoral theologians."[16] As hospital chaplain Martha Jacobs points out, they must maintain a "dual-track mind-set and heart-set" that allows them to simultaneously "remain connected to their own theology while also supporting and enabling another's theology."[17] This personal approach to theology invites the chaplain to hear and reflect on "a sense of 'call'…and to *choose* to respond affirmatively to this call."[18] Having accepted the call, chaplains then ask how their faith informs that response and points to the core values and qualities they will use to transform the theory of pastoral care into action.

---

12 Forster-Smith (2013), p.xvii.
13 Schipani (2013), p.2.
14 Schipani (2013), p.3.
15 Schipani (2013), p.3.
16 Schipani (2013), p.6.
17 M.R. Jacobs (2012) "Creating a Personal Theology to Do Spiritual/Pastoral Care," in *Professional Spiritual and Pastoral Care: A Practical Clergy and Chaplain's Handbook*, p.8.
18 D.B. Plummer (2012) "Creating a Personal Theology to Do Spiritual/Pastoral Care," in *Professional Spiritual and Pastoral Care*, p.12. Emphasis his.

It is in light of all of this that we invited 27 chaplains, scholars, and other important voices in the arena—most of them Hindu—to join us in reflecting on the theology and practice of Hindu chaplaincy. The body of the volume comprises three sections. In Part One, *Foundations of Care*, we provide 11 explorations of the theological and metaphysical roots of Hindu chaplaincy, examining the way in which it is informed by sacred texts, teachers, or practices. We begin with Rita Sherma's argument for "The Necessity of a Hindu-American Chaplaincy." In a sense, Sherma's piece offers us the foundation to our project: we cannot delve into the roots of Hindu chaplaincy without first exploring, albeit in brief, *why* we ought to care about this topic in the first place. Sherma is in an especially good position to do this, in that—in addition to her own scholarship—she is helping to develop a viable track for Hindu chaplains wishing to pursue study at the Graduate Theological Union. Varun Khanna takes us one step further, mining Hinduism's textual and commentarial wisdom to provide "theoretical foundations" for spiritual care. Likewise, scholar Anantanand Rambachan eloquently puts forth a theology of care from an Advaita Vedanta perspective, while Shaunaka Rishi Das (Hindu chaplain for Oxford University) does so from a Vaishnava Bhakti-focused tradition. All three of these authors play the role of constructive theologian, drawing from rich sources within their respective lineages while also articulating fresh insights.

Next, in "Body, Mind, and Breath," Christopher Key Chapple brings us to an exploration of yoga and its practical application to chaplaincy. As the director of a graduate program in Yoga Studies at Loyola Marymount University, Chapple is no stranger to the idea of yoga "off the mat" and in this volume he makes a compelling case for yoga's efficacy as a pastoral care framework. Princeton University Hindu chaplain Vineet Chander echoes Chapple by proposing *kriyā-yoga* as a paradigm for college chaplaincy. As Chapple and Chander look to the *Yoga Sūtras of Patañjali*, Viraj Patel seeks to locate a theological root for chaplaincy in another beloved Hindu text—the Bhagavad-Gita. His chapter points to lessons on Hindu anthropology in the Gita, and then offers Krishna as exemplar of pastoral care.

The next three essays consider Hindu resources for coping with loss and grief. Ramakrishnan Parameshwaran's "Rama in the Forest: A Hindu Framework for Grief Resolution from the Valmiki Ramayana" takes a fresh look at a poignant episode from the epic to suggest a Hindu approach to the concept of self-compassion. Parameshwaran combines his background in medicine with his current training in chaplaincy to build bridges between theology and clinical psychology, making useful comparisons between Hindu approaches and western models but also pointing out divergences. Gopal K. Gupta's "Does God Really Care? A Hindu Response to the Problem of Suffering" examines the problem of suffering—a common challenge that chaplains are tasked with responding to. Gupta interrogates the Bhagavata Purana to offer a Vaishnava theodicy that seeks to reconcile a personal relationship with a loving God with the reality of the devotee's suffering in this world. Rachel Fell McDermott approaches this same question from the lens of Hinduism's Goddess-centered traditions in "How Does the Goddess Help Us Handle Pain and Suffering? A Shakta Theological Foundation for Hindu Chaplaincy." McDermott combines her vast knowledge of Shakta theology with fieldwork—including moving historical and contemporary examples of people grappling with suffering—to explore the way devotees of the Divine Mother might approach the problem of pain. Our first section concludes with pastoral insights gleaned from the Upanishads, explained by college chaplain Madhu Vedak Sharma. Sharma wisely chooses to focus her examination on the *Katha* and the *Isha* Upanishads, two of contemporary Hinduism's most beloved texts, to draw out practical lessons that can be applied in a number of contexts.

Part Two, *Care in Context*, focuses on issues around Hindu chaplaincy expressed in particular locations. We begin with a reminiscence by Swami Sarvaananda (a disciple of Swami Satchidananda)—the first Hindu ever to be credentialed by the Board of Chaplaincy Certification Incorporated (an affiliate of the Association of Professional Chaplains). Swami's story, told in a straightforward and yet endearing way, highlights several important facets of what it means to formally serve as a Hindu chaplain. Fittingly, her piece is followed by a reflection on hospital chaplaincy by Shamā Mehtā—the second Hindu ever to be so certified. Healthcare is an arena in which the presence of Hindu chaplains is especially needed, and Mehtā's piece presents us with a helpful snapshot of this world. Also within the hospital context, Joseph Ghanashyam Caruso's heartfelt and moving essay reflects on his experience as a Hindu offering end-of-life care to non-Hindu patients.

We journey from the hospital to seats of higher education, as our next four authors consider university chaplaincy from various perspectives. Scholar Jeffery D. Long's "Hindu Chaplaincy as Karma Yoga in the Tradition of Sri Ramakrishna and Swami Vivekananda," based on an interview with MIT chaplain Swami Tyagananda, sets the tone for our examination of this context. This is fitting, perhaps, since the lineage of Sri Ramakrishna and Swami Vivekananda was likely the first Hindu tradition to engage in college chaplaincy in the West. Against this backdrop of history, we turn to Brahmachari V. Sharan's reflection on being a Hindu chaplain at Georgetown University—a Jesuit institution. Brahmachari's position, modeled as it is on the Jesuit ideal of the scholar-practitioner, calls him to play many roles in his work: pastor, ritual priest, teacher; he engages with these in his thoughtful essay. Yale University's Hindu chaplain Asha Shipman then explores the issues involved in transforming a campus space for Hindu spiritual purposes. Shipman's piece beautifully integrates her training as an anthropologist with her on-the-ground experience in helping to design and inaugurate Hindu prayer space at Yale. Of course, creating sacred space is one aspect of a larger effort by college chaplains to create a home-away-from-home on campus. Tahil Sharma's account of building Hindu community at USC gives us a fascinating look at this dynamic in action. Colleges and universities have a storied history of chaplaincy, though the presence of Hindus is a relatively new piece of this history.

Are there opportunities for spiritual caregiving in the workplace as well? Ramdas Lamb—a former monk who brings his monastic training to his work—writes on spiritual caregiving in the context of prisons. He reflects on years spent as a spiritual counselor to inmates, sharing techniques he employed and lessons he learned along the way. Rasanath Das, another former monk who brings his monastic training to his work, shares his approach to the relatively new domain of corporate chaplaincy. As a coach who helps individuals and organizations develop in terms of spiritual and emotional wellness, he draws on his deep study of wisdom texts and his experiences as a monk.

Part Three, *Care at Crossroads*, examines expressions of Hindu pastoral care offered in settings not typically associated with "chaplaincy." Thus, we have Murali Balaji on Hindu academics as spiritual caregivers. Balaji draws on his work as an education consultant to unpack the need for, and possibilities of, pastoral care in the academy. Pulin Sanghvi next shares a Hindu approach to vocational counseling. He brings to this nuanced exploration his experience working on career and life visioning at Princeton University and Stanford University, as well as in high-profile corporate spaces like McKinsey and Company. Raja Gopal Bhattar then examines intersectionality in the chapter "Hindu Spiritual Care of

LGBTQ People." Bhattar—formerly Director of the LGBTQ Center at UCLA; formerly Assistant Vice Provost and Executive Director of the Center for Identity and Inclusion at the University of Chicago—suggests that Hindu wisdom provides us with a rich and complex paradigm that allows for fluidity and affirmation.

With Vaishali Gupta Chandrashekar's reflection we are treated to the perspective of a former college chaplain who has found a new mode of spiritual care—cooking for people, helping them to discover wellness and nourishment on physical and spiritual levels.

Next, Amrutur V. Srinivasan shares thoughts on pre-nuptial and nuptial counseling by and for Hindus. Srinivasan literally wrote the book on officiating Hindu weddings in the West! His guidebook on the subject has become the seminal textbook for officiants in North America, so he speaks from a wealth of experience here.

Gopal D. Patel's "Hindu Approaches to Climate Trauma" offers us a fascinating and timely glimpse into the pastoral dimensions of environmental activism. Patel is well at home at this intersection—he served as a university chaplain and now directs The Bhumi Project, an environmental non-governmental organization (NGO) rooted in Hinduism.

The final piece in the volume is Shrestha Singh's heartfelt and moving essay on Hindu care and emotional healing. Singh draws from her personal experiences, as well as her role as a university chaplain, to share guidance for reinterpreting classic Hindu narratives to extract lessons in healing from post traumatic stress disorder (PTSD) and other trauma.

We hope this book will be of value to working chaplains, chaplaincy educators, students of chaplaincy and related modes of professional spiritual caregiving, and anyone interested in spiritual caregiving from Dharmic (rather than more typically presented Abrahamic) perspectives. While most of its contributors come from North America and work in the US, we hope readers in the UK—and elsewhere—will find it helpful too. Moreover, it is our belief and hope that readers will see this volume, not as the final word on the subject, but as the start of a dynamic and developing conversation.

A Note on Language

Most of our contributors prefer full diacritics on transliterated Sanskrit words. However, we realize that our readership includes many who are unfamiliar with that practice. Furthermore, some Sanskrit terms—particularly names of people, deities, and sacred texts—are now in common use in written English discourse. As a compromise, therefore, use of diacritics in this book is—for the most part—limited to Sanskrit names and terms not in common use in English-language discourse.

Part One

FOUNDATIONS OF CARE

The Necessity of a Hindu-American Chaplaincy

Rita D. Sherma

A New Kind of Dharma Leadership[1]

For American culture to fully exemplify *E Pluribus Unum*, three elements need to coalesce: (1) the acknowledgment of certain commonly held foundational principles for the wellbeing of all, enshrined in law and the collective consciousness; (2) the acceptance of various expressions of such values in different cultural and religious forms; and (3) the evolution of American forms of the world's religions.

Without the affirmation of pluralism as a value, America's claim to represent human liberty is compromised. But without moral and spiritual common grounding, the US will become a nation of "many solitudes"—with fragmented identities and brittle boundaries between its many communities. Just as many generations of Jewish Americans have forged different forms of American Judaism, and new systems of American Buddhism have begun to take hold, there may yet be a day that opens to the emergence of an American Hinduism (henceforth, Hindu *dharma*).

Do Hindus Need Chaplains?

The Hindu diaspora is a largely well-educated, law-abiding, and financially comfortable community in the US. Therefore, a sense of invulnerability

---

[1] First published by the online journal *The Interfaith Observer* on September 6, 2013 (https://interfaith-observer.squarespace.com/journal-articles/2013/9/6/the-necessity-of-a-hindu-american-chaplaincy.html, accessed on October 6, 2018). As offered here, the essay has undergone slight revision by its author and is included in this volume with permission of *The Interfaith Observer*.

exists, especially amongst those blessed with good fortune. But everyone, regardless of status, suffers illness, old age, infirmity, and bereavement. Many encounter additional trauma such as discrimination, divorce, and natural and personal disasters.

Christians, Jews, Muslims, and Buddhists can turn to religious communities who are equipped to help individuals transition from what I call "grief to grace." But to whom does a Hindu in America turn? Throughout Hindu history, networks of relationships provided security. In India, there existed, for most, various psychological, material, financial, informational, and relational networks composed of extended families, multi-generational contacts, ashrams (retreat centers), and the support of religious groups associated with one's family.

In the diaspora, many of these traditional support systems are either missing or inaccessible. This can be due to time constraints from heavy work schedules; family discontinuity (separation, divorce, and the loss of connection with relatives); community ruptures; geographic distance, and resource limitations in the nuclear (rather than extended) family. These realities particularly impact second, third, and future generations, as well as those who marry outside the confines of the community.

To be sure, many spiritual resources are available within the American Hindu *dharma* to heal the body, mind, and spirit. Yet, without a human hand to hold when life's tribulations strike, and a trained guide along the way, it is difficult to access this richness of traditional resources. Swamis who arrive on these shores offer wisdom about life and liberation. They are not meant to serve as counselors for life's myriad and diverse trials and traumas. Priests who come from India and are employed by temples (*mandirs*) serve a useful function; but their task is to perform complex rituals of worship, devotion, celebration, rites of passage, sacraments, and so forth.

These leaders are not at all trained in family counseling, grief and bereavement assistance, or providing support for addiction recovery work. The success of the Hindu community leaves an appearance of immunity from problems—as if Hindus float through air as they go through life. So when Hindu Americans experience crises and catastrophes, particularly later generations, they have nowhere to turn except for their elderly parents, who may themselves be in need of care. Who is there to help diaspora Hindus now, on new and distant shores?

From such reflections the idea of Hindu chaplaincy has arisen. Hindu chaplains can be priests who take additional training, retired persons who seek to offer service (*sevā*), and those who would like to step forward as new examples of spiritual leadership among American Hindu communities. There will always be a need for priests, as well as gurus, monks (*swamis*), and other religious teachers. But the vacuum of intensive personal care, compassion, and counseling from spiritual leadership that lies at the heart of the Hindu community in the American diaspora can only be filled by properly trained Hindu chaplains. These individuals would study foundational rituals; Hindu philosophy, ethics, principles and practices; and care and counseling for those in need.

What Is a Trained Chaplain?

A professional chaplain is a representative of a particular religious tradition with skills in counseling and spiritual care for those in need or undergoing crisis, a solid background in basic principles of clinical psychology, along with the wisdom, philosophy, and spiritual practices of his or her particular tradition. Chaplains thereby can assist individuals, couples, families, and faith communities in coping with and surviving difficult or painful circumstances. In the US, one finds not only Christian chaplains, but also Buddhist, Jewish, Muslim, Native American, and Pagan chaplains, amongst others.

Building on those models, one might say a properly trained Hindu chaplain would be educated in an accredited institution that offers:

- APC (Association of Professional Chaplains) requirement for a 72-unit accredited theological degree in Hindu Theology (a Master of Divinity equivalence)
- the training in spiritual care needed for the application of Hindu scriptures, theology, ethics, and practices to pastoral care and chaplaincy
- instruction in prayer and worship proper to the tradition (e.g., *prārthanā* or Hindu prayer, *pūjā* and *vandana* or worship, mantra recitation, or the ability to use sacred sounds in a pastoral context).

If ordained, the chaplain must also be able to officiate at sacramental rites such as marriage, life-cycle rites, and protective or benedictive ceremonies (*saṃskāras* and *pūjās*).

An Evolving Hindu Dharma in America, and Its Care

The American Hindu temple can no longer serve only as a place of worship and social religiosity. It needs to become the primary sanctuary for the Hindu heritage community as a whole. This long-range challenge will take decades, but it must be initiated now. The development of Hindu chaplaincy is an important step in that direction. Hindu chaplains would not only serve as sources of solace in difficult times and counselors in life crises, but as resources for individuals and families who need to be connected to resources, institutions, and persons who can help with all sorts of questions, issues, and activities.

Additionally, the presence of professionally trained Hindu chaplains will allow for a new kind of Hindu presence at the American interfaith table and in government agencies, educational institutions, and other important organizational bodies. Chaplains can represent their traditions for a host of political, social, interreligious, and charitable functions. For Hindu *dharma* in the US, this task is now often filled by non-ordained individuals or by ordained priests from India who are unfamiliar with the cultural and linguistic norms of the West. As a result, Hindus have a diminished religious voice in America.

So while respecting the role, dedication, and professional capacity and commitment of traditional priests, an American Hindu chaplaincy would still push forward the progressive and global edge of the *dharma* by opening new doorways to religious leadership by women, people of different ages, *jatis*, ethnicities, professions, and to future generations of Hindus. A chaplaincy program that is comprehensive and well-conceived could provide intellectual and pastoral space for the application of Hindu principles to contemporary problems and needs, in India as well as the diaspora.

Theoretical Foundations for Hindu Chaplaincy in Advaita Vedanta

Varun Khanna

In this chapter I will propose that not only does Hinduism have the provision for spiritual care (and more broadly, social engagement) theoretically, it is in fact a necessary and often overlooked component of Hindu tradition that must be extracted and developed to meet the demands of modern-day society. The adaptation of Hindu practice has been a feature of Hinduism for millennia, with the creation of new theories, practices, and even sects over the years adding to the plethora of traditions within Hinduism, which has contributed to the survival of the overarching tradition and the vast and diverse range of philosophical and practical expressions therein. Of course, one must acknowledge that spiritual care in Hinduism does already exist—not, perhaps, in the form of "chaplaincy," *per se*—but as a component of the traditional guru-*śiṣya* (teacher–student) relationship, or within the role of a "family guru," or even within the role of a priest at the local Hindu temple. However, the point is not only to acknowledge where it already exists as an ancillary component within these traditional roles of Hindu practice, but to extract that component and develop it as an independent role adding to the scope of traditional Hindu leadership.

What Is Hindu Chaplaincy?

To understand Hindu chaplaincy, one must understand what it means to be Hindu, and what it means to be a chaplain, and why this combination is a necessary one within the framework of Hinduism. There has already been so much academic and popular work on what it means to be Hindu that to reproduce it here would be amiss. However, for the purpose of this chapter, I propose to think about Hinduism as an overarching term comprised of several distinct and diverse traditions, which are growing in number even today.[1]

With this in mind, it would seem that for almost every Hindu view, there appears to be another opposing view that is equally Hindu. To even use the name "Hindu" for all of these views together—and to accordingly call oneself Hindu, then—is to acknowledge the oppositional nature of many of these views, while recognizing an inherent thread that is nevertheless identifiable as Hindu. To be Hindu, for the purposes of this chapter, means to identify with one (or multiple, or sometimes none) of these diverse traditions, acknowledging that one's path is not the only path, but one among many valid paths, as the philosopher Jonardon Ganeri succinctly argues in his short piece on the tree of knowledge being a banyan, and not an apple or an oak.[2]

Having stated this, we come to the point about "chaplaincy." Exactly what chaplaincy is has been and is the subject of discussion and debate to this day.[3] Still, words that describe chaplaincy today—such as care, healing, presence, listening, spiritual, and support—offer us insight into an (albeit difficult to pin down) "essence" of chaplaincy. In my conversations with a Board-Certified Hindu Chaplain, I have come to understand that a chaplain seeks to offer spiritual care and support, as well as to assess and address spiritual needs of those who are experiencing distress through their life circumstances, irrespective of the recipient's identification with any religion, race, gender, sexual orientation, and so on. Chaplaincy seeks to identify and address one's experience and relationship to self, other, family, community, society, nature, and the significant or sacred.

---

1 I refer here to the inclusion of the Akṣara-puruṣottama philosophy of the Swaminarayan path, officially recognized as a valid and complete philosophy among the gamut of Vedantic philosophies by a majority vote of scholars present at the most recent World Sanskrit Conference held in Vancouver in July 2018, accompanied by a release of a complete commentary by Bhadreshdas Swami on the *prasthāna-trayī*, the tripartite corpus of foundational Vedantic textbooks, namely the Upanishads, the Bhagavad-Gita, and the Brahma-Sutra.

2 J. Ganeri "The tree of knowledge is not an apple or an oak but a banyan." Aeon.com. https://aeon.co/ideas/the-tree-of-knowledge-is-not-an-apple-or-an-oak-but-a-banyan, accessed on September 23, 2018.

3 Upon searching for a succinct definition of "chaplaincy" and not finding one, I concluded that it was open to interpretation to some degree, which grants one great freedom to explore within the field, but also invites the danger of straying away from the essence of chaplaincy. Nevertheless, I offer in this chapter a working idea of chaplaincy for the purpose of establishing the opportunity and need for "Hindu chaplaincy."

A Hindu chaplain, to put it all together, is someone who, rooted in a Hindu tradition, engages in the active pastoral care of others in the context of institutions like hospitals, prisons, universities, the army, and even corporations. The rest of this chapter will look inward, as it were, to extract from within the tradition, if possible, an argument that makes the case for not only the validity but also the necessity of Hindu chaplaincy, drawing on the previously existing teachings of Advaita Vedanta, urging the tradition to accept the possibility of chaplaincy as a role specifically, and social engagement more generally.

Why Advaita Vedanta?

But why Advaita Vedanta? Today, Advaita Vedanta appears to be a (if not *the*) dominant paradigm of Hindu thought, thanks to the teachings of several important figures of the nineteenth and twentieth centuries who happened to be exponents of Advaita in some form or another. These include Ramakrishna Paramahamsa (1836–1886), Swami Vivekananda (1863–1902), Sri Aurobindo (1872–1950), Ramana Maharshi (1879–1950), Sarvepalli Radhakrishnan (1888–1975), and Swami Chinmayananda (1916–1993), among others. As a result, Advaitic views on meaning and the world have also dominated the discussion among scholars and practitioners of Hinduism.

The Problem with Advaitic Interpretation Today, and the Two Paths for a Seeker

The overwhelming consensus among scholars of Advaita—according to Anantanand Rambachan, in his *The Advaita Worldview* (2006)—is that the world is devoid of meaning and value.[4] As such, the only path for an Advaitin to follow seems to be the path of the *sannyasin* (renunciate), letting go of all material attachments, engaging in *nivṛtti dharma* (the path of renunciation) defined below. But in fact the Advaita tradition recognizes two paths: one for the practitioner who is committed to realizing his or her oneness with *brahman*,[5] and one for the practitioner

---

4 A. Rambachan (2006) *The Advaita Worldview*. Albany, NY SUNY Press, p.67–69.
5 Brahman is most often defined as *sat-cit-ānanda*, "existence-consciousness-bliss." It is the basis for everything, infinite, all-pervading, immortal, and the ultimate cause of the universe. Realization of and abidance in one's own identity as *brahman* is the goal of Advaitic practice. This identification with *brahman* is said to be the cause of unending happiness, the goal of all life, and the motivation for any action.

who is not yet committed to this realization.⁶ These paths are called *nivṛtti dharma* and *pravṛtti dharma*, respectively, and are prescribed according to one's stage in the development of one's distinguishing ability (*viveka*) between real (Self, *brahman*, *ātman*) and unreal (non-Self) and the resulting dispassion from the world (*vairāgya*). The *pravṛtti* path is prescribed for one who feels that there is meaning and value in the world. This is our default state, the Hindu tradition understands, and it proceeds to lay out a path for action in the world, called *pravṛtti dharma*, or more commonly, *dharma*. Shankara writes in the introduction to his commentary on the Bhagavad-Gita:

> There are two types of *dharma* as stated in the Veda: *pravṛtti* and *nivṛtti*. That which is the cause of the maintenance of the universe and is directly responsible for the elevation, prosperity, and liberation of living beings is *dharma* when practiced by all classes of people, [especially] those who are seekers of the highest good... Both types of *dharma* as described by the Lord [Krishna] have been captured here by the holy all-knowing Veda Vyāsa in this text, known as the *Gita*, of 700 verses.⁷

Pravṛtti dharma is characterized by Advaita as focusing on karma, or action in the world, with each action being dedicated to a higher altar (and not one's personal gain). This technique is said to develop dispassion from the world because of the world's unfulfilling nature in the absolute sense, naturally resulting in the turn away from the world and towards the *nivṛtti* path. *Nivṛtti dharma* is characterized as focusing on *jñāna*, or knowledge of self, that is, undergoing the threefold process of *śravaṇa* (understanding the essence of the Upanisadic teaching, or knowing about the oneness between *ātman* and *brahman*), *manana* (removing doubts about one's nature as *brahman*, or intellectually believing oneself to be *brahman*), and *nididhyāsana* (removing the subtle conditioning that prevents one from feeling like *brahman*, or practicing identifying with *brahman*). But while a person still seeks happiness from the world, the world having meaning is the default state for that person.

---

6   See Śaṅkara's commentary on *Īśāvāsya* Upanishad verse 2.

7   Found in Śaṅkara's upodghāta bhāṣya (introductory commentary) on the Bhagavad-Gita. The text reads: *dvividho hi vedokto dharmaḥ pravṛttilakṣaṇo nivṛttilakṣaṇaśca. jagataḥ sthitikāraṇaṁ prāṇināṁ sākṣāt abhyudaya-niḥśreyasa-hetuḥ yaḥ sa dharmo brāhmaṇādyaiḥ varṇibhiḥ āśramibhiḥ ca śreyo'rthibhiḥ anuṣṭhīyamānaḥ...taṁ dharmaṁ bhagavatā yathopadiṣṭaṁ vedavyāsaḥ sarvajño bhagavān gītākhyaiḥ saptabhiḥ ślokaśataiḥ upanibabandha.* Translation is my own.

The problem in the final Advaitic teaching arises when a seeker asks the question: liberation may be my goal; but, given that only knowledge of Self can remove the ignorance that prevents me from my own liberation, and despite hearing the teaching over and over again, do I actually *feel* like I am infinite, immortal, in eternal consciousness bliss? Or do I still feel like I am a finite, limited, sorrowful being? It is due to the problem of this tenacious perceived limitation and the fact that while we are in the world we cannot avoid action in it, as Krishna points out to Arjuna,[8] that the philosophy of Advaita Vedanta deigns to acknowledge and reckon with the lived human experience and may suggest *pravṛtti dharma* for the practitioner. Shankara clearly writes in his commentary on *sūtra* 1.1.4 of the Brahma-Sutra, "Until one is fully convinced of one's identity as *brahman* and abides totally in that identity, all means of knowledge related to the world are acceptable and valid."[9]

The *nivṛtti* path, often simply called Advaita, appears to have become the dominant strand of Advaitic teaching, and it has stifled conversation about Hindu forms of social engagement, because its focus is fundamentally on the nature of and methods for achieving individual *mokṣa*, or liberation from the cycle of birth and rebirth. This gives rise to a particular cognitive dissonance within the mind of a lay Advaitin, who naturally sees meaning and value in the world and derives happiness from it, but who is also simultaneously taught that the giving up of the world is the only way to happiness, resulting in a self-contradictory approach to the world, both in the pursuit of material pleasure and in thinking that the world is not the source of one's happiness. But Advaita is not a path that only caters to those who are ready for *mokṣa*, as I have argued, and includes within it an often-overlooked provision for meaningful action in the world while the world still holds value and the potential for happiness for a seeker, called *pravṛtti dharma*.

The Nature of Pravṛtti Dharma

It is the possibility offered by the utilization and revitalization of *pravṛtti dharma* that is essential in the development of a Hindu approach to social engagement, and therefore also Hindu chaplaincy. So exactly

---

8   Bhagavad-Gita 2.47.
9   Shankara writes: *laukika tadvadevedamaukika tadva"tmaniścayāt* (*BhāKed, Brahma Sūtra* 1.1.4). Translation mine.

what is *pravṛtti dharma*? It is characterized, as stated above, by one's focus on karma, and its purpose is to develop within an ordinary seeker two requirements for pursuing the path of renunciation, which leads one to *mokṣa*, the stated goal of Advaita Vedanta: *cittaśuddhi* (purity of mind) and *cittaikāgratā* (single-pointed focus of mind). Once these two requirements are gained, then the trifold path of *śravaṇa-manana-nididhyāsana* as defined above, which constitute *nivṛtti dharma*, are a fruitful endeavor, leading one to the establishment in one's own identity as *brahman*.

What does it mean to focus on karma? There are five types of karma as identified in Vedantic literature. These are:

1. *Nitya* karma: performance of prescribed daily action. While this type of karma normally refers to daily Vedic rituals—like the *agnihotra* fire ritual, or *sandhyāvandana*, the daily ritual worship of dawn and dusk inviting the day and night, respectively—in modern times it also has come to include daily activities like bathing, brushing one's teeth, etc.

2. *Naimittika* karma: performance of prescribed circumstantial action. This type of karma refers to rituals that are not performed daily but are performed based on a particular circumstance—such as a particular day of the fortnight, or the death anniversary of a family member.

3. *Prāyaścitta* karma: performance of penance in order to reduce the negative effects of previous karma. This is usually the performance of extended *japa* (repetition of a mantra or sacred name) or other elaborate ritual that causes difficulty in order to ward off anticipated karmic retribution for one's negative deeds.

4. *Kāmya* karma: performance of action with a particular desired result in mind; desirous action. This type of karma is the performance of ritual or other action that is done with a desired result in mind; for example, the performance of the Jyotiṣṭoma sacrifice for the achievement of heaven, or the *putrakāmeṣṭi* sacrifice for the achievement of a son.

5. *Niṣiddha* karma: prohibited action. This type of karma is never allowed under any circumstances, and must be avoided as much as possible because it incurs negative results.

The seeker is advised to perform only *nitya, naimittika,* and *prāyaścitta* karma as the content of *pravṛtti dharma*. This is essentially the performance of one's duties without the expectation of reward (the removal of *kāmya* karma, most notably, means to no longer perform actions in order to gain a particular result). It is a complete detachment from the results of one's actions, and complete engagement in duty. This mode of action is also known as karma yoga and is designed to develop the two prerequisites for embarkment on the *nivṛtti path*—*cittaśuddhi* (purity of mind) and *cittaikāgratā* (single-pointed focus of mind).

As Krishna points out to Arjuna in the well known Bhagavad-Gita verse 2.47, "You only have control over [your] actions, never [over] the results [of your actions]. [Therefore] do not be one who acts for the sake of the result. [But also] do not be [one who is] attached to inaction."[10] This verse, often cited as the essence of the entire Bhagavad-Gita, indicates that desireless action is the ultimate mode of action, understood in the context of *pravṛtti dharma* as performing only *nitya, naimittika,* and *prāyaścitta* karma.

The Case for Hindu Chaplaincy

Any person who identifies as *dharmic*, then, according to Advaita Vedanta—so long as that person is engaged in action in the world, thinking the world to be meaningful and valuable—is enjoined to follow the path of *pravṛtti dharma*. It is not only a *provision* within the Advaitic framework, but a *prescription* entailing a meaningful mode of operation within the world, should the seeker be interested in the ultimate goal of *mokṣa*. The ideal way to enact this is to act selflessly, engaged always in the service of others, performing one's duties without the desire for particular results. The role of a chaplain, as defined earlier in this chapter, is as though designed with exactly this in mind. A Hindu chaplain, then, is not only a *good* role to play as an Advaitic practitioner, but an almost *inevitable* one. If one looks for an ideal mode of action in the world, aligned with the framework of *pravṛtti dharma*, it would be difficult at best to deny the neatness of the configuration of chaplaincy as a profession to fit such an ideal.

In effect, the theory of Advaita Vedanta enjoins us all, in some way, to be chaplains. Given that *mokṣa* is the stated goal of Advaita Vedanta,

---

10 Krishna says: *karmaṇy evādhikāras te mā phaleṣu kadācana; mā karmaphalahetur bhūr mā te sangostv akarmaṇi* (Bhagavad-Gita 2.47). Translation mine.

it must be noted that to be a chaplain creates not only the conducive conditions for the pursuit of *mokṣa* in the individual by promoting purity and focus of mind, but also the conducive conditions for the pursuit of *mokṣa* societally as well, by promoting the external peace and stability required in the larger system for any individual to be prepared to pursue the final goal of life.[11] It is not far afield, then, for the Hindu tradition to accept and even enjoin chaplaincy as a legitimate and venerated profession and role in society.

Conclusion

Through an analysis of the two types of *dharma* offered in the Hindu tradition of Advaita Vedanta—namely *pravṛtti dharma* (path of engagement) and *nivṛtti dharma* (path of detachment), and their placement not opposed to each other but rather on a continuum of development of the seeker—I have shown, I hope, why Hindu chaplaincy is not only a possibility but a necessity. I first acknowledged the need to understand what it means to be Hindu, what it means to be a chaplain, and what it means to be a "Hindu chaplain." I then considered why being a Hindu chaplain in particular—and social engagement in general—is an acceptable and even necessary mode of action within the Advaitic framework. The often-overlooked potential of *pravṛtti dharma* is where I envision the future discussion regarding Hindu chaplaincy to lie. This framework holds the key, I submit, not only to Hindu engagement in society as chaplains, but also to the envisaging of many more as yet unthought of roles in society for Hindus to involve themselves in for the achievement of individual *mokṣ* as well as the simultaneous betterment of society as a whole.

---

11 Elsewhere, I will argue in more detail about the two-fold social engagement required of a practitioner of Advaita Vedanta to truly be engaged in *pravṛtti dharma*. This is the performance of *dharma* at the individual level, characterized by all actions one takes to bring one closer to one's own *mokṣa*, by cultivating *cittaśuddhi* and *cittaikāgratā*, but also the performance of *dharma* at the societal level, which is about the optimization of society such that each individual is taken care of (in terms of food, shelter, peace, and other basic needs) to the point that they can begin to pursue *mokṣa*, should they desire to, given that *mokṣa* is the Advaitic goal of life.

An Advaita Vedanta Theology of Spiritual Care

Reverence, Diversity, and Detachment

Anantanand Rambachan

The Tradition of Advaita Vedanta

Before proceeding to outline an Advaita theology of spiritual care, it will be helpful, very briefly, to identify the place of the Advaita tradition within the diverse family of Hindu traditions. Advaita refers to one of several Hindu traditions that are grounded in the recognition of the four Vedas (Rg, Sama, Yajur, and Atharva) as sources of valid knowledge (*pramāṇa*). The fundamental teachings of Advaita are derived from the exegesis of the Vedas and, more specifically, from the last sections of the Vedas, referred to as the Upanishads. The Upanishads are religious dialogues between teachers and students discussing the fundamental questions of human existence such as the nature of self, the causes of suffering, and liberation. For this reason, the tradition is more accurately described as Advaita Vedanta (lit. "end of the Veda") to acknowledge the specific authoritative significance of the Upanishads.[1] Although looking to the Upanishads as the highest source for its teachings, the Advaita tradition also recognizes the Bhagavad-Gita and the Brahma-Sutra as authoritative sources.[2]

---

1 Vedanta is a compound of Veda and *anta*, meaning "end." It signifies primarily the location of the Upanishads at the end of the Vedas, although there are interpreters who understand "end" to mean the highest teaching or culmination of the wisdom of the Vedas.
2 The Brahma-Sutra is attributed to Badarayaṇa (c.400BCE). In this work the author attempts a systematic exposition of the Upanishads in the *sūtra* style of short condensed statements.

Advaita acknowledges a line of distinguished teachers for the exegesis, clarification, defense, and transmission of its teachings. The principal systematizer, exponent, and apologist for Advaita is Shankara (ca.788–820). Shankara's legacy to the tradition is his commentary on the Bhagavad-Gita, the Brahma-Sutra, and on ten of the Upanishads (Isha, Kena, Katha, Prashna, Mandukya-Karika, Mundaka, Aitareya, Brihadaranyaka, Chandogya, and Taittiriya). He is also credited with the authorship of many independent works.

The word *Advaita* literally means "not-two," and identifies the tradition's distinctive mode of characterizing the relationship between the infinite *brahman*, the world, and the self. Describing this relationship as "one" or "two" is not, according to Advaita, appropriate. It is because the relationship between *brahman* as cause and world as effect is asymmetrical. The world, as an effect, originates from *brahman* and is dependent upon *brahman* for its existence. It is finite and subject to change. The existence of *brahman*, on the other hand, is independent and *brahman* is not limited by the finitude of the world. *Brahman* is immanent in the world, while also transcending it. The relationship between *brahman* and the world is not "two" since *brahman* constitutes the ultimate ontological ground of the world and the self, even as clay is the truth of all clay objects and water the truth of all waves. *Brahman* exists equally and identically in all beings as the self (*atma*).

At the heart of the human problem is ignorance (*avidyā*) of *brahman* and its nature as the ground of all that exists. This ignorance is the root cause of human suffering and discontent. It is the source of the human sense of inadequacy, anxiety, and want. Liberation (*mokṣa*) is synonymous with the overcoming of ignorance (*avidyā*), and the birth of a radically new understanding of *brahman*, world, and self. In a liberative understanding, the world and other beings do not cease to exist, but their ontological unity and inseparable existence from *brahman* is affirmed and celebrated. Liberation is possible here and now. It is not an end that must await the death of the body. The ideal is referred to as living liberation (*jīvanmukti*).

Although my contribution draws in a special way from Advaita Vedanta, it is by no means limited to this theological tradition. The religious traditions of India are not homogeneous and have never existed in impermeable compartments. Advaita shares many of the theological assumptions of other traditions and exists in relationships of mutual giving and receiving with these traditions.

A Theology of Reverence

An Advaita theology of spiritual care is one that is grounded in respect and reverence for every human being. The Upanishads, which are the primary sources for Advaita, speak of *brahman* as "That from which all beings originate, by which they are sustained and to which they return" (Taittiriya Upanishad 3.1.1). Chandogya Upanishad (6.2.1-2) speaks of *brahman* as the indivisible and uncreated One from which the many are created. These texts also affirm, unequivocally, the equal existence of *brahman* in all beings. Isha Upanishad (1) begins with the famous call to see everything in the world of movement as pervaded by Isha (God). There is no life outside of God and there is nothing that exists which is not sustained by God.[3]

Some of the most eloquent verses on this teaching occur in the Bhagavad-Gita. According to Bhagavad-Gita (13:28), "One who sees the Supreme God existing equally in all beings, the imperishable in the perishable, truly sees." This verse affirms the presence of God in the world and characterizes this presence in two very important ways. The first is by the use of the word "equally (*samaṁ*)". The second is "in all beings (*sarveṣu bhūteṣu*)." These words admit no exclusions or distinctions. Put simply, God exists equally in all beings. The divine presence is not limited by anything—nation, gender, ethnicity, age, or religious affiliation. This is not unusual for the Bhagavad-Gita and other Hindu texts that always speak of the divine presence in terms of equality and inclusivity. The Bhagavad-Gita (18:61) returns to this insight in the final chapter with the teaching that God abides in in the heart of all beings.

Seeing the imperishable and indivisible in the perishable and divided is consequential. It is commended in this verse as true seeing because it is the seeing of that which is ultimate and which therefore has ultimate value. The imperishable evokes reverence and that reverence extends to all humanity. Such reverence finds expression in care, compassion, and respect for the other's freedom; it excludes the exploitation and instrumentalization of others to satisfy one's own needs.

This teaching about divine immanence is a powerful inspiration for a theology of spiritual care. Swami Tyagananda, a Hindu monk from the Ramakrishna order, states it succinctly. "If God dwells in me and in everyone and everything in the world, then no matter who I am dealing with and who I am working for, I am really dealing only with God and

---

3   I translate *Isha* as God, cognizant of theological differences about divine nature.

working only for God."[4] Speaking to his disciples on one occasion about the meaning of compassion, the famous Hindu teacher, Shri Ramakrishna (1836–1886), guru of Swami Vivekananda (1863–1902), explained that they should see the service of others as the service of God. "No, no; it is not compassion to *jīvas* (living beings) but service to them as Shiva (God)." Ramakrishna obviously wanted his students to understand care as a privilege and honor that must be exercised in humility as a worshipful act. His words had a powerful impact on his young disciple, Vivekananda, who vowed, "I'll proclaim everywhere in the world this wonderful truth I have heard today. I will preach this truth to the learned and to the ignorant, to the rich and the poor, to the Brahmana and the Chandala."[5] The Ramakrishna Mission, founded by Swami Vivekananda, uses the word *sevā*, translated as "service," instead of compassion (*dayā*).

The Sanskrit word that best articulates a theology of care based on divine immanence is *sevā*. The caregiver is a *sevaka*. *Sevā* comes from the root *sev* which has an array of rich meanings including "to stay near," "to serve," "to honor," or "to worship." *Sevā* is used to describe traditional worship in Hindu temples in which a series of hospitality offerings (*upacāras*) are made to the divine present in the *mūrti* (icon). These are about 16 in number and include the invitation to receive worship, the invitation to a seat, the washing of the feet, and acts of adoration through the offering of flowers, the burning of incense, the waving of lights and food. Each offering is accompanied by the recitation of sacred words (mantras) and done mindfully and reverentially. There is a consciousness of the divine being present and graciously receiving each offering. It is profoundly significant to note that Hindu worship is a form of caregiving to God.

Spiritual caregiving becomes a mode of worship when offered with a knowledge of the divine present in the one we serve and done with attitudes of reverence, respect, and regard for the dignity of the recipient. The caregiver's (*sevaka*) disposition is one of gratitude for the privilege of rendering service. It is the very opposite of aloofness or arrogance and enriches the meaning of compassion by adding reverence for the one who is served. The sacred value of the human being is not diminished by a need. The Bhagavad-Gita (9:27) commends the transformation of

---

4   S. Tyagananda (2014) *Walking the Walk*. Kolkata: Advaita Ashrama, p.52.
5   Cited in S. Saradananda (1952) *Sri Ramakrishna: The Great Master*, Vol. II, trans. Swami Jagadananda. Mylapore, India: Sri Ramakrishna Math, pp.939–940. The translations in parenthesis are my own. Brahmana and Chandala refer to members of the highest caste and the lowest.

every act into a worshipful one ("Whatever you do, whatever you eat, whatever you offer in worship, whatever you give, do it as an offering to me") and spiritual caregiving is no exception.

A Theology of Diversity

An Advaita theology of spiritual care will be one that is deeply cognizant of human diversity and especially of the diversity of human religious needs. The most meaningful spiritual care is offered individually in a deep personal and dialogical relationship between caregiver and receiver. Caregiving becomes irresponsible if the caregiver is indifferent to, presumes, or misunderstands the needs of the receiver. The Bhagavad-Gita 3:26 counsels, "Let not the wise person confuse the unwise who are attached to selfish action; by devotion to action, the wise should inspire others to act." The point here is that it will be inappropriate to commend the renunciation of action for someone who is attached to action. The more appropriate teaching and example for such a person is one that inspires action free from greed and oriented to the service of the world. The caregiver, according to the Bhagavad-Gita 3:25, must model what she commends. "As the unwise act from selfish attachment to action, O Bharata, so should the wise act without selfish attachment intent on the good of the world." The final chapter of the Bhagavad-Gita, 18:67, returns to the point of appropriate and inappropriate sharing and caregiving: "This teaching is not to be shared by you with anyone who is without discipline or devotion, who has no desire to listen and who denounces Me." Caregiving is a mutual process requiring receptivity and, in this specific instance, love and discipline.

This regard for offering appropriate care manifests in many places in the tradition. Shankara interprets the Vedas as catering to a diversity of religious needs, reflecting various human interests and desires. For Shankara, the first or the ritual section of the Vedas provides scripturally approved methods for pursuing and attaining finite goals such as wealth, power, fame, pleasure, and heavenly worlds of enjoyment. The tradition does not condemn those who pursue such ends, religious or secular, once this is done with attentiveness to ethical norms and especially the concern to avoid causing harm and suffering to others. It recognizes that many, in all religions, look to their traditions to support and enhance their attainment of such goals. When one comes to understand the limits of such finite goals, one is directed then to the second or wisdom section of the Vedas (the Upanishads) where the focus is on the knowledge of the infinite (*brahman*). The aspirant for the ritual section is someone who has not yet understood the limits of finite gains created by action. He has not yet grasped the fundamental human problem, described by Shankara as the longing for the infinite. The student of the wisdom section has grasped the limits of such ends and understands that her true search is for the infinite. A skilled caregiver must invest time in learning of these needs and in offering help. The Upanishads offer answers but these are not meaningful without questions being asked. Traditionally, Advaita teachers waited for the questions before offering answers.

Bhagavad-Gita 7:16-18 speaks of four types of religious persons with distinct needs: the distressed, the seeker of security and pleasure, the one who desires to know God, and the one who knows God. Although commending the knower of God, the teacher does not condemn the others; they are, in fact, praised as doers of good actions. Another example in the Hindu tradition of recognizing and celebrating different ways of being religious is the well known classification of the five dispositions (*bhavās*) that obtain in human relationships with God. The first is *śanta bhava*, a relationship of quiet contemplation with little outward emotional expression. The second is *dāsya bhāva* in which one relates to God as servant to master. The third, *sakhya bhāva*, is more intimate: God is viewed as a trusted personal friend, always near. The fourth is *vātsalya bhava*, in which God is loved and adored as child. This relationship is present in those Hindu traditions that teach a doctrine of God's incarnation and it becomes prominent when the birth anniversaries of persons such as Rama and Krishna are celebrated. Conversely, one may choose to think of oneself as child and of God as father or mother. The most intense relationship is *madhura bhāva*, in which God is thought of as cosmic lover. The famous Hindu teacher Sri Ramakrishna, who had disciples with a variety of needs, likens both God and the teacher to a mother who ensures that every child has his or her favorite dish.

> The mother cooks different dishes to suit the stomachs of her different children. Suppose she has five children. If there is a fish to cook, she prepares various dishes from it—pilau, pickled fish, fried fish, and so on—to suit their different tastes and powers of digestion.[6]

---

6   *The Gospel of Ramakrishna*, trans., Swami Nikhilananda (New York: Ramakrishna-Vivekananda Center of New York, 1942, 1948, 1958), p.81. Used by permission of the Ramakrishna-Vivekananda Center of New York.

Ramakrishna's example is a beautiful and suggestive one for spiritual caregiving. The ability of the caregiver to cater to a diversity of needs is an act of profound love comparable to that of a parent's loving concern to provide for the different preferences of each child.

This is a teaching with implications for spiritual caregiving across religious traditions. Later on, in one of his addresses at the Parliament of World Religions (1893), Ramakrishna's disciple Swami Vivekananda will say to his religiously diverse audience, "The Christian is not to become a Hindu or a Buddhist, nor is a Hindu or a Buddhist to become a Christian. But each must assimilate the spirit of the others and yet preserve his individuality and grow according to his own law of growth."[7] The aim of the caregiver is not the conversion of the other, but his spiritual growth and flourishing. Obviously, this is an important challenge when offering spiritual care in a context of religious diversity.

A Theology of Optimism

An Advaita theology of spiritual care will be deeply informed by the tradition's understanding of the fundamental human problem. As noted above, this problem is described in the language of ignorance *(avidyā)*. This ignorance is centered on the nature of the self *(atma)* which is erroneously regarded as existing separately from *brahman* and every other self. Its ontological identity with *brahman* and its fullness is concealed by ignorance.

The consequences of this ignorance are not to be underestimated. It expresses itself in a persistent and gnawing sense of inadequacy, in greed, and in the multiplication of desires that have as their fundamental aim the overcoming of this deep sense of self-lacking. Every finite gain, however, provides only a momentary satisfaction, leaving our sense of want to return again and again. In the teaching of Advaita, the only enduring solution to this existential problem is the overcoming of ignorance by transformative knowledge *(jñāna)* of the truth of the self. Ignorance does not change the fundamental nature of the self, even as clouds in the sky do not alter the nature of the sun.

---

7   S. Vivekananda (1893) *Address at the Final Session of the Parliament of Religions*, Chicago, September 27. In S. Nikhilananda (1953) *Vivekananda: The Yogas and Other Works*. New York: Ramakrishna-Vivekananda Center of New York. Copyright 1953 by Swami Nikhilananda, Trustee of the Estate of Swami Vivekananda. Used by permission of the Ramakrishna-Vivekananda Center of New York. See also: www.ramakrishna.org/chcgfull.htm, accessed on July 20, 2018.

The implication of the Advaita understanding of the human problem is a deep optimism about human nature. There is indeed a major predicament, but this is never articulated as an intrinsic flaw or defect in human nature. It is contrary and contradictory to the most fundamental teachings of the Advaita tradition to denigrate, demean, or condemn human beings in the name of caregiving. Swami Vivekananda, in one of his addresses at the Parliament of World Religions, refused to use the word "sinner."[8] "It is a sin to call a man so; it is standing libel on human nature," said Vivekananda. Advaita caregiving is always done with a vision of the highest truth of the human being and with optimism.

The tradition affirms that ignorance can be removed by caregiving that takes the form of right teaching, with the consequence that one owns oneself as a full being, free from the anxiety of incompleteness. The caregiver as teacher, knowing the truth of the human being, offers care with the long-term aim of removing ignorance, but does so with patience and compassion. Teaching is offered in response to a request and this particular teaching speaks meaningfully to a person who has carefully examined life's experiences and understands the limits of the finite. Though rooted in a specific theology, the Advaita teacher is aware that teaching cannot be forced and ought never to be offered in ways that are arrogant, militant, and without appreciation for the particular needs of the receiver. Good teaching and caregiving is individually oriented and always dialogical.[9]

Caregiving that excludes arrogance, militancy and which is oriented to the individual requires a deep humility on the part of the caregiver. I would suggest, also, that such caregiving must be offered with detachment. The detachment that I regard as fundamental to good caregiving is described repeatedly in the Bhagavad-Gita as the renunciation of the fruit of actions (karma *phala tyāgaṁ*).[10] It does not signify the offering of care without compassion or with an attitude of indifference to the outcome. It calls for the offering of care with the understanding,

---

8   S. Vivekananda (1983) *Paper on Hinduism*, read at the Parliament on September 19. In S. Nikhalananda (1953) *Vivekananda: The Yogas and Other Works*. New York: Ramakrishna-Vivekananda Center of New York. Copyright 1953 by Swami Nikhilananda, Trustee of the Estate of Swami Vivekananda. Used by permission of the Ramakrishna-Vivekananda Center of New York. See also: www.ramakrishnavivekananda.info/vivekananda/volume_1/addresses_at_the_parliament/v1_c1_paper_on_hinduism.htm, accessed on April 25, 2019.

9   I have discussed Advaita methods of teaching in *The Advaita Worldview: God, World and Humanity* (Albany: State University of New York Press, 2006).

10 See, for example, Bhagavad-Gita 18:2.

according to Bhagavad-Gita 2:47, that the outcome of one's efforts can never be guaranteed. According to the Advaita teacher, Swami Dayananda Saraswati (1930–2015), it is important that we accept our limits as human beings.

> What the result will be depends on so many unknown factors that it is always a question mark. Whether what you want from a particular karma will happen as you expected is anyone's guess. Since you do not have a complete choice over the results of action, you had better recognize this limitation. Limitation here is not helplessness. Helplessness is felt only when you do not accept the limitation and, therefore, it has a negative connotation, whereas acknowledging the limitation is being objective.[11]

Realism about outcomes is a very important disposition for caregivers. Acknowledging the absence of control over results is an anxiety-relieving approach that prepares the caregiver for coping with uncertainty and unanticipated outcomes. It helps the caregiver direct her energies where it really matters, namely on the means. It shifts energies from the future to the present. Detachment from the results of action is an empowering teaching that liberates the caregiver from the fear of failure that is so often a deterrent to engaging in action. Detachment from results is also conducive to clear-mindedness. On the whole, detachment promotes mental and emotional balance and contributes to the overall wellbeing of the caregiver that is vital to the work of offering care. Care that is healing and wholesome requires a caregiver who is emotionally and mentally healthy and balanced. Detachment from the results of action promotes such health while also respecting the freedom of the person in one's care.

One of the finest examples of such caregiving is the approach of Krishna in the Bhagavad-Gita. Arjuna sought his spiritual guidance on the battlefield and, with great patience, Krishna responded to every question of Arjuna, even when a question seemed repetitive. It is also clear what is Krishna's own preference for Arjuna. However, at the conclusion of the text (18:63), he leaves the choice and the outcome in Arjuna's hands: "Thus the knowledge that is more secret than all that is secret has been taught to you by me. After fully reflecting on this, do as you wish." In this single verse, Krishna embodies reverence, detachment, and respect for freedom, fundamental virtues to good spiritual caregiving.

---

11 Swami Dayananda Saraswati (2011) *Bhagavadgita*, 9 volumes. Chennai: Arsha Vidya Research and Publication Trust, Vol. 2, p.247. Included here with the written permission of Arsha Vidya Research and Publication Trust.

A Theology of Spiritual Care from a Bhakti Tradition

Shaunaka Rishi Das

In Ireland, when asking directions, I have often been graced with the helpful observation, "Well, I wouldn't start from here." In attempting to discern a theology of spiritual care for Bhakti traditions I hear voices echo the same advice. Where to begin, and how to represent the diversity of practice and interpretation inherent in these traditions? I propose therefore to focus on the tradition of my practice, the Gaudiya Vaishnava tradition, and work from there, hoping not to misrepresent the depth of even this small sample. I have organized this chapter in two parts: the first defining terms and proposing a context; and the second presenting values which could be helpful for the practice of Vaishnava care.

Part one gives us our *darshana*, our way of seeing the subject. *Darshana* is a Sanskrit word often translated to mean philosophy, but more appropriately it means "to see." We are interested here to understand how the Vaishnava sees God, sees those they care for, and how they see themselves. Part two offers six principles from the Bhagavad-Gita, which might serve as meditations on caring behavior. They may also more generally form a basis for developing an Applied Theology of Hindu Care, as they are not specific to Vaishnavas.

Krishna Bhakti and Care

Care is at the heart of Bhakti—and of Vaishnava theology. Bhakti means to share, an activity which involves at least two people, and hints at a mood of service from one to the other. The ideas of personal relationship and service offered with love are the very foundations of

Vaishnava understanding. The Bhagavat Purana, a book sacred to Gaudiya Vaishnavas (who more often refer to it as the *Srimad Bhagavatam*), offers a definition of the ultimate *dharma*. Although sometimes translated as religion, law, or duty, the term *dharma* appears to be more subtle than these translations might suggest. One *sloka* (verse) goes as follows:

> The supreme occupation [*dharma*] for all humanity is that by which one can attain to loving devotional service unto the transcendent Lord. Such devotional service must be unmotivated and uninterrupted to completely satisfy the self. (BP. 1.2.6)[1]

Aside from defining the supreme *dharma* this *sloka* clarifies the object of our service—the Supreme Lord, and the nature of that service as being without expectation of reward, and constant. It thus defines the nature of love, and specifically the love shared between the individual and the supreme individual. And such a love, the verse offers, completely satisfies our desires, ambitions, and our need to love and be loved.

Our understanding of the Supreme is individual. A popular Hindu understanding is that the Supreme is one, although manifest in many different ways—hence the number of Avatars (manifestations of the Supreme)—and that each person must choose their *Ishtadeva*, the form of the Supreme that appeals to their heart. This is good as far as it goes but we can also include the possibility that the Supreme also has a choice. It is a relationship after all.

The specific object of love for Gaudiya Vaishnavas is Krishna, evidenced as follows, again from the *Srimad Bhagavatam*: "All of the above-mentioned incarnations are parts of the Lord, but Lord Sri Krishna is the original Personality of Godhead" (BP. 1.3.28).[2] Here is meant not just any form of Krishna, but specifically Krishna as found in Vrindavan. This is significant for our deliberation, as Krishna in Vrindavan is surrounded by love and concern. The stories of Krishna are full of his feelings of compassion, care, and love, even for those who try to hurt him.

Bhakti is about love for the Supreme, never for another. It seems exclusive in this regard. We don't share Bhakti between ourselves but with Krishna—and Krishna is a beautiful, funny, and extraordinary child

---

1 *sa vai pumsam paro dharmo | yato bhaktir adhok dhar | ahaituky apratihata | yayatma suprasidati.* In this chapter, all passages from the Bhagavata Purana are according to A.C. Bhaktivedanta Swami Prabhupada (trans.) *Srimad Bhagavatam* (The Bhaktivedanta Book Trust International, 1987). Texts courtesy of The Bhaktivedanta Book Trust International, Inc. www.Krishna.com. Used with permission.

2 *ete camsa-kalah pumsah | krsnas tu bhagavan svayam.*

who is full of love for us, and whom one day we may kiss. In the *Srimad Bhagavatam*, Gopis (milkmaids) discuss the love shared between Krishna and the inhabitants of Vrindavan—including the cows.

> Another Gopi said to her friends, "My dear friends, the cows are also charmed as soon as they hear the transcendental sound of the flute of Krishna. It sounds to them like the pouring of nectar, and they immediately spread their long ears just to catch the liquid nectar of the flute. As for the calves, they are seen with the nipples of their mothers pressed in their mouths, but they cannot suck the milk. They remain struck with devotion, and tears glide down from their eyes, illustrating vividly how they are embracing krishna heart to heart."[3]

Thus, we see that love of Krishna is not dependent on *dharma*, philosophy, and culture as we know it, certainly not as cows know it. It is not even dependent on knowing that Krishna is the Supreme. It is more personal. The cows love Krishna simply because they love Krishna.

Having some experience of our loving relationship with the Supreme how do we then treat all the other living beings we bump into? In the late nineteenth century Bhaktivinod Thakur, a noted Vaishnava scholar, addressed this as follows:

> The tenderness of the heart experienced towards Krishna is known as Bhakti. All other jivas (living beings) are servants of Krishna. When one experiences tenderness of heart towards them, it is known as daya, compassion. Therefore, compassion is included within Bhakti.[4]

Compassion is included. It is not the goal, but a symptom of one who is infused with Bhakti. The goal of the devotee *sādhu* (a devoted or holy person) is the love of the one who can love us unreservedly, who is behind everything and connected to everything. This goal includes the love of everything connected to that one, to Krishna—which is everything. It then becomes very personal—with everyone. Of primary concern is not others' family background, their religion, their politics, or which type of body they inhabit. Of primary concern is the recognition that others are connected with Krishna eternally, and that all living beings share a

---

3   A.C. Bhaktivedanta Swami (1970) *The Krishna Book*. Alachua, FL: Bhaktivedanta Book Trust, Chapter 21. Text courtesy of The Bhaktivedanta Book Trust International, Inc. www.Krishna.com. Used with permission.

4   B. Thakur (1998) *Jaiva Dharma*, part one. Mathura, India: Gaudiya Vedanta Publications, p.179.

profound need to love and be loved. This is also the focus of the Vaishnava chaplain, who offers help regardless of distinction.

The *sādhu* who lives this type of spiritual life is later defined in the *Srimad Bhagavatam* as follows: "The symptoms of a *sādhu* are that he is tolerant, compassionate, and friendly to all living entities. He has no enemies, he is peaceful, he abides by the scriptures, and all his characteristics are sublime" (BP. 3.25.21).[5] The qualities of tolerance and compassion are the basis of a Vaishnava theology of care, first as they are experienced by the devotee in relationship with Krishna, and then as they are shared with others.

This is certainly not a tick-box exercise, where we happily claim that some of our best friends are of another ethnicity, of another religion, disabled, or gay, or where we are legally compelled to be nice to people. Rather, the deep concern for others comes as a realization of the deep concern Krishna has for all. Affection will be shown because one has experienced that it is the only remedy for the heavy heart. Sacrifice of time, energy, and resources will be made because those things are so much less valuable than the care of a person. The vocation of care, temporal and spiritual, will be a natural expression of the heart when the heart has an experience of the soft touch of Krishna's kindness; and the vocation is to share that kindness with others.

An Applied Theology of Vaishnava Care

There are a number of principles, values, and virtues discernible in scripture which can be explored and applied to a theology of care in the Vaishnava traditions. Discernment and interpretation is always individual. What serves as a good value to apply in one context may not serve in another, and what once served us as a foundational understanding may transform as we develop our understanding, and our relationship with the Supreme. Ultimately, we have to choose the values that serve us as principles, the values behind the values, which mean most to us, and then follow them. Otherwise we cannot even respect ourselves. Let us give detailed consideration to six principles discernible in the Bhagavad-Gita.

---

5   titiksavah karunikah | suhrdah sarva-dehinam | ajata-satravah santah | sadhavah sadhu-bhusanah.

1. Sama Darshana *(Equal Vision)*

In the Gita, equal vision means seeing the equality of all living beings and respecting all life regardless of race, gender, caste, creed, or species. The energy we call life is not considered temporary or material but eternal and spiritual. Krishna says that the wise see a saint, a laborer, a dog, and an elephant with equal vision, and—while acknowledging their material differences—see in them a spiritual equality. This vision awards personhood to all, links everyone with Krishna, and consequently with each other. Therefore, civilization would ultimately be defined by its regard for all life, not just human life, for the dignity of all life, not just human dignity. This is considered basic Vedanta vision.[6]

Whereas the Gita speaks of spiritual equality, in the material circumstance in which we live it proposes equity. The Gita, as with all Hindu texts, recognizes that materially there is no equality. Our bodies and their mental and intellectual gifts are different, some more excellent than others. Therefore, respect for all life should form the fundamental basis of our relationships, social, political, legal, environmental, and religious. Treating others equitably is thus both respectful and practical.

In caring terms, this way of seeing gives us the spiritual basis for seeing all whom we meet, all for whom we should care with an equal vision, regardless of their identity in this world. This is put very well in an assertion attributed both to Pierre Teilhard de Chardin S.J. and C.I. Gurdieff: "We are not human beings having a spiritual experience. We are spiritual beings having a human experience." The human experience can be a terrible experience for some, thus the need for concern, compassion, and care. For a Vaishnava, the notion of respecting the spiritual core of all, and the idea that we are equally servants of the Supreme, allows for care of all—serving equitably. This vision serves as a rational basis of Bhakti, and for Vaishnava chaplaincy.

2. Iccha *(Choice)*

Choice is a natural conclusion of understanding the freedom of being eternal by nature. The Gita begins with Arjuna choosing to seek guidance from Krishna. It concludes with Krishna recognizing that after he has offered his opinion Arjuna will do as Arjuna desires. Krishna has spoken to Arjuna openly, truthfully, and with affection. He has not been demanding

---

6   See Bhagavad-Gita 5.18.

or dogmatic. By leaving the choice to Arjuna, Krishna has acknowledged this freedom. Thus, Arjuna can freely choose his relationships, his service, and his responsibilities. The Gita establishes that choice is a basis of respect and love.[7]

In the first instance the Gita exemplifies that, whether in family dealings, in politics, in business, or in spiritual life, forcing others, manipulating their behavior, or obscuring their freedom to choose is unhelpful to all parties. These approaches are touched by cruelty, and do not belong to one who cares.

Vaishnavas also cherish choice for its positive personal implication. In the first text of teaching in the Gita, a text offering the basis of *sama darshana*, Krishna reminds Arjuna of his eternal freedom to choose: "Never was there a time when I did not exist, nor you, nor all these kings; nor in the future shall any of us cease to be."[8] In Vaishnava understanding, this text says that Krishna, Arjuna, and all the people on the battlefield are eternal, without beginning or end. Krishna is saying that he did not create Arjuna. He certainly provided the ingredients to create Arjuna's body, his mind, and intellect but not the more substantial person, the eternal living person. This grants Arjuna absolute freedom to choose. He is not bound by having to worship his creator. At the Gita's end Krishna asks Arjuna to deliberate on what Krishna has said and do as he desires—as he chooses. Without such freedom Arjuna could not truly choose—to love, as it turns out.

With Krishna extending himself so generously, how can his devotee fail to extend the same grace to others? Others choose what may seem to us to be strange identities as they journey through this world, sometimes very strange indeed, we may conclude. But every identity, save that eternal proposition of being Krishna's servant, is just a passing phase in Vaishnava understanding. We may take these identities seriously for some time, fighting for our nationalism, our religious ideals, our notions of *me* and *mine*, or our gender, but a Vaishnava will not allow these identities to be barriers to relationship, or will be motivated to find a solution where kindness can be found or offered. The Vaishnava carer, counsellor, guru, and chaplain consciously choose their path, and recognize that others will choose their paths. All of this is acknowledged by Krishna, and his devotee.

---

[7] See Bhagavad-Gita 18.63.
[8] See Bhagavad-Gita 2.12: *na tv evaham jatu nasam | na tvam neme janadhipah | na caiva na bhavisyamah | sarve vayam atah param.*

3. Ahimsa *(Without Harm)*

Ahimsa becomes an obvious lifestyle when considering *sama darsana* and *iccha*. It is the beginning of putting such a worldview into practice. *Ahimsa* means to act in a way that causes the least harm. In the Mahabharata, Krishna says that all *dharma*, all good acts, will depend on this principle. The context of the Gita, a battlefield, helps us appreciate that *ahimsa* does not equal pacifism. Nevertheless, a life of *ahimsa* does include avoiding violence, employing cruel words, distressing or confusing others, withholding knowledge or insight, or being neglectful of ourselves. In the Gita Krishna asks us to consider *loka-sangraha* (the welfare of the world) and *sarva-bhuta-hita* (the welfare of all beings).[9]

We have spoken of the Supreme *dharma*. Here we speak of the multitude of other *dharmas* which are not necessarily dependent on a theistic understanding. *Dharma*, in this sense, includes our sense of what is good and what is the common good. In this context *ahimsa* is a value that informs all our behavior and all our relationships, and which defines our character and integrity.

For a Vaishnava, *ahimsa* has another aspect, which is theistic. The Vaishnava will not take another life, not only for the *dharmic* reason—that it is cruel—but also because it displeases Krishna. From another perspective, as we pray for mercy and kindness, yet do not extend that to others, we betray hypocrisy and a lack of compassion.

In terms of a vocation of care, minimizing harm begins with the carer. Taking care of oneself, leading a balanced life, avoiding harmful influences and embracing healthy ones help us respect ourselves. Not only does this lead to a life minimizing our negative influence on the world but it nurtures thoughtful and positive interactions. *Ahimsa* vision is the beginning of a caring culture. We become more attentive to others per se, to their physical, emotional, and spiritual wellbeing. We also become awake to symptoms of self-harm, substance abuse, and mental illness in others. Rather than being a value of weakness it takes incredible self-confidence to take the focus off our needs to care for the needs of others. *Ahimsa* is a sign of courage and strength, the qualities a carer needs to act in the world with tolerance and compassion.

---

9   See Bhagavad-Gita 6.21, 12.15, 13.8, 16.1-2.

4. Acharya *(Teaching by Example)*

The word *acharya*, from the Sanskrit *char* (to act), means one who leads and teaches by example. The *acharya*, by behavior, shows what should be done, what can be done, and how it could be done. The *acharya* sets standards by practical action. Teaching by example is the essence of education. Leading by example is the essence of government. Exemplifying one's principles is the basis of respect, dignity, and trust.[10]

The psychologist Alfred Adler is quoted as saying, "It is always easier to fight for one's principles than to live up to them."[11] Attributed to Groucho Marx is a rather cynical quip, "I've got principles, and if you don't like them, I've got other ones." Neither position, although insightful and jolly, is encouraging. To see someone honestly try to practice their principles is encouraging. We tend to judge others by their lack of cruelty, their kindness, and their thoughtful behavior. We judge ourselves by the same measure and all parties are often found lacking. Yet every honest endeavor to follow our values takes us one step forward and itself serves as a good example. To try to act according to our own values shows that we respect ourselves and others and shows that we can be trusted. A teacher, leader, carer, all at times attributes of the work of a chaplain, must be trusted to be able to do their service. This is not an optional extra, but central to a good relationship—and caring is about relationship (in case I did not mention that enough).

To be an *acharya*, aside from being a value we aspire to, is also a quality of our person. It is not inherited or awarded. It manifests through our thoughts, words, and deeds. The old story which exemplifies this has been attributed to a number of *sādhus*, including one on the political spectrum, Gandhi. It goes:

> A mother once took her child to the *sādhu* and asked him to tell her son to stop eating so much sugar. The *sādhu* asked the mother to return in three days. She returned and the *sādhu* did as he was asked. The mother wanted to know why she had to return in three days and the *sādhu* replied that he needed time to stop eating sugar himself before he could admonish the child.

---

10   See Bhagavad-Gita 3.21.
11   P.Bottome (1939) *Alfred Adler: Apostle of Freedom*. London: Faber and Faber, Chapter 5.

5. Amanitva *(Humility)*

If being one who teaches by example inspires trust, nothing does it more than humility. Humility in the Gita is a virtue that is seen in behavior but that rests on understanding. Humility means not being anxious to be honored. Humility helped Arjuna understand himself and what to do in the greater scheme of things. Humility is not weakness. It nurtured Arjuna's self-esteem, self-confidence, and courage. It allowed him to know, love, and serve God. Humility perfumes our communication, is the jewel of the broad-minded, and is the key to a spiritual life. It is the most attractive quality we can possess.[12]

Humility is to know our place in the scheme of things. At times we need to be independent, dependent, and interdependent, and humility is the power of discernment which helps us act in our best interest. In our relationships it helps us listen, cooperate, create connections, reach agreement, stand firm, and achieve balance. For a Vaishnava it is the most precious of all values. The *Shikshastakam* of Sri Chaitanya speaks of being as humble as a blade of grass being trodden underfoot. It always bounces back, never taking offence, and is uncomplaining. Humility is not about thinking less of ourselves; but rather, thinking about ourselves less.

The Gita begins and ends with humility. Arjuna is humble enough to ask for help, and Krishna displays humility by reminding Arjuna of his choice. This is an excellent example of the relationship between a chaplain and one who seeks their help. The courage and humility it takes to ask for help must be matched by the humility of one qualified to offer help. I say courage because humility does not imply a passive, docile, or relaxed attitude. Arjuna, having made his choice, fought valiantly in the battle. We will all be called to stand up on occasion, to advocate for *ahimsa*, to suggest other choices, to consider the dignity of all living beings. The honesty necessary for humility to rise in our minds and hearts also requires much strength, a strength we gain by the very act of self-examination.

6. Priti *(Affection)*

Humility will open the door to the last of these values. In the Gita, Arjuna listens to Krishna's advice and makes his choice because of his love for Krishna. Equally Krishna has shared his knowledge with Arjuna

---
12 See Bhagavad-Gita 11.55, 13.8, 16.3.

because of his love for him. The Gita draws attention to the importance of nurturing affection in all that we say or do—of being kind. Our ability to care is enriched when graced with a concern born of affection; it is made excellent by our ability to offer and receive affection. Our affection for Krishna and others should be apparent by the kindness of our dealings—as the nature of a rose is apparent by its scent.[13]

In this value caring is not dependent on philosophy, nor a mission statement, nor the prospect of gratitude, wealth, position, fame, or power. All of the values we have mentioned are influenced by our ability to share affection with others, and with ourselves. *Priti* is the oil that makes both managing our self and managing others possible. We can't be kind to others if we can't be kind to ourselves. We can't share love with others if we don't first love ourselves. If we understand our own value—that we are loved by Krishna—we gain greatly in confidence and self-esteem. We can also appreciate that others are equally loved by Krishna and thus are lovable.

Our confidence in Krishna's love encourages our compassion for anyone suffering in this world. A Vaishnava is distressed to see others distressed. We all share the advantages and disadvantages of this world; but they all become different degrees of suffering without kindness, affection, and love. A Vaishnava endeavors to share even the modicum of love they possess to relieve the distress of others. This is the motivation of the Vaishnava chaplain.

Affection infuses all the other values with excellence and our work with kindness. It helps us forgive, to be more caring, inclusive, and peaceful. It nurtures in us a culture of benevolence, well-wishing of others, and of greater social concern. Our ability to be compassionate and tolerant is nourished by our ability to share affection. For the Vaishnava chaplain to care for others is an expression of affection born of love for Krishna and is always offered with kindness.

A Lack of Conclusion

I don't think there is really a conclusion to a theology of care for the Vaishnava traditions, as Krishna's love and care is dynamic, ever expanding, and filled with increasing joy. In attempting to discern a theology of care for a Bhakti tradition I hope this small effort can act as

---

13 See Bhagavad-Gita 4.12, 6.32, 12.13, 16.1.

an inspiration to think more broadly and more deeply about the vocation of care. Deliberate on it as we will, we can truly appreciate the kindness of a Vaishnava when we experience it—heart to heart.

Body, Mind, and Breath

Yoga as a Framework for Integrative Spiritual Care

Christopher Key Chapple

The practice of yoga provides a way of spirituality for millions of people worldwide. With the globalization of cultures, yoga has emerged as a readily adaptable technique that provides solace and a sense of purpose. Its various techniques integrate body, breath, and mind. Defined as "the stilling of the fluctuations of the mind," the experience of yoga offers respite from both the tedium and the frenzy of modern life.

Yoga as a tradition developed over the course of many centuries in India, spreading with Buddhism throughout all parts of Asia and, since the nineteenth century, to Europe and the Americas. The term yoga means "to yoke." In the Rig Veda (ca. 1500BCE) yoga referred to the process of connecting horses to a chariot. Eventually this physical action became a metaphor designating the yoking of the body and senses to a controlled mind. This metaphor finds iconic representation in the image of Krishna counseling the confused warrior Arjuna. Both stand in the middle of battle on Arjuna's chariot, with Arjuna holding the reins of five horses that represent the senses and organs. By controlling his intention through the advice of Krishna, Arjuna manages to find stability in the midst of chaos. A yoga class holds a similar promise: by engaging in yoga, the practitioner retreats from the world into a place of higher wisdom. Yoga allows one to take control of the reins that govern one's life.

The Upanishads, Buddhism's Pali canon, and the earliest texts of Jainism—all hailing from the second half of the first millennium before the common era—articulate aspects of yoga recognizable today. The Katha Upanishad speaks of control of mind, as do Buddha's teachings and the ethics of Jainism. By the middle of the first millennium of the common era, a non-denominational yoga was articulated by Patañjali, codified in 196 terse statements known as the Yoga Sutras. Using language and practices common to all three traditions, Patañjali organizes yoga into four aspects, dedicating a chapter to each: Contemplation/Meditation (*Samādhi*), Practice (*Sādhana*), Powers (*Vibhuti*), and Freedom (*Kaivalyam*). In the first section, one comes to understand the mind and learn various techniques to focus and purify one's mental and emotional landscape. The second section describes how karma operates and lays out eight primary steps for undertaking yoga: ethics, observances, posture, breath control, inwardness, concentration, meditation, and the state of being absorbed (*samādhi*). The third section describes various benefits and powers of yoga. These include understanding the link between intention and action. The text states that with regular yoga practice one can become virtuous, empathetic, beautiful, and discerning. The fourth chapter reiterates the role of each person in shaping her or his own reality and encourages the yogi to ascend to a state of abiding freedom.

Patañjali designed his text to be understandable to all without being tied to one particular theological view. By invoking an eightfold path and the idea of entering a cloud of virtue, this yoga appealed to Buddhists. By requiring adherence to a strict fivefold code of non-violence, truthfulness, not stealing, sexual propriety, and non-possession it spoke directly to the Jains. By introducing the practice of choosing one's own favorite deity as a focal inspiration, it echoed Hindu multivalence. By grounding these insights and practices within the landscape of human psychology, yoga came to develop a universal appeal.

By the end of the first millennium, yoga philosophy came to be augmented with a new yoga physiology. The Yoga Sutras hint at and name the energy centers in the body (*cakras*) that become well known in the texts of Tantra. The *Yoga Shastra of Hemacandra*, a Jain manual of the twelfth century, describes non-seated yoga poses (*āsana*) and many variations of breath control (*prāṇāyāma*). The *Dattatreya Yoga Shastra* (circa thirteenth century) elaborates on these practices in greater detail and by the middle of the second millennium, 84 standard yoga postures had been identified and illustrated, as well as dozens of breathing techniques. Yoga and yogis became associated with the acquisition of power and most of the hundreds of kings and queens of medieval India would employ yogis to enhance their personal and political power, a practice that continues into the modern era. Mahatma Gandhi took yoga lessons from Swami Kuvalyananda and Paramahamsa Yogananda. Prime Ministers Indira Gandhi and Narendra Modi have very publicly embraced yoga personalities and practices.

Swami Vivekananda famously brought yoga to Chicago's Parliament of the World's Religions in 1893. Paramahamsa Yogananda built an enduring worldwide yoga organization in Southern California, working tirelessly from 1920 until his passing in 1953. With the change of US immigration laws in 1965, influenced by the Civil Rights Movement, it became possible for a new wave of yoga to spread throughout the US as teachers from other lineages established themselves in America. Whereas the work of early two-thirds of the twentieth century promulgated a religiously themed yoga practice, in the last third of the century the new teachers also emphasized the more physical aspects of yoga, specifically *āsana* and *prāṇāyāma*. Yoga shifted from church-like temples to the newly invented yoga studio, a more neutral space that generally eschews identifiably religious trappings. Transcendental meditation and its use of a personal mantra similarly emphasizes physiological and emotional benefits rather than couching its practice in religious categories. Simultaneously, Americans who had studied Buddhist meditation in Southeast Asia began to develop retreat centers that introduce a secular form of meditation sheared from its religious denotations. Increasingly, the two movements of yoga and meditation share commonality and many individuals participate in cross-training between the two.

Yoga Chaplaincy

A chaplain faces many situations that require an open ear, an open heart, and an open mind. Hospital chaplains must deal with persons who are ill, perhaps terminally ill. Chaplains in the armed forces must deal with the large issues of life such as war and peace as well as deal with trauma inflicted by the challenges of gender as well as experiences of fighting and maiming and seeing death and facing one's own death as well as survivor's guilt. Increasingly, educators also serve as chaplains and social workers, taking on the responsibility of the wellbeing of their students at all levels, from pre-school through professional and even doctoral studies.

Death and dying, harassment and killing, stress and doubts about self-worth all confront a chaplain. How might yoga be useful in each of these situations? How might the yoga teacher be an adequate resource?

How also might a yoga teacher manage sufficient self-care to not buckle under the responsibility of tending to vulnerable human souls?

Death and Dying

Yoga traditions offer several instructive narratives in regard to death and dying. The Buddha, who as Prince Siddhartha was sheltered from the realities of old age, illness, and death, was catapulted onto the spiritual path when he directly encountered these three grim inevitabilities. On his deathbed he urged his grieving disciples to maintain their composure. He reminded them that all things are made of parts, even the human person, and eventually those parts fall apart. This wisdom continues to inspire thoughtful persons to seek understanding and acceptance regarding the final days of life.

The Jain tradition developed an art of embracing death that requires many decades of preparation. Jains generally fast at least twice a month and attempt a much longer fast of seven days each fall. This allows them to minimize the harm committed to life during those days of sacred suspension of the alimentary process. Eventually, as they reach the last third of their expected lifespan, many Jains become increasingly attentive to their vegetarian diet, eliminating foods such as green beans that harbor many seeds that could potentially sprout into new life. When illness sets in and one is no longer able to attend to one's basic needs, the community supports the gradual withdrawal of nutrition and liquids over a 40-day period, easing the soul to separate from the body with acceptance and calm. This process, known as *sallekhana* or *santara*, stands in stark contrast to the over-medicalized approach to death that has come to suffuse allopathic practice. During the course of the Jain final fast, one is reminded of the eternality of the soul through the chanting of mantras and regular supportive visits from members of one's family and the religious community.

In the Bhagavad-Gita, Arjuna laments that it would be better to die than to kill his relatives. Krishna reminds Arjuna repeatedly that neither Arjuna nor his relatives can ever be killed. He states that the soul is eternal. At the point of death this body takes on another body just as a person changes clothes. "Winds cannot dry it, rains cannot wet it, weapons cannot slay it." He further counsels Arjuna that all occurrences have a beginning, a middle, and an end. Why lament over the inevitable?

Krishna teaches that through the Yoga of Knowledge one gains serenity and acceptance and freedom.

Harassment, Rape, and Killing

Gender comes into high relief in military situations. Historically, highly masculinized young men were pressed into military service by government authorities, required to defend the honor of nation or ideology out of a sense of patriotic duty. In some instances, mercenary soldiers made fighting their profession. At times of war men often assault women through organized campaigns of rape. Assertion of power through force yields violence of all sorts and leaves many casualties. Women entering military service often find themselves vulnerable at the hands of their fellow soldiers. The aggression associated with war causes many forms and intensities of trauma resulting from harassment, rape, and killing.

How might yoga help unravel the difficulties that arise from these horrific circumstances? First, many victims of trauma dissociate from their bodies. It is very common for victims of rape to imagine themselves as out of the body and visualize what is happening as if from above. Such dissociation can result in profound feelings of disconnect and mistrust. To restore a connection with the body through the breath and simple movement can effect profound healing, though trauma specialists advise moving carefully in choice of language and yoga posture and breathing sequences to avoid triggering painful memories.

The Buddha told many stories of women who, having killed their would-be rapists and bandits, repented for their violence they committed. These despairing persons sought and found forgiveness in the Buddhist community, practicing the Buddhist vows and meditation to expiate for their deeds. Many a yoga teacher has created safe space that allows an exploration and recovery of the body, with emotional releases that might include uncontrollable weeping or shaking. An insightful yoga teacher will also advise counseling, just as many psychotherapists recommend the practice of yoga and meditation.

Survivors of war often have a very difficult time reintegrating into society. A large percentage of the homeless population, men and women, completed several years of military service. After World War One, such persons were deemed shell-shocked: unable to re-enter civilian life effectively, often living out their years in a sanitarium. Such persons are now diagnosed with post-traumatic stress disorder (PTSD). Many veterans now receive wrap-around services that include supportive housing and instruction in yoga and meditation. The psychological substratum of yoga recognizes that actions of the past leave residues known as *saṃskāras* that condition one's experience of the present and the future. Many of these residues take root in the body, which can become tight and contorted, and in the breath, which can become irregular and shallow. Yoga practices work at healing and releasing body and breath, which in turn improves mental outlook and emotional state.

Stress and Self-Doubt

With the rise of concern about sexual identity, social status, and economic uncertainties, the level of stress has risen throughout the globe. Many people, when they compare themselves to others on social media at the micro-level or mass media on the macro-level, feel inferior, thinking others to be more powerful, more good looking, more wealthy, and more worthy. This comparing-mind syndrome can lead to states of depression, frustration, and anger toward oneself and others. Many of the mass shootings of recent decades were committed by radically estranged individuals whose loneliness turned to hatred. Loneliness and alienation are widespread in modern industrialized cultures. In simpler times, families operated in three spheres: home, work/school, and church. This created a three-fold personal and societal safety net. Now, many homes are not safe or supportive. Work and school have been driven by quantitative outcomes with less concern for the wellbeing of an individual. The rapid decline in church attendance and in community organizations has removed an important source of meaning-making. Today, teachers often play the role of substitute parent, social worker, and pastor.

Educators see the benefits of in-class yoga and meditation practices at the level of primary and secondary school. Universities increasingly offer yoga and meditation both as a curricular and extracurricular offering. Yoga and meditation teach check-in skills, tools that can promote connectivity with the body and breath and a calming of the mind. This experience can help ameliorate some of the most damaging effects of feeling less than worthy. Similarly, yoga and meditation have become mainstays at rehabilitation centers that treat addictions.

Yoga Therapy and Chaplaincy

Studies have demonstrated the benefits of yoga for a wide range of troubled populations. Loyola Marymount University (LMU) has trained yoga therapists and yoga teachers who have delivered yoga instruction to diverse populations, often serving as de facto chaplains and life guides.

Recognizing the need for greater knowledge about yoga among the growing numbers of yoga teachers who received 200 hours of teacher training instruction within the framework established by Yoga Alliance, LMU instituted an 120-hour training in Yoga Philosophy in 2002. This training includes 20 hours of Sanskrit language, 20 hours on the Yoga *Sūtra*, ten hours on the *Sāṃkhya Kārikā*, ten hours on the Bhagavad-Gita, ten hours on the Upanishads, and five elective ten-hour courses, including offerings on other yoga texts such as the *Haṭha Yoga Pradipika*, as well as aspects of Buddhism and Jainism. Just as lay Christian pastors often immerse themselves in the study of the Bible, these yoga teachers receive grounding in the foundational theologies that undergird yoga. Equipped with new vocabulary and insight, many leaders within the yoga community have been able to enrich their class and teacher training offerings with this knowledge base.

In 2004, Larry Payne established what became a four-year sequence for training yoga therapists at LMU in accord with the requirements of the International Association of Yoga Therapists, a regulatory body that emerged at roughly the same time. This sequence, which meets one weekend per month for 11 months over the course of four years for a total of 44 meetings, includes learning about the muscular and skeletal components of the human body, common maladies that can be addressed through the practice of yoga, proper yoga regimens, and supervision as a yoga therapist in training. In conjunction with Venice Family Clinic, the nation's largest provider of medical services to the underserved and disenfranchised—including many homeless people—free six-week sessions are offered to a variety of populations. Remarkable results were seen. One distraught, recently widowed, overweight woman who spoke only Spanish lamented that with her diabetes and high blood pressure she was at risk of dying alone. Within one session that focused primarily on alternate nostril breathing, her blood pressure was brought into normal range, sustained through the follow-up visits.

In 2013, LMU welcomed its first class of candidates for the Master of Arts in Yoga Studies. Combining both the physical practices of yoga with its psychological, spiritual, and philosophical aspects, students took up an array of final projects, many of which fall loosely into the category of chaplaincy. In the spring of 2015, the students in that program and a faculty member took up a six-week residency at Covenant House in New York City, providing daily yoga and meditation sessions for previously homeless youth aged 18–24 along with the staff, the maintenance crew, and volunteers. With support from the Fred Lenz Foundation, sustained outreach to prisons and shelters in Los Angeles was established. Graduates have created yoga training programs at universities and community colleges. They have also opened studios nationwide that teach an integrative approach to yoga.

Yoga and the Intent of Chaplaincy

For yoga to be administered in a spirit of chaplaincy, several aspects can be emphasized. First, the philosophical foundation of yoga rests upon the articulation of an ongoing relationship between two ways of being human. The human person houses a place of silent awareness (*puruṣa*) that remains untouched regardless of circumstance. The realm of activity (*prakṛti*) presents a wide range of experiences to that consciousness along with the opportunity to unravel the ups and downs that obscure awareness. Yoga claims that the key to freedom lies in sorting out these two aspects, one from the other, through the repeated entry into states of absorption (*samādhi*). Defined as a moment where the distinction between subject and object collapses, the ensuing states of bliss serve to recondition prior inclinations, tending toward self-improvement.

A second factor within yoga practice entails the cultivation of ethics. Most teachers of yoga are familiar with the two foundational principles espoused by Mahatma Gandhi: *ahimsa* (non-violence) and *satyagraha* (holding to truth). The first accords well with the universal golden rule: do unto others as you would have done unto you. Because of the adoption of Gandhian principles by Martin Luther King, Jr. and Nelson Mandela, the humanistic aspect of observing non-violence carries a broad appeal. The dietary aspects of non-violence have also become widely accepted and even expected within American and European cultures which have been quick to embrace both vegetarianism and veganism. Truthfulness, when seen within the arc of cultivating authenticity within one's life, can easily be communicated by yoga teachers without seeming overly moralistic. A third aspect of ethics holds great relevance for contemporary life:

non-possession (*aparigraha*). In keeping with the yoga precept of minimizing attachments, yoga teachers can gently remind their students that things do not define a person, including clothes, automobiles, and all the accoutrements that come with the computer-mediated world of social media. By gently inviting yoga students to release their identification with all externals while in the protected space of the yoga class, the teacher also implicitly invites students to shift the focus of their world away from ownership and selfishness toward concern for others and selflessness. A life of service can bring happiness. A life of self-obsession leads to difficulty and disappointment for oneself and others.

Breath supports life. Thoughts and emotions ride on the waves of the breath. Introductory meditation exercises in the Buddhist tradition entail counting the breath: one on the inhale, two on the exhale, up to ten, and then repeating. This rhythmic breathing when practiced for 20 minutes generates a brain wave pattern that brings calm and a sense of abiding in the center. Other breath-related techniques include a body scan, letting the breath relax the various areas of the body progressively, from the toes and fingers to the shins and forearms, the knees and elbows, the thighs and upper arms, the pelvic floor and lower abdomen, the middle abdomen and chest, the throat and jaw, the cheeks and eye sockets, the ears and forehead, up to the scalp. To facilitate full body relaxation and energization, more advanced breath control (*prāṇāyāma*) includes the three contractions of the pelvic floor, chin to neck, and stomach contraction (*tribandha*) and alternate nostril breathing and other techniques. These practices have been proven to lower respiration rate and blood pressure, increasing a body feel of wellbeing.

The Upanishads offer a handy formula for abandonment of ego: recitation of the phase "not this, not that" (*neti, neti*). When the Buddha announced, one by one, the enlightenment of the 500 disciples who reached the Arhant state of freedom, he pronounced that they had seen and experienced and were forever changed by adopting the worldview "I am not the ego, I am not the doer, I own nothing" (*nāham, nāsmi, na me*). The same phrase appears in the *Sāṃkhya Kārikā*, the text paired with Patañjali's *Yoga Sūtras*. Patañjali states that knowledge arises when one surrenders attachment to permanence, impurity, unhappiness, and ego. By moving away from defining oneself in terms of externals one can arrive at a state of inner contentment, reversing realms mired in attachment.

Yoga Āsana can stretch and strengthen the body, releasing pent-up tightness and weakness that results from chronic negativity and feelings of self-loathing. The aim is not to glorify the body for the sake of vanity but to lighten the body of its inertia. B.K.S. Iyengar and Swami Sivananda brought physical yoga techniques to the world stage in the twentieth century, implicitly instructing people in an experience of the body-breath-mind connection now practiced daily by millions daily. As mentioned above, therapists and chaplains work regularly with yoga teachers and encourage their clients to seek out instruction in yoga and meditation. Additionally, many therapists and educators receive dual credentialing that authorizes them to teach these techniques.

Conclusion

Happiness in times of trouble can be elusive. Chaplains face the difficult task of counseling clients about how to find meaning in a seemingly meaningless world. Historically, chaplains brought solace by reminding the bereaved of the truths and comfort offered by their childhood religious instruction. In many cases, this remains sufficient, particularly for persons who have been reared in a particular tradition. In times of crisis, one can suspend disbelief and feel comfort and assurance from a pastoral authority.

The world has become a complex place. Belief systems have shifted. A significant percentage of Christians now believe in reincarnation. Persons of all faiths and no faith can be found in nearly every urban hospital and school and workplace. For a Hindu, words from the Bhagavad-Gita and the chanting of Om can bring solace. For a Buddhist, remembrance of the impermanence of life can serve a similar function, as words about the undying nature of the soul can calm a troubled Jain.

Yoga, practiced by a person of any faith or no faith, works to enhance physical, respiratory, emotional, and psychological wellbeing. Regular practice can help caregivers find a space of safety and stability. Persons who cultivate yoga on a daily basis will be better equipped to recognize symptoms of stress, including shortening of the breath and tightness in the stomach. The tools of yoga allow one to lengthen the breath and to relax the musculature that contracts and contorts one's posture and overall comportment. Yoga teaches an important human skill: the ability to recognize adversity, feel it in one's body and mind and breath, and use the body, thoughts, and the breath itself to move into a space of calm and acceptance.

The Yoga Sūtras of Patañjali in the Context of College Chaplaincy

Vineet Chander

My appointment as Princeton University's Coordinator for Hindu Life—which marked me as the first full-time Hindu chaplain at an American college or university—offered me the opportunity to craft a model of collegiate chaplaincy that is at once grounded in and faithful to my Hindu tradition, open to adopting and adapting insights from outside of Hinduism, and relevant to the needs of those I am charged with caring for. In the years since, I have found that Hinduism's classical yoga tradition provides a useful paradigm for such spiritual caregiving. In this chapter, I demonstrate how the path of *kriyā-yoga*—or, the "yoga of action"—as defined in the opening *sūtra* (aphorism) of the second chapter of the *Yoga Sutras of Patañjali,* offers Hindu chaplains serving in collegiate contexts a theological basis for, and an effective model of, spiritual or pastoral care.

Kriyā-Yoga as a Framework for Pastoral Care

The *Yoga Sutras of Patañjali*, compiled early in the Common Era, is regarded as the seminal text for classical yoga—one of the six schools of orthodox Indian philosophy. It comprises the sage Patañjali's systematization of pre-existing traditions and teachings of meditative practices and techniques ubiquitous in ancient India. In style, each passage is a "terse and pithy philosophical statement in which the maximum amount of information is packed into the minimum number of words." *Sutras* are designed for commitment to memory and evocation of larger, more subtle philosophical concepts—typically unpacked in conversation with a teacher. Indeed, a rich commentarial tradition has grown around the text to facilitate that.[1]

The text's first chapter defines yoga as the quieting of the mind and seems to address those yoga adepts who have already disciplined the mind to be able to remain fixed in practice and dispassion. In the second chapter, to those desirous of spiritual growth but still struggling with distractions and obstacles, Patañjali offers a more action-oriented approach: *kriyā-yoga*—a practicable and accessible method for approaching the goal of self-realization. I suggest that *kriyā-yoga* is effective as a framework for pastoral care for three main reasons. First, the three component practices of *kriyā-yoga* offer one the opportunity to develop *sattva* (clarity) by engaging in behavioral, intellectual, and devotional spheres of activity.[2] The three work together to assure a holistic and balanced approach to spiritual practice. Moreover, these practices provide the aspirant with a structure and categorical scheme, but also leave open the possibility for diverse application and individualization.

Second, *kriyā-yoga* might serve as a sort of short-hand for a multivalent approach to spiritual paths that resonates strongly with contemporary, popular Hinduism—particularly in the diaspora. To be clear, the Yoga *Sūtras* is not a primary sacred text for the average Hindu. Most Hindus are much more likely to study (and hold in high regard) the epic literature and narratives (principally the Ramayana or Mahabharata and the Bhagavata Purana), a handful of the most well known Upanishads, and the Bhagavad-Gita—which, for a variety of reasons, seems to have emerged as a singularly important text for contemporary diasporic Hindus. The *Gita* outlines, in broad strokes, three paths: *karma-yoga* (the path of selfless engagement and duty for duty's sake), *jñāna-yoga* (the path

---

1 E.F. Bryant (2009) *The Yoga Sūtras of Patañjali*. New York: North Point Press, p.xxxiii.
2 *Sattva*—one of three primal states of energy (*guṇas*) in Hindu metaphysics—is difficult to define with one English word. It suggests a state of clarity, wholesomeness, goodness, purity, balance, and even sustainability. The internal competition for dominance among the *guṇas* is key to understanding Hinduism's view of the spiritual practitioner's struggle. When *sattva* predominates, the individual manifests peacefulness, wisdom, detachment, discrimination, or lucidity. When *rajas* (the second *guṇa*) predominates, the practitioner's disposition tends toward attachment or yearning and is expressed as passion, striving, restlessness, or creativity. *Tamas* (the third *guṇa*) is the least conducive to yoga or meditative practice; when it is dominant, the practitioner is disposed toward lethargy, sleepiness, disinterest, delusion, or ignorance. Not surprisingly, then, one of the implicit goals of yoga practice is to enhance *sattva* in one's mind while minimizing *rajas* and *tamas*. In this essay, I suggest that this might be a useful way of articulating the objective of college chaplaincy as well.

of intellectual study, renunciation, and introspection), and *bhakti-yoga* (the path of performing action in devotion to *Īśvara*, or God). The traditional commentators seem to regard the three components of *kriyā-yoga* as evoking these three paths. *Kriyā-yoga* seems to synthesize the three paths as a single, but fluid, integrated practice.[3]

As much as the three components of *kriyā-yoga* echo the framework of the Gita and thus resonate with the paradigm of contemporary Hinduism, they also speak to more universal themes. A third reason, then, to consider this approach as suitable for a Hindu theology of spiritual care is that it strikingly mirrors and complements existing models of pastoral care from outside the Hindu context. Turning to the three components of *kriyā-yoga*, I see *tapas* as enabling ministry to the embodied being at the behavioral level; *svādhyāya* as facilitating a way to offer pastoral care in the intellectual and introspective sphere; and *Īśvara-praṇidhāna* as creating a powerful forum for transformation and connection on the devotional, or transpersonal, level. Let us consider each in detail.

Tapas: *Cultivating Clarity*

As I have noted, the over-arching project of *kriyā-yoga* is to produce clarity and purity of the mind-body complex. This is perhaps most apparent in its first component; *tapas* (self-discipline) represents, perhaps, the most tangible and external aspect of *kriyā-yoga* practice. In one sense, *tapas* is all about regulating and disciplining how the individual engages with the exterior world. When engagement is unregulated, one loses touch with the inner self and seeks short-lived happiness and fulfillment through sensual engagement with external objects. This, however, only reinforces an over-identification with the body which, in turn, ingrains habits of attachment to pleasure and avoidance of discomfort in one's psyche. One is then trapped in a seemingly endless cycle of expectation, frustration, and further alienation from true contentment and clarity. *Tapas*, the commentators suggest, is designed to break this vicious cycle and purify the mind and senses.[4]

Unlike more ascetically oriented approaches to *tapas* in Hindu texts— which tend to understand the concept as *austerity* and generally associate it with practicing severe bodily penance or hardship, undertaking extreme fasts or vows, and other methods of radically championing the will over

---

3   Bryant, pp.172–173.
4   Bryant, pp.170–171.

the body or senses—the approach taken by *Yoga Sūtras* commentators tends to be gentler and more pragmatic, seeking to increase the clarity of the mind without unduly disturbing it. Their emphasis seems to be on cultivating an awareness of the mind's habituated tendency toward prioritizing sensual pleasure, and intentionally disciplining or restraining it by modifying one's behavior. The commentators offer various examples of how a yogi might do this—for instance, by regulating one's diet, one's sexual activity, the quality of what one reads or listens to, or the content and appropriateness of one's speech. A common thread through the examples is intentionality in sacrificing the immediate sensual pleasure for the sake of cultivating a more morally grounded and introspective—that is, *sattvic*—lifestyle. While the particular application tends to vary according to context or individual commentator, they concur, emphatically, that such a lifestyle is non-negotiable: without practicing *tapas,* there is no yoga.[5]

As a Hindu chaplain, this idea of *tapas* as the cultivation of clarity through self-discipline is fundamental to my theology of caring for persons in their wholeness. My theology begins, in one sense, by being grounded in twin assertions: that all living beings are, at core, divinely spiritual beings; and that, as embodied beings, we must also contend with engagement with, and invariable identification with, the material world. How do we negotiate this tension? My theology—informed by texts such as the Yoga Sutras and the Gita, nourished by my teachers and guides, and affirmed by my own experiences and realizations—orients me to believe that our individual and collective misidentification with the body and mind, and our relentless pursuit of happiness in external objects and objectifying relationships, results in alienation, frustration, and ultimately suffering (*duḥkha*).[6] As a spiritual caregiver, I feel called to assuage suffering—be it tangible physical pain, or emotional distress, or the more subtle existential malaise. I believe that to facilitate and encourage *tapas* in others, I must live and model it myself.

I see *tapas* as especially relevant, and badly needed, in the collegiate context. According to Hindu ideals, places of learning are, by definition, meant to be bastions of *sattva*; ironically, in a contemporary context, they are too often cauldrons of *rajas* (passions) and *tamas* (imbalance) instead. I see my role as a chaplain as helping students to articulate their own morality. As a Hindu chaplain I can (and, in some sense, I must)

---

5   Bryant, pp.170–171.
6   See, e.g., Bryant, pp.203–212, 229–236.

draw from my theology of *sattva* in order to suggest how one is to make life's choices.

For me, the concept of *tapas* informs the *why* of spiritual caregiving. Might it also help me to theorize *how* I am to care for the students I am called to serve? Rather than adopting the traditional guru-disciple posture, in which the teacher gives directives and holds the student morally accountable, as a chaplain I use the teaching around *tapas* to return to the question of shared responsibility. I seek to offer students a way to take on questions of meaning, purpose, and identity. To do so, I draw on teachings about enduring life's dualities and aspiring for work based on duty for duty's sake. I appropriately push students to embrace the challenging and daunting project of self-discipline, while I resist the temptation to be prescriptive or judgmental. Rather—and especially since so many college students struggle with self-acceptance and perfectionism—I strive to encourage students to cultivate clarity in their lives while simultaneously providing an environment in which it is safe to err or to fall short. Thus I reinterpret *tapas* to represent a larger process of self-development—including stumbles and apparent failures, especially if they are accompanied by reflection and learning. While I might assist in this process of reflection, I see active and compassionate *listening* to be the most valuable skill I might bring to the exchange.

Svādhyāya: *Facilitating Study*

If *tapas* weans us off our misidentification of the self with the body and mind, then *svādhyāya* (the second component of *kriyā-yoga*) seeks to positively engage us in acquiring knowledge about, and realization of, the true Self. *Svādhyāya* (self-study) may be understood as "studying the self" (introspection), "study about the self" (sacred text study), or "one's own study" (a curriculum customized and relevant to the individual). In the Yoga Sutras, commentators suggest there is an overlap between the three possible meanings.[7]

While such study is sure to engage and develop the intellect, it is not meant to be a mere cerebral exercise. The student is specifically advised to study sacred texts whose subject matter is liberation—ultimate freedom from the misidentification, with the aim of replacing the desire for things worldly with things spiritual. This, in turn, nourishes and invigorates

---

7 Bryant, p.273. Bryant notes that, just as the commentators linked *tapas* to *karma-yoga*, they tend to frame *svādhyāya* as practice of *jñāna-yoga*. See Bryant, p.171.

one's meditation practice. The commentators see an explicit connection between *svādhyāya* and developing one's theistic orientation. The texts to be studied give the aspirant glimpses of *Īśvara*, a somewhat generic term Patañjali seems to equate with a supreme deity that is capable of bestowing grace on his devotee and is present, sonically, in the sacred syllable *oṁ*. The dual practice of recitation of the sacred syllable and study of scriptures brings the devotee closer to a particular form of *Īśvara*. But, to be clear, as a practice, *svādhyāya* is much more spiritual than academic.[8]

Because my theology of spiritual care includes *svādhyāya*, in many ways I see myself as a pastoral educator. My theology also informs me, however, that knowledge is not an extrinsic substance to be poured into the empty vessel that is a student. Rather, I believe that as eternal, spiritual beings we are all fundamentally full of knowledge in the truest sense of the term—indeed, we *are* pure knowledge or awareness.[9] And yet, as a Hindu chaplain serving in an educational institution, I occupy a uniquely privileged role and bear a responsibility to assist students in their study of sacred texts and their practice of meditation. I seek to approach this apparent paradox by viewing myself as a facilitator of study, a creator of learning environments, and a possible conduit to the development of knowledge and the building and deepening of faith that the Yoga Sutras suggest.

I understand *svādhyāya* to be an incredibly personal and complex process of spiritual education and formation. As we have touched upon, the student is expected not only to engage his or her mind in study, but to also open the heart to personal and theological transformation. As a Hindu chaplain working predominantly with Hindu-American students, my delicate role entails helping those students to navigate intricacies of ritual, culture, history, and more—in a space that requires they engage with both their identities as Hindus (if indeed they identify as such) and as students in an essentially non-Hindu space. For many students, college provides their first opportunity to explore and establish their spiritual lives as Hindus—and their concerns are many, complex, and urgent! My understanding of *svādhyāya* does not necessarily equip me to answer all of these questions (or even suggest that I am the person to answer them), but impels me to always engage with, often clarify, and sometimes

---

8   Bryant, pp.253, 273, 275.
9   Here I have in mind, for instance, the Vedantic theological principle that the self is *sat-cid-ananda*—pure beingness, pure knowledge, and pure bliss.

re-frame students' questions. I feel called to facilitate student exploration of the benefits of integrating study of sacred texts and meditation into their lives.

Rather than view *svādhyāya* as a single discrete activity, I interpret it as a body of practices—some more formal or regulated, and others more occasional or personalized. When I seek to put *svādhyāya* into practice, then, I consider a number of avenues. For instance, I facilitate a weekly study group dedicated to discussing the Bhagavad-Gita—we approach the text, not through the lenses of literary analysis or memorization, but with the express aim of applying its teachings to our day-to-day lives. At the same time, I also support students to engage in more ritualized engagement with sacred texts and traditions, by means, for example, of small-group and individual recitation of prayers or narratives. I encourage students to adopt meditation practices, particularly with regard to the repetitive chanting (*japa*) of mantra. I stress the importance of cultivating quietude. Accompanying all of these programs or recommendations is my invitation to students to reflect on their practice and its impact on their lives.

The role of *svādhyāya* in my theory of pastoral care is not without challenges. For one thing, Hinduism enjoys vast internal diversity—an umbrella under which reside significant theological, cultural, regional, and linguistic differences. How can I do this while maintaining a sense of cohesion and inclusion in the pluralistic community under my care? There is no easy answer; but I know that it will entail active listening.

A second challenge: by making study and meditation a focus of pastoral care, I may force students to face their own ignorance with regard to Hindu belief or practice—and for some students, this may be a deterrent. A chaplain is challenged to mitigate students' feelings of inadequacy while simultaneously helping them gain fresh perspective, knowledge, and wisdom—confident that they will indeed find that they "belong" and that, through study and meditation practice, they can find joy and meaning.

Īśvara-praṇidhāna: *Connecting to Divinity*

Patañjali suggests that the natural result of *svādhyāya* is a spontaneous attraction to a particular *iṣṭa-devatā*—a manifestation of divinity that serves as one's chosen deity. Although the text does not explicitly state it, the context suggests a correlation between the concept of *iṣṭa-devatā* and the notion of *Īśvara*, thus linking the second component of *kriyā-yoga* to the third, devotion to God and the dedication of all action to him.[10] In this, Patañjali seems to draw an intentional parallel to the *karma-yoga* of the Bhagavad-Gita.

The Gita initially proposes *karma-yoga*—action purely out of a sense of *dharma* and not for self-interest—as a viable means to approach transcendence, but ultimately favors "an alternative but overlapping path to *karma-yoga*, namely *bhakti-yoga*" instead. Action performed for the sake of duty is surpassed by, and culminates in, action performed as an offering to *Īśvara*. Likewise, the Yoga Sūtras commentators take the third component of *kriyā-yoga* in this *bhakti* sense, and suggest that the *karma-yoga* flavored practice of *tapas* finds its fulfillment in the more devotionally-oriented *Īśvara-praṇidhāna*.[11] Seen in this light, taking *Īśvara-praṇidhāna* to its natural conclusion invites an explicitly personal and devotional practice: rather than merely cultivating an abstract sense of selflessness, the practitioner is enjoined to offer his or her very self to *Īśvara*. This suggests a profound—perhaps even radical—re-orienting of one's life and sense of self: the practitioner sees him- or herself, primarily and ultimately, in obedient relation to *Īśvara*. Moving beyond duty for duty's sake, the devotees care nothing for duty except for the exclusive duty to devote themselves to *Īśvara*. As a practical matter, of course, they act dutifully—but do so out of devotion.[12]

Īśvara-praṇidhāna is at the core of my personal theology of spiritual care, and represents, to me, the fullest expression of that care. I believe that we are fundamentally relational beings, and that the fact that we seem intrinsically drawn to connection evinces our natural state as one of loving union with our Divine source. My particular theology is informed by the stance that God is both perfectly imminent and fully transcendent; one with us in spirit but eternally and infinitely greater; at once omnipresent and all-pervading, intimately present within us as the indwelling supreme Self, and our perennial refuge and beloved object of worship.[13] I thus

---

10 For a thorough argument that *iṣṭa-devatā* refers to *Īśvara*, and not a minor Vedic deity or secondary god who bestows temporary material boons, see Bryant, pp.274–275.
11 Bryant, p.172. These commentators explicitly cite several Gita verses which are commonly understood to demonstrate the primacy of *bhakti,* for instance BG. IX.27, V.29, IX.23, and XVIII.66.
12 Bryant, p.172.
13 My theology is primarily informed by the Caitanya Vaisnavite strand of Hinduism, a *bhakti*-oriented Vedantic tradition. For a concise and approachable overview of this theology, see R. Swami (2015) *The Journey Within: Exploring the Path of Bhakti*. San Rafael, CA: Mandala Publishing.

understand *Īśvara-praṇidhāna* as the act of re-awakening our most essential connection and accessing Divine grace—and, through the gift of this grace, the ability to see the true Self. I do not see *Īśvara-praṇidhāna* as merely one of three components making up *kriyā-yoga*, then, but as the culmination of that process. I interpret the self-discipline of *tapas* and the study and reflection of *svādhyāya* as helping us to develop the clarity, knowledge, and inspiration needed to best connect with *Īśvara* and the openness to receive his grace.

To the question of why one should engage in pastoral caregiving, *Īśvara-praṇidhāna* is, for me, the simplest and most profound response. I see all beings as yearning for reconnection, and I believe that the fullness of connection comes from re-orienting one's life to be in alignment with God's grace—I feel called to play a role in facilitating that connection. Like many of my Christian, Jewish, and Muslim counterparts, I feel moved, as one Christian puts it, to "join with God in being present to those suffering…in the passionate pursuit of truth and wholeness."[14]

As I move from *why* to *how*—from a theology of care to the practical actualization of that care—I must confront the challenges posed by engaging with *Īśvara-praṇidhāna* in a contemporary, multifaith, and largely secular space. My theology impels me to foster connection with Divinity as I understand that practice. And yet, I must bear in mind that it would be a violation of the sacred trust placed in me—indeed, an act of spiritual violence—for me to approach caregiving by pushing my particular picture of *Īśvara* onto others. While I might find appropriate and welcomed opportunities to share that picture, there is, I believe, no place for proselytizing in the exchange. How do I relate, for example, to the student whose conception of God is grounded in a monism that appears to be at theological loggerheads with my own? What might I offer a student who is in need of pastoral care, and yet also expresses agnosticism or doubt of God's existence? In each instance, I might ask "Who or what is *Īśvara* for them?"

As a chaplain, I must meet the student to whom I am offering care where that student is; I must base my application of *Īśvara-praṇidhāna* on that student's own belief as to who God is. While being open to that, I cannot help but use my own connection to *Īśvara-praṇidhāna* as I understand and practice it and pray on my students' behalf. In this respect, Patañjali himself serves as something of a role model. He clearly

---

14 D.S. Schipani (ed.) (2013) *Multifaith Views in Spiritual Care*. Kitchchener, Ontario: Pandora Press, p.10.

promotes *kriyā-yoga* as a theistic method of spiritual practice; at the same time, he seems not to be dogmatic. An astute and mature devotee, he resists the urge to insist upon his own vision of the Deity. He seems to leave the particulars of *bhakti* praxis up to the individual practitioner.[15]

As a chaplain working predominantly with students who self-identify as Hindu, I might use *Īśvara-praṇidhāna* as a way of explicitly connecting pastoral care with religious and cultural identity. After all, one might argue that contemporary popular Hinduism is very much the expression, through *bhakti* traditions, of various forms of *Īśvara-praṇidhāna*.[16] Many Hindu students, therefore, are likely to have some frame of reference for the practice—at least in terms of specific rituals or liturgical components it might involve. At the same time, however, my role as a chaplain and my own experiences as a Hindu-American call me to complicate the sometimes simplistic ways in which Hindu students might approach religious and secular aspects of their lives. By framing *praṇidhāna* as "connection with Divinity," I might push students to explore the possibility of integrating their Hinduism into the fullness of their lives. I give myself and the students permission to bring the ancient rituals, texts, and traditions of Hinduism to life in our current context. It is my conviction that *Īśvara-praṇidhāna* is a living, dynamic, and whole-life-encompassing practice that allows me to do this.

Final Reflections

Throughout this chapter, I have explored *kriyā-yoga* as a dynamic, integrated, holistic, and especially good framework—both theologically and pragmatically—for Hindu chaplains in collegiate contexts. I suggest that *kriyā-yoga*'s tripartite make-up mirrors the multivalent nature of popular contemporary Hinduism—in particular, by including *karma-yoga*, *jñāna-yoga*, and *bhakti-yoga* approaches. Thus, it lends itself well to chaplains addressing spiritual care at the interpersonal, personal, and transpersonal levels. Nonetheless, I would be remiss not to acknowledge that this framework—like any framework—has its limitations, as well.

---

15 Bryant, pp. 278, 280–281. Here Bryant notes the possibility that Patañjali was simply aware of the development of "sophisticated and extensive theologies" of *bhakti*; so, rather than duplicate these efforts, limited his own project to the metaphysics of yoga and directed his students to these already existing resources.
16 Bryant, p.282.

First, I must recognize that in my project of applying portions of the *Yoga Sutras of Patañjali* to chaplaincy, I am necessarily taking these passages out of their cultural, historical, and religious contexts and projecting them on to a very different landscape. Likewise, I admit that in the act of viewing chaplaincy through the lens of yoga metaphysics and praxis, I must decontextualize, reimagine, and reinterpret concepts such as pastoral and spiritual care. To be sure, neither the traditional commentators examining Patañjali's treatise, nor the pioneers of the pastoral care movement or the famous college chaplains of previous generations, could have dreamt that they would be brought together in this way—and had they known, they probably would have protested the attempt! I realize, then, that there is a very real danger in divorcing concepts from their contexts. However, I do not think that this danger ought to prevent us from attempting to build bridges between cultural paradigms or applying old wisdom to new canvases.[17]

While I believe that *kriyā-yoga* is a particularly helpful and effective resource, I realize that it is simply that: a resource, an instrument, one tool among many. It must never become a substitute for the authenticity and presence that is, perhaps, at the heart of what it means to be a chaplain. While it might be tempting to apply the framework to others and thus forego developing one's own pastoral authority, I strongly believe that chaplains must resist this temptation if we are to do justice to our calling. Being a spiritual caregiver requires that I have a spiritual life myself. If I do not, however sincere my intention and however efficacious my framework, my attempts to offer care will likely ring hollow and fall flat. Moreover, I run the risk of incongruity and even hypocrisy. How can I help students to engage with *tapas* if my own life is devoid of self-discipline and attempts at selfless action? How can I expect students to enter into the intimate and profound space of loving connection with *Īśvara* if I am not dwelling in that space already, constantly working on my own relationship with the Divine and modeling how to give and receive love?

None of this is to suggest that a chaplain need be flawless in his or her spiritual practice. On the contrary, I believe that, as chaplains, we are called to honestly embrace the messiness, humility, and vulnerability of our own shortcomings. We strive, not for effortless perfection, but for authenticity.

---

17 See A.R. Jain (2014) *Selling Yoga: From Counterculture to Pop Culture*. Oxford: Oxford University Press.

The Bhagavad-Gita's Theological Anthropology as a Foundation for Hindu Pastoral Care

Viraj Patel

In November 2017, I learned that I would soon need open heart surgery. Shortly after, I attended a service at the BAPS Shri Swaminarayan Mandir in Bartlett, Illinois, commemorating the birth anniversary of their late guru Pramukh Swami Maharaj.[1] In the assembly, some congregants recalled how in 1998, during a visit to New York, Pramukh Swami Maharaj was told that he would need emergency quintuple coronary bypass surgery. He faced the news with serenity, remaining unmoved from his constant prayer and trust in God. Throughout his treatment, his doctors marveled at how he dealt with pain so stoically, without suffering, leading them to surmise that his sense of self seemed transcendent of his physical body.

A year later, Mahant Swami Maharaj, who would eventually succeed him as guru, also had coronary bypass surgery. He later explained that, while some people may find it difficult to actualize the doctrine of a radical distinction between the *atma* (self) and the body during times of great physical and mental distress, during his own post-op recovery, loving recollection of his guru had also alleviated his suffering.

---

1   The following two incidents were part of the celebration programs. While examples of Swaminarayan Hinduism are used in this chapter, the principles about the body, self, and God drawn from them apply to Hinduism broadly. Full citation: BAPS Devotees (2001) "Pramukhji Aapnu Roon Chukvu Hu Sha Vade." Presentations for the birth anniversary of Pramukh Swami Maharaj. BAPS Shri Swaminarayan Mandir, Bartlett, IL, December 2.

Discussion of these former and current gurus' approaches to their heart surgeries helped me mentally, emotionally, and spiritually prepare for my own. These gurus appear to have lived the wisdom about the body, self, and God taught in Hindu scriptures that allowed them to transcend suffering. In what follows, I aim to uncover some of the scriptural foundations of this wisdom in order to articulate Hindu theological anthropology and a theology of pastoral care grounded in it.[2]

Hindu Theological Anthropology

Before we exegete these theologies, we must understand what it means to be human within Hindu contexts. Hindu ideas of theological anthropology differ from those of Abrahamic traditions on the themes of humanness, the aims of life, and how those aims are achieved. Clarifying these themes will help us understand how Hindu anthropology should shift contemporary models of Hindu pastoral care. In order to do this, we must understand two differentiating presuppositions of Hindu anthropology: *punarjanma* (rebirth)[3] and *moksha* (freedom from *punarjanma*).

Presuppositions: Punarjanma and Moksha

These two presuppositions lead to the divergence of Hindu anthropologies from the Abrahamic anthropologies that undergird contemporary models of pastoral care. Furthermore, recent efforts in the field to incorporate "lived," "embodied," or "contextual" theologies exacerbate the pitfalls of these contemporary models by building upon anthropologies that do not account for Hindu presuppositions. Appropriate Hindu pastoral care therefore starts by building an anthropology within the context of *punarjanma* and *moksha*.

The doctrine of *punarjanma* asserts that there are 8.4 million lifeforms in the world, all of which are animated by individual *jīvas* (selves) that

---

2   Despite its Christian connotations, I use the term "pastoral care" instead of "spiritual care" because the latter engages with religious difference while the former does not. This chapter clarifies Hindu themes that should be understood before engaging religious difference, so "pastoral care" is more appropriate.

3   *Punarjanma* has traditionally been translated as "reincarnation." However, I intentionally use *punarjanma* instead of *reincarnation* in this chapter because the former reflects a more precise understanding of this Hindu doctrine. Literally, *punarjanma* translates to "rebirth," and implies with it a continuous cycle in which individuals successively inhabit all forms of life, not just human.

transmigrate from one body to the next in a constant cycle of death and rebirth.⁴ The often-overlooked implication of this doctrine is that each *jīva* has animated all types of life: human, animal, insect, and plant. The uniqueness of human life is that it offers the opportunity for freedom from *punarjanma*. Such freedom from *punarjanma*, in which the *jīva* enjoys unhindered devotion to God, is called *moksha*.

Insofar as the ultimate aim of each individual *jīva* is *moksha*, Hindu pastoral care should be teleological. Humans may enjoy secondary aims, such as maintaining health, amassing wealth, or cherishing relationships with loved ones, but these secondary, worldly aims, whether fulfilled or unfulfilled, can distract one from the ultimate aim of *moksha* in which the *jīva* enjoys the unhindered bliss of God. When one is distracted by such worldly aims, Hindu pastoral care reminds care-seekers that "of all of the pleasures found in this world, none of them are without misery."⁵ While the aphorism acknowledges that this world can be pleasurable, it reminds us that this-worldly pleasure feels hellish compared to the bliss of God. In this way, Hindu pastoral care reminds care-seekers that their ultimate aim is *moksha*.

These presuppositions—*punarjanma* and *moksha*—lay out the preamble to a Hindu anthropology and theology of pastoral care. To explain these theologies, I turn to the *Śrīmadbhagavadgītā Svāminārāyaṇabhāṣyam*, a commentary on the Bhagavad-Gita by Bhadresh Swami, a world-renowned theologian of the Swaminarayan Sampraday.⁶ This commentary is grounded in the teachings of Bhagwan Swaminarayan, as taught in the Vachanamrut, a collection of sermons he delivered from 1819 to 1829. The commentary discusses Hindu anthropology in a way that also illuminates a theology of pastoral care. Upon completing the exegesis, we will return to the gurus' examples cited above to analyze how they embodied these pastoral concepts.

---

4   S. Paramtattvadas (2017) *An Introduction to Swaminarayan Hindu Theology*. Cambridge: Cambridge University Press, p.213.
5   S. Vato (trans.) (2006) *Sadhu Amrutvijaydas*. Shahibaug, Amdavad, India: Swaminarayan Aksharpith, p.52.
6   B. Swami (2012) *Śrīmadbhagavadgītā Svāminārāyaṇabhāṣyam*. Shahibaug, Amdavad, India: Swaminarayan Aksharpith.

The Self and the Body

The Bhagavad-Gita can be seen as a pastoral conversation in 700 verses between Krishna and Arjuna just prior to the war of the Mahabharat. Arjuna's crisis of faith in anticipation of the war offers Krishna an opportunity to engage in pastoral care. The conversation helps us understand Hindu anthropology as well as the mechanics of pastoral assessment and care.

Hindu anthropology describes a radical distinction between the self and body. The self is called either the *jīva* or the *atma* and is "uncuttable, unpiercable, immortal, [and] formed of consciousness... It pervades the entire body from head to toe."[7] When the *atma* wants to see something, "it does so *through* the eyes...[hears] *through* the ears...smells *through* the nose," and so on.[8] The body is therefore an instrument of the *atma*, and yet it remains ontologically distinct.

Furthermore, Hindu anthropology states that each *jīva* has *three* bodies: the *sthūla* (gross), which is the physical body; the *sūkṣma* (subtle), which is comprised of mind and the senses; and the *kāraṇa* (causal), which "stores the *jīva's* karmas and is the form of ignorance, [and] therefore the cause of *punarjanma*."[9] All three of these bodies are described in the Bhagavad-Gita, and Krishna incorporates this into his pastoral care.

Arjuna experiences distress in the beginning of the Bhagavad-Gita,[10] and he relays this experience to Krishna through a description of its impact on his gross body in verses 1.29–1.30: "My limbs are exhausted, and my mouth has gone dry. My entire body is shaking, and my hair is standing on end...and my skin is flush. I can't even stand up." Though Arjuna is describing somatic symptoms, it is clear that they are of psychological origin. This is because the "gross body provides the physical support system for the senses, mind, etc. of the subtle body to function."[11]

The "subtle body" consists of, among other things, the mind and the five cognitive senses: sight, hearing, touch, taste, and smell. These senses are not the sense *organs* but the cognitive ability to receive the organs' input. The subtle body includes the mind and its abilities of thought,

---

7   BAPS Sadhus (trans.) (2001) *The Vachanāmrut*. Shahibaug, Amdavad, India: Swaminarayan Aksharpith, Jet. 2. 610–693.
8   Ibid.; emphasis added.
9   For a full discussion on these bodies, see Swami Paramtattvadas (2017), pp.214–217.
10 Unless otherwise noted, all passages from the Bhagavad-Gita are according to my own translation.
11 Paramtattvadas (2017), p.214.

reason, contemplation, and affirmative identity.[12] Arjuna describes the impact of his distress on his subtle body next, "Krishna, my head is spinning, and I see evil omens" (BG 1.30–1.31). "I no longer want to win this war. I don't want my kingdom, nor the pleasures it entails" (BG 1.32). The Bhagavad-Gita's narrator tells us that Arjuna "sits down in [his] chariot, dejected, *with a mind afflicted by sorrow*" (BG 1.47).

Though Arjuna is describing psychological symptoms, Hindu anthropology asserts that they are of karmic origin, rooted in the "ignorance" of his causal body. The causal body "stores" karma whose effects will be felt later and thereby binds the *atma* in *punarjanma*. This body through the karmas it stores acts like a "veil" over the *atma* insofar as it enshrouds the *atma's* ability to apprehend itself and worship God. Because Arjuna is ignorant of his true self as the *atma*, and identifies with the three bodies, he is bound to experience psychological and attendant somatic distress. Arjuna fails in his effort to liberate himself from this distress as he is unable to directly apprehend the causal body, but Krishna, as a manifestation of God, describes its effects in his pastoral assessment.

Krishna's Pastoral Care
Assessment

Krishna makes his pastoral assessment in terms of Hindu anthropology: he describes Arjuna's gross body in the phrase "eyes irritated because by crying," subtle body as "grief-stricken," and causal body as "overcome by compassion."[13] Krishna acknowledges Arjuna's physical and mental distress with just one verse: "How has this depression afflicted you? It does not befit you, Arjuna. Get rid of it, [for you are] a vanquisher of your enemies" (verses 2.2–2.3). In doing so, Krishna affirms Arjuna's crisis, and reminds Arjuna of his own strength and agency.

Krishna sees the root of Arjuna's distress in terms of the causal body insofar as Arjuna has lost sight of *punarjanma* and *moksha*. The *Śrīmadbhagavadgītā Svāmīnārāyaṇabhāṣyam* states that Arjuna's distress "is characterized by delusion born of love for one's [bodily] relations."[14] The commentary describes what Krishna sees in Arjuna's self-assessment: "a being whose self is veiled by *mahāmoha*."[15]

---

12 Paramtattvadas (2017), p.215.
13 *aśrupūrṇākulekṣaṇam, viṣīdantam*, and *kṛpayāviṣṭam*, respectively from verse 2.1.
14 Swami (2012), p.18.
15 *mahāmohavyāptātmatattvaḥ*. Ibid. See verses 1.26–1.28.

Mahāmoha (alternatively called *mahāmāyā*) is defined as "the ignorance that shrouds [sentient] beings...the root cause of the soul's incessant transmigration through various life-forms, attended to by suffering, sorrow and disappointment."[16] Arjuna has forgotten that, according to Hindu anthropology's ideas about the *atma*, his present body and its relationships are ephemeral. He should instead focus on his true self as *atma* and his connection with God. To remedy this loss of focus, Krishna teaches him the difference between the three bodies and the *atma* from verse 2.11 to 2.39.

Framing Principles: Samkhya and Yoga

In verse 2.39, Krishna frames this teaching with two pan-Hindu terms: "I just explained samkhya to you, now listen to what yoga is. With this knowledge of yoga, you will become free of the bondage of karma." Samkhya stresses that knowledge of the ontological distinction between the body and *atma* is necessary for freedom from the karmas that lead to *punarjanma*.[17] Arjuna's distress is born of the causal body, which prevents him from turning to God at his time of crisis. So, Krishna first teaches him to differentiate himself from the three bodies.

With yoga, Krishna teaches that samkhya is actualized only with simultaneous attachment to God. The commentary shows that the Bhagavad-Gita's entire system of pastoral care turns on an exegesis of *yoga* in verses 2.39–2.40. In these verses, *yoga* and *dharma* are taken as synonymous, on exegetical grounds, to mean attaching oneself to God.[18] With this perspective, we read verse 2.40 as "even a little bit of that *dharma* (qua *yoga*) protects one from great distress."[19] The commentary clarifies this distress as "fear of adharma, death, and *mahāmāyā* [the

---

16 Paramtattvadas (2017), p.245.
17 Swami (2012), pp.38–39.
18 Swami notes that there are two definitions of "dharma" in the Gita. The first refers to *varṇāśramadharma*, and the second to faith in the form of God (yoga). The second definition applies in verse 2.40. This is substantiated by the context and on grammar grounds: *dharma* in this context refers to yoga because of the word *asya*—which, as a pronoun, must refer to an antecedent. The best antecedent for *dharma* is found in verse 2.39—and is yoga. For an explication of this and notes on where each definition of *dharma* is utilized in the Gita, see Bhadreshdas, pp.38–50. For an English language explication of this argument, see Sadhu Aksharananddas (2017) "Svāminārāyaṇa's Interpretation of 'Dharma' as It Appears in the Shrimad Bhagavad Gita." Unpublished Doctoral Thesis, University of Lancaster, Lancaster, UK.
19 For a full exegesis of this phrase, *svalpam api asya dharmasya trāyate mahato bhayāt*, in Swaminarayan's own words, see *Vachnamrut Gadh*. II-9 (386–390). Furthermore, Swaminarayan directly states that *both* samkhya and yoga as defined here are necessary in *Vachanāmrut Gadh*. I:61 (117–119).

cause of *punarjanma*]." Samkhya will only get Arjuna so far, but even a little bit of *yoga* would alleviate the distress that he experiences.

Pastoral Teaching: Sthitapragya toward Brahmabhūta

Krishna's teaching on yoga culminates near the end of the Bhagavad-Gita in verse 18.54 "*Brahmabhūta prasannātmā...*" with Brahman as the exemplar. The commentary on this verse describes a state "similar to that of [Akshara] Brahman's" insofar as the self transcends the three bodies, is unperturbed by the world, and offers perfect worship to the form of God (*nārāyaṇasvarūpaparābhakti*).[20] This state is a recapitulation of *moksha*, as it was described in terms of samkhya and yoga. Between verse 2.40 and 18.54, Krishna's pastoral care instructs Arjuna to become like Brahman.

Krishna describes this state of Brahman throughout his teaching. The *sthitapragya* (regarding a stable intellect) verses from 2.54–2.72 are useful for a theology of pastoral care because they show how Krishna's teaching on Brahman can be embodied by describing an exemplar whom care-seekers can learn to emulate. Krishna stated that one needs to focus all of one's energy on God; that is how one remains unperturbed amid distress. Having picked up on this, Arjuna asks for an example of such a person in verse 2.54, "What are the characteristics of one who has a stable intellect? How does he speak? How does he sit? How does he walk?" Based on this question, and Krishna's lengthy response, we see that Arjuna is asking about a human person, and we infer that human beings can attain such a state. In fact, there are likely such beings on earth if Arjuna is asking for an observable example.

A second practical concern asks how to make meaning of life events. Verses 2.56–2.57 state, "He who remains unperturbed amid *both* extreme joy and sorrow, he who is free of desire, fear, and anger is said to have a stable intellect. He who is unattached to anything or anyone [other than God], who experiences both good and evil and responds with equanimity has a stable intellect." Times of joy and sorrow, extreme expressions of desire, fear, and anger are precisely the times that we find ourselves administering pastoral care. The *sthitapragya* verses remind one that Hinduism views these events as realities of embodied life. Despite situations that might cause all of these extreme emotions, one who is *sthitapragya* remains free from their perturbations. This is accomplished by yoga, an attachment to God which precludes all other desire.

---

20 Swami (2012), pp.18–19; 360–361.

Guru as Pastoral Caregiver

In the BAPS Swaminarayan tradition, the state of Brahman to which Krishna refers is exemplified by the guru, presently Mahant Swami Maharaj. In fact, Mahant Swami Maharaj's authority is deeper than an institutional designation as guru. It is grounded in the belief that he is the ontological manifestation of Aksharabrahman, who is the ideal disciple of Parabrahman, or God. As Brahman, the guru is free from the perturbations of *maya* and focused completely on God. For this tradition, then, the guru's Brahmic state is the state to which all devotees aspire.

The guru as Brahman is also the primary source of pastoral care. The guru–disciple relationship that develops is based on the theological idea that since the guru is Brahman, disciples learn to become free from *maya* through his living example. Of course, the guru's teachings are a primary source of pastoral care; however, disciples also learn to form their lives in accordance with the guru's by studying his life and those of past gurus. Specific examples from their lives, such as the heart surgeries described in this chapter's introduction, help disciples visualize and work toward "*Brahmabhūta prasannātmā...*" The practice of applying scriptural doctrines occurs through the medium of exemplars.

Conclusion

This chapter's primary aim has been to draw out scriptural foundations for Hindu pastoral care. This was possible only after describing the particularity of Hindu theological anthropology. The Bhagavad-Gita provided the theoretical frameworks for this work, but it would have remained incomplete without an eye to practice. The practice of pastoral care was actualized for the purpose of this chapter in exemplars of the scriptural doctrines described. For example, the gurus' reactions to major heart surgeries gave me a vocabulary to communicate my Hindu identity to the medical professionals and chaplains who cared for me.

For pastoral care in a Hindu context, I see a dialectic between scriptural foundations and how they are lived today. Sometimes authority is diffuse, while at other times, as with respect to an Aksharabrahman guru, there is a deep theology of how scripture ought to be applied. These nuances, both scriptural and how scripture is embodied, are easily overlooked in healthcare, campus ministry, and multi-religious spiritual care. This is especially the case in Hinduism due to the diversity of its sub-traditions. The role of a pastoral caregiver, in my opinion, is to learn to identify both scriptural and embodied sources—for Hindus usually possess both. The best among caregivers will use both sources and assist in their application to the individual in their care.

Rama in the Forest

A Hindu Chaplaincy Framework for Grief Resolution from the Valmiki Ramayana

Ramakrishnan Parameshwaran

Spiritual caregivers are often called on to assist people with the experience of grief or loss. How might a Hindu scriptural text offer caregivers a framework with which to do this? In what way would such a framework echo or resonate with modern Western clinical diagnostic tools? How might it diverge from these tools, and thus challenge our paradigm of grief resolution? In this paper, I examine a section of the Valmiki Ramayana detailing Rama's grief in light of the stages of grief delineated by Elisabeth Kübler-Ross, and suggest that Rama's deep and empathic communion with nature in this episode illustrates a framework for grief resolution. I locate this framework as rooted in a Hindu theory of emotional states and interpersonal relationship, known as *rasa* theory. I argue that this *rasa*-based framework has much to offer the field of chaplaincy, even as it differs significantly from conventional clinical conceptions of notions such as "empathy," "projection," or "compassion."

Rama's Grief: An Overview of the Episode

The Ramayana, a beloved Hindu epic attributed to the poet sage Valmiki, describes the divine activities (*līlā*) of the prince Rama. Faithful believers worship him as an *avatāra*, a fully-human-fully-divine personality, and see him as a source of inspiration in their lives. In the book's *Araṇya Kāṇḍa* (literally "the forest volume") Valmiki narrates the extreme challenges faced by Rama, his loving wife Sita, and his brother Lakshmana in their wilderness exile. This section culminates in Sita's abduction by the demon king Ravana, while Rama and Lakshmana have been tricked into being elsewhere in the forest. Valmiki describes Rama's discovery of Sita's absence, and his subsequent emotional breakdown following this traumatic loss, with acute clinical precision. We turn now to this episode to examine Rama's process of working through his grief and consider what this might suggest to us.

Valmiki uses his poetic skills to project Rama's sadness on to non-human beings such as animals and trees, and even inanimate objects, in the episode's forest setting. He depicts Rama experiencing his own feelings as reflected in these objects, while also feeling compassion *for* them. Might this suggest, then, that Rama experienced self-compassion—and healing of his own pain—through the act of projection?

One might recognize, in Valmiki's description of Rama's initial feelings during his grief period, a state of shock and despair. In Sita's absence, Rama perceives the natural world as devoid of movement or meaning, in a way that is strikingly reminiscent of the testimonies of patients who have lost a loved one and can see no beauty or life in their surroundings.

From his initial shock, Rama seems to turn to emotional expression. Valmiki describes his response to Sita's absence vividly:

> "Oh great-armed Lakshmana, do you see my beloved anywhere? Oh my beloved, my Sita, where can you have gone?" So, Rama lamented on and on as he ran from wood to wood. (58.35, 345)

> When Rama, son of Dasharatha, found the *ashram* empty, the leaf hut vacant, the seats in disarray; when he found Vaidehi missing and had looked everywhere for her, he stretched out his novel arms and wailed. (59.1, 347)[1]

In this state of emotional turmoil, Valmiki discloses, Rama communes with the natural world. For instance, Rama asks the trees near their hermitage:

> "Have you seen my beloved, *kadamba* tree? She loved you so much. Tell me what happened to my beautiful Sita. Perhaps you, *arjuna* tree—she loved you, too—perhaps you can tell me about my beloved, whether or not the shy daughter of Janaka is still alive." (58.10, 343)

---

1 This and all quotations from The Ramayana in this essay are according to the Valmiki Ramayana translation project coordinated by Prof. K.V. Rāmakrishnamacharyulu and Prof. P. Geervani: www.valmiki.iitk.ac.in, accessed on July 18, 2019.

Here Rama seems to approach the trees—which Sita tenderly cared for—as fellow sufferers, imagining them to be as grief-stricken as he is. Thinking of how much they must have loved Sita too, he feels compassion for them.

> "Tiger, if you have seen Maithili, my moon-faced love, speak out in full confidence; you have nothing to fear." (58.20, 343)

In this verse, by asking a tiger not to be fearful, Rama may be projecting his own fears—the possibility of Sita being devoured by cruel animals, for instance—and is thus telling himself not to fear that such a drastic end has befallen Sita. At the same time, one may also observe how even in the midst of his own fears, Rama is asking a wild and cruel man-eater not to fear; he asks that the tiger offer him some clue as to Sita's whereabouts and reassures the beast that he will not retaliate or become angry with him.

Valmiki writes of Rama's particular sensitivity to the sadness he observes in the deer:

> "The fawns that used to play with you so trustingly, dear Sita, are lost in worry, teary-eyed at your absence." (59.1, 347)

> "Lakshmana, these herds of deer filled with tears in their eyes seem as if they are telling me that she is eaten by nightwalkers." (3.62, 9)

Again and again, Rama associates the deer with tear-filled eyes and an urgency to express themselves. While it is entirely possible that these animals did appear to be teary-eyed and anxious, might it not also suggest that Rama is indirectly articulating his own state of great sorrow and perhaps an inability to become self-reflective in his intense grief that steals one's metacognitive skills? It is also telling that deer factor in the story in a number of ways. Sita's delicate beauty is compared to that of a deer, evoking a sense of her vulnerability within the forest. At the same time, a "deer" was the cause of Rama and Lakshmana being absent from the hermitage when Sita was taken: they went to chase a demon in the guise of an enchanted golden deer. Could Rama's seeing tears in the eyes of the deer, and his sense that they wish to speak to him, indicate subtle feelings of anguish and pangs of guilt? As with the trees, Rama seems to regard the deer as compatriots and feels compassion for them. He sees them through his own tear-filled eyes.

Rama's pleas to the natural world are met with silence. He then seems to go into the anger phase of his grief and threatens to destroy the mountains, forests, river, and animals in his rage. In response, his younger brother Lakshmana is quick to pray to Rama, reminding him of his original nature of compassion towards all creatures:

> At the sight of such rage in Rama as he had never seen before, Lakshmana cupped his hands in reverence and addressed him through a mouth gone dry with fear. "You have always been mild in the past, self-restrained, and dedicated to the welfare of all creatures. Do not abandon your true nature, yielding to rage." (3.61.1.361)

As if, to inform us that Lakshmana's counseling had indeed impacted Rama, Valmiki describes how Rama addresses the inanimate elements of nature such as the wind and sun as personified and divine beings, praying to help him find his beloved:

> "O Sun! you are the knower of all that is committed and omitted in the world. You are the witness to all true and false deeds of people. Please tell me where my Sita has gone or been taken away? I am in the grip of sorrow."

> "O wind god! you always pervade all over the worlds. There is nothing you know not. You may tell me about that lady of noble race. Tell me whether she is abducted, dead or moving on the way." (3.63.17)

Personifying elements of nature and addressing them as deities, while perhaps a bit strange to a modern clinician, is not unusual in the context of Hindu theology. What is striking here, however, is how Rama approaches them with a grief-driven desperation to know the whereabouts of Sita. It seems that Rama is struggling with uncertainty; his grief is not just in being separated from Sita, but in not knowing her fate at all. That he asks, "Is she abducted, dead, or moving," seems to suggest that he would rather have closure (even if the outcome is tragic) than not to know at all. Rama's struggle with not knowing is also significant in light of his simultaneous divinity and humanness, a theme that the Ramayana and Hinduism generally wrestle with. Is it possible, therefore, that Rama's assertions that the sun and wind are omniscient is a statement on his own tension between knowing all and yet, in this episode, not knowing, representing his humanity?

It can be understood that, with the religious and/or spiritual change that dawned in him following Lakshmana's counseling, Rama meets the deer in a more empathetic way, i.e., without judgmental thoughts and worries:

Rama, the tiger among men, on seeing the deer with his sight clouded by tears, looked at them and in reply to their gestures asked them "Where is Sita?"

O Lakshmana of great courage! These deer are again and again looking at me, indicating me by their signs as if they wish to tell me something. (3.64.15-16)

With these verses it can be understood that Valmiki may be informing us how a deeper empathetic approach towards those deers could have helped Rama read their minds in a positive way, as if they were pointing him at the direction in which he can find Sita. Along with Lakshmana, Rama continues to search, and they find a few flowers fallen on a forest trail which Rama identifies as the same that he had lovingly presented to Sita earlier on that day. Further ahead, they find broken pieces of a chariot and then a mortally wounded, anthropomorphic bird named Jathayu who was growling in pain, breathing with difficulty and counting his last moments of life. After talking to Jathayu and learning that the cause of his mortal injuries is due to his heroic act of trying to save Sita from Ravana, Rama feels greatly indebted and respectful of Jathayu's valor and selfless act. Rama realizes that his loss is not as great a loss as that of Jathayu, who has given up his life for the sake of Sita. Rama shares these feelings with Lakshmana as follows:

"He was born a long time ago and had lived for many years, and now he lies here slain—how inescapable is doom." (64.20, 375)

"Dear brother, slayer of enemies, my sorrow over Sita abduction has not been so hard to bear as the death of this vulture in my cause." (64.25, 375)

After recognizing that his loss is less than that of Jathayu, Rama starts to gain control over his emotions more effectively in this chapter of Ramayana. Rama resumes his responsibilities starting with conducting the funeral rites for Jathayu and proceeds to search for Sita. Thus, one may say that Rama has had a successful resolution of his grief episode.

Western Paradigms of Healing, Empathy, and Projection

It is not difficult to hear echoes of the grieving process as articulated by Elizabeth Kübler-Ross and others, as well as other clinical paradigms for dealing with loss, in this short episode of Rama's grief in the forest. Remarkably, Valmiki describes Rama's engagement with these stages (though not necessarily in the order conventionally cited in the Kübler-Ross model) in relation to Rama's natural surroundings. Rama's initial shock, perhaps even coupled with denial, is mirrored by the surreal scene of the vacant, lifeless winter-like forest hermitage. He imagines the trees and deer in a state of depressed silence. He relates his fear to the tiger's fear and bargains with the tiger, assuring the wild creature of his protection in exchange for some information about Sita. He similarly pleads with the sun and wind. His grief expresses itself as anger directed to the natural world. Finally, his recognition of the sacrificial act of Jathayu—another creature of nature—offers Rama an opportunity to accept the situation and move forward constructively.

All through this episode of grief, Rama is able to see external non-human objects, such as trees and animals, to be reflecting back his sadness, fear, and other emotions. He is not only able to project his grief on to those trees and animals around him but also responds empathetically—he shows them a caring-compassion for "their loss" of Sita. In situations of loss, interpersonal connectedness can diminish and with it, one's compassion and empathy can be lost. For healing to take place, this interpersonal connectedness needs to be nurtured on an ongoing basis.[2]

Notwithstanding our cultural biases or tendency to judge Rama's behavior of talking to a tree as "irrational," interpersonal communication skills are considered to be one of the spiritual tools of self-care. Clinically depressed patients are reported to be lacking in such tools. Such patients frequently complain of feeling disconnected with their environment.[3] It is striking to compare clinical patients' inability to connect with their surroundings and Valmiki's description of Rama's emotional communication with the animate and inanimate objects around him. Whereas the patients generally report that nothing in them gets touched by the external world, Rama not only believes that the trees are able to experience his emotional pain and grief, but he is also able to empathize with them. The anhedonic feelings expressed by clinical patients may be comparable to the initial feelings of Rama during his shock, but Rama goes on to commune with the trees with empathy.

---

2   See L. López and A.J. Dyck (2009) "Educating physicians for moral excellence in the twenty-first century." *Journal of Religious Ethics 37*, 4, 651–668.
3   See K. Aho (2013) "Depression and embodiment: phenomenological reflections on motility, affectivity, and transcendence." *Medicine, Healthcare, and Philosophy 16*, 4, 751–759, at p.755.

Of course, one may argue that the fawns, deer, and other animals are likely indifferent to Sita's absence. It is Rama who is sad and tearful, and as he interacts with these animals, he projects his sadness on to them. He then externalizes *his* feelings, now reflected on them, and then empathizes with them. In this process, Rama is indirectly empathizing with his own self. Thus, Valmiki illustrates Rama's ability to be self-reflective even in the midst of his grief and stress. Such self-empathy is being recognized as the therapeutic element in a spiritual care process.[4] Self-compassion, though projected on to external objects, helps Rama to process and recover from his grief. Loving-kindness, interpersonal empathy, and connectedness along with mindful self-awareness have been identified as factors leading to intrapersonal satisfaction, restorative healing, and growth.[5] Empathy and compassion are the qualities of healthy interpersonal connectedness; when attributed to caregivers they turn out to be tools for healing.

Successful resolution of grief is signified by resuming responsibilities and effectiveness in one's social and occupational role despite those periodic recollections of the loss and its associated feelings of sadness.[6] Poor integration with one or more stages of grief leads to chronicity of the grief leading to various mental illnesses.[7] A successful recovery from grief is signified by the dawn of rational thinking, and the individual starts to accept the loss despite the pain. According to Elisabeth Kübler-Ross and David A. Kessler, individuals may move back and forth between the stages of grief before actually arriving at this stage of acceptance. They measure their loss relative to their rest of their own life's worth and to that of the loss in others' lives; by asking themselves questions about their loss they are able to move beyond the solely emotional aspects.[8] Rama's empathetic

---

4 See C.W. Hall, K.A. Row, K.L. Wuensch, and K.R. Godley (2013) "The role of self-compassion in physical and psychological wellbeing." *Journal of Psychology* 147, 4, 311–323. See also, C.K. Germer and K.D. Neff (2013) "Self-compassion in clinical practice." *Journal of Clinical Psychology* 69, 8, 856–867.

5 See C.L. Woods-Giscombé and A.R. Black (2010) "Mind-body interventions to reduce risk for health disparities related to stress and strength among African American women: The potential of mindfulness-based stress reduction, loving-kindness, and the NTU Therapeutic Framework." *Complementary Health Practice Review* 15, 3, 115–131. See also J.E. Van Sant and B.J. Patterson (2013) "Getting in and getting out whole: Nurse-patient connections in the psychiatric setting." *Issues in Mental Health Nursing* 34, 1, 36–45.

6 See E. Kübler-Ross and D.A. Kessler (2005) *On Grief and Grieving: Finding the Meaning of Grief Through the Five Stages of Loss.* New York: Scribner Publications, p.25.

7 See M.K. Shear, A. Ghesquiere, and K. Glickman (2013) "Bereavement and complicated grief." *Current Psychiatry Report* 15, 11, 406.

8 Kübler-Ross and Kessler (2005), p.11.

communing with nature is, perhaps, an example of such questioning and eventually leads to his acceptance of the loss.

Still, one might argue that Rama's apparent empathy is, in fact, not empathy but projection. Projection is generally understood to be one of Ego's immature defense mechanisms that is expressed most commonly as a symptom of paranoia in mental illnesses. It is described as the behavior of attributing the self's aggressive feelings onto others and reacting to those projected feelings/thoughts as if they are arising from the other person. Thus far, projection has been used only in association with pathological states of mind. It is rarely discussed as having any positive attributes; and it is generally not considered beneficial to the individual using such an ego defense mechanism.

Having defined empathy as "a perception-like exploration of others' experiences that develops progressively through certain styles of interpersonal interaction,"[9] philosopher and psychologist Matthew Ratcliffe asserts: "However close the association between empathy and projection might be, empathy is not projection; there is empathy without projection and projection without empathy."[10] I think that such a distinction, while valuable in many ways, falls short when applied to a Hindu theological framework such as the one found in the episode of Rama's grief. Instead, I argue that the complex phenomena of projection and perception of emotions involved in empathy between individuals can be better explained using a Hindu theory of emotional states and interpersonal relationship, known as *rasa* theory.

Emotional Aesthetics: *Rasa* Theory

Rama's emotional breakdown can be re-examined through the lens of the *rasa* theory. This theory developed by the dramaturge and sage Bharatamuni in the Natyashastra, or sacred texts describing drama and aesthetics, provides us with a new framework of understanding.[11]

A fuller description of *rasa* theory is beyond the scope of this paper, but for our purposes we might understand it as a framework for articulating inner and outer feeling. While psychology is understood as the study

---

9   M. Ratcliffe (2013) "The phenomenology of depression and the nature of empathy." *Medicine, Health Care and Philosophy* 17, 2, 7.
10 Ratcliffe (2013), p.11.
11 See P. Kumar (ed.) (2006) *Natyasastra of Bharatamuni*: Text with commentary of Abhinavabharati and English translation. Delhi: New Bharatiya Book Corporation, pp.219–313.

of human behavior, *rasa* theory may be understood as the study of our behavioral interaction with surroundings. According to Bharata, *rasa* is the experience of an emotion manifested outwardly; *sthāyī-bhāva* is one's innate or instinctual emotional state. Analogizing to food, we may observe that just as an external olfactory or gustatory stimuli (the smell and taste of a dish) triggers the experiential emotions attached to tasteful food, with proper external stimuli (*vibhava*), the innate sentiments or instinctual emotions (*sthāyī-bhāva*) within the subject may be aroused. Further, this arousal can be as a voluntary (*vyabhicāri* or *sanchāri-bhava*) or an involuntary and reflexive reaction (*anubhava*).[12] The *bhāva* (innate emotion), when expressed well by an actor or writer, will arouse similar *bhāvas* (emotions) in the spectator or reader—which in turn arouses an appropriate and corresponding *rasa*.[13] According to Hindu theologian Abhinavagupta, *rasa* that arises from a combination of *vibhavas* (external emotional stimuli), *anubhavās*, and *vyabhichārins* (voluntary and involuntary emotional reactions) is not a fixed mental state, but is an ongoing form of relishing, which develops out of a response of the heart and from our identifying with the portrayed character or message. "It is only through the *rasa* that we enter the hearts of princes and so instruct them."[14]

An experience corresponding to grief and painful stimuli is called *karuṇa rasa*, or pathos. Pathos is described as an emotion that is "capable of arousing sympathetic sadness and compassion"[15] or "having a capacity to move one to either compassionate or contemptuous pity."[16] It is this *rasa* which is most clearly evoked in the episode of Rama's grief and its resolution. The symptoms demonstrated by Rama in his grief—lamenting uncontrollably, weeping or crying loudly, fainting, going limp, and so on—are all considered voluntary grief-related *vyabhichāri bhāvas*. His grief reactions such as wailing could be viewed as emotional stimuli

---

12 It is also called *sattvika bhavas* and is of eight types: feeling stunned, swearing, thrill, break in voice, trembling, pallor, tears, breakdown. This includes dejection, lassitude, suspicion, jealousy, infatuation, fatigue, laziness, helplessness, anxiety, confusion, remembrance, boldness, bashfulness, fickleness, pleasure, excitement, heaviness, pride, sorrow, impatience, sleep, forgetfulness, dream, awakening, intolerance, dissimulation, ferocity, desire, disease, insanity, death, fear, and guessing.

13 That is: *shringar* (erotic), *karuna* (pathetic), *raudra* (furious), *vira* (heroic), *bhayanaka* (terrible), *hasya* (comic), *bibhatsa* (odious), *adbhuta* (marvelous).

14 A. Rangacharya (1996) *The Natyasastra*: English translation with critical notes. New Delhi: Munshiram Manoharlal Publishers, p.55.

15 www.thefreedictionary.com/pathetic

16 www.merriam-webster.com/dictionary/pathetic

(*vibhava*) to Lakshmana and the animals who were witnessing his grief; this, in turn, could have provoked an *anubhava* of grief in them. Such complementary feeling within the hearts of two individuals is called *sahrudaya*. We can imagine human beings demonstrating an *anubhava* of grief-emotions after witnessing a person in grief; stretching our imaginations, perhaps, we might also accept that animals can have an *anubhava* of grief-emotions after witnessing a person in grief. In this episode, however, even inanimate beings are posited as witnessing and having an *anubhava* of Rama's grief. While we can see it as an illustration of Rama's externalizing his own grief-emotions onto an array of objects in the natural world, believing them to be *sahrudaya*, this study is also meant to provoke a curiosity about the divinity of Rama. What is the meaning of being divine? What qualifies Rama to be "fully divine while being fully human?" Is the ability to stay empathetically connected to oneself and his/her surroundings be understood as the aspect of the divine? Is that what we should learn from Rama when we look up at him as a role model or worship to regain our strength when we are in despair?

Rama's externalizing of his grief is not a "projection" in the sense of an ego defense mechanism as described by Sigmund Freud, but rather a valid application of *rasa* theory. Rama's *sthāyi-bhāva* was of *śoka*, or grief, following the abduction of Sita. According to *rasa* theory, this grief should evoke *karuṇa* (pathos or compassion) in the observer. For instance, the audience members who watch an actor demonstrating grief will naturally have feelings of compassion aroused within them. But how does one evoke *self-compassion* or even *self-empathy*? By externalizing his own *śoka-bhāva*, or feelings of grief, on to the animals, plants, and elements of nature around him, Rama could play the role of "observer" to *their* grief and could thus invoke *karuṇa rasa*, compassion, within himself for them. As a result, he was able to offer this compassion reflectively towards himself. This episode suggests that, while being surrounded by empathetic individuals during a crisis is important, it is also important for the individual dealing with grief to be able to *feel* compassion— for others as *sahrudaya* and, through the other, for oneself.

Valmiki Ramayana's Contribution towards Hindu Chaplaincy

One should consider Lakshmana's counseling as the beginning of the chaplaincy process in this narrative of Rama's grief. Valmiki describes in several verses (not shown in this paper) how Lakshmana is also severely distressed with Rama's loss, as a *sahrudaya* should be. Clinical chaplains are trained to reflectively feel the pain and suffering of his/her patient as a first-person experience and yet stay empathetically connected to and tending to patients' pain and suffering, without distracting away from it. In addition, just as Lakshmana knew how and when to direct Rama to become self-reflective, clinical chaplains are trained to facilitate patients' self-reflective engagement with their externalized grief and chaplain's empathy. The chaplain's empathetic communion with patients would assist them to reflexively and unconsciously become empathetic to themselves (*anubhava*). Thus, they experience their own healing.[17] The spiritual caregiver plays an active role, intervening to help a patient to move through grief stages without becoming overwhelmed. In this episode, for instance, Lakshmana's intervention as a counselor was quite appropriate from a clinical point of view, allowing Rama to become mindful of his anger and then reminding Rama of his *sthāyi bhāva* (innate nature) of compassion.

Getting reconnected to his premorbid empathetic self was the key event in Rama's process of grief that led to its eventual resolution. Contrasting this, as psychologist Matthew Ratcliffe notes, clinical symptoms continue when depressed patients are characterized by a "loss of capacity for interpersonal relatedness."[18] Psychologist William James quotes a depressed patient, who says: "I see, hear, but the objects do not reach me, it is as if there is a wall between me and the outer world."[19] Clinical chaplains are trained to facilitate the patients to become mindful of their emotions and get connected with their empathetic-self through interpersonal empathy.

Rama's continued connectivity with his surroundings further leads him to believe that the animals and plants around him share his grief. When it comes to real-life or clinical situations, however, one may find it more difficult to arouse emotions within oneself or the others. This is another context in which a spiritual caregiver can be critical—as

---

17 See P. Ramakrishnan (2015) "Theory and practice of chaplain's spiritual care process: A psychiatrist's experiences of chaplaincy and conceptualizing trans-personal model of mindfulness." *Indian Journal of Psychiatry 57*, 1, 21–29. See also P. Ramakrishnan (2015) "'You are here': locating 'spirituality' on the map of the current medical world." *Current Opinion in Psychiatry 28*, 5, 393–401.
18 Ratcliffe (2013), p.1.
19 W. James (1990) *The Principles of Psychology*. New York: Henry Holt, p.299.

emerging research on the contemplative neuroscience of clinical spiritual care process reveals.[20]

Conclusion

In this chapter, I have explored ways in which the episode of Rama's grief in the forest illustrates behavior that resonates with modern Western clinical diagnostic tools and methodology, but also complicates it. I suggest that *rasa* theory is a useful framework to better understand a process of evoking self-compassion that involves expressing compassion to individuals and objects external to oneself. This might provide an alternative to the conventional understanding conveyed by the psychological term projection, which carries negative connotations and is seen as an ego defense mechanism or tool of avoidance.

Researchers are coming to understand the ability to establish interpersonal compassion and empathy as vital aspects of spiritual care and healing. An approach to spiritual caregiving based on *rasa* theory has much to offer us. Understanding *rasa* theory as an underlying mechanism in the clinical spiritual care process lends us the tools to study theological concepts in Hindu scriptural texts with the current research in contemplative neuroscience. Such an approach might be especially helpful in contexts of working with Hindu patients—or patients from other non-Western cultures—for whom self-compassion might otherwise seem like an alien concept.

---

20 See, for example, K.A. Bingaman, (2011) "The Art of Contemplative and Mindfulness Practice: Incorporating the Findings of Neuroscience into Pastoral Care and Counseling" *Pastoral Psychology 60*, 3, 477–489. See also, Y. Y. Tang and M.I. Posner, (2012) "Tools of the trade: Theory and method in mindfulness neuroscience." *Social Cognitive and Affective Neuroscience 8*, 1, 118–120.

Does God Really Care?
A Hindu Response to the Problem of Suffering

Gopal K. Gupta

The Bhagavata Purana's narrative opens as a continuation of the Mahabharata's central narrative, which deals extensively with the problem of suffering. After the battle of Kurukshetra, Yudhishthira, who has ascended to the throne, is in a condition of immense agony, overcome by guilt, regret, and loss. Accompanied by sages, his brothers, and Krishna, Yudhishthira proceeds to the now-quiet battlefield to seek consolation from Bhishma, the powerful grandsire of the Kuru dynasty, who is lying on a bed of arrows that had been shot through his body. Indeed, all the survivors of the terrible battle were distraught by the great loss of life, but the Bhagavata specifically draws attention to the suffering of Yudhishthira because he was the son of the god Dharma, the very embodiment of righteousness. Surely the Pandavas, who understood all the intricacies of *dharma* (righteous action) and lived by them, were the least deserving of suffering. The Purana expresses this sentiment in the words of Bhishma who shows great sympathy for the Pandavas' misery: "Oh sons of Dharma! Alas how painful! How unjust! You, who have always taken shelter of brāhmaṇas, *dharma* and Acyuta (Krishna) do not deserve to live such a miserable life" (1.9.12).[1]

As an early scene in the Bhagavata, this exchange between Yudhishthira and Bhishma signals the text's concern to engage with perennial questions of human suffering. Why must people suffer so much? Why doesn't God seem to care? Why isn't escape from suffering any easier? A chaplain will invariably wrestle with these and other questions concerning suffering

---

[1] In this essay, my translations of the Bhagavata are largely based on Ganesh Tagare's translation, unless otherwise stated.

and tragedy. This essay explores a Hindu response to the problem of suffering, and in so doing provides unique insights that a chaplain may find useful.

The Bhagavata Purana is one of the most highly regarded and variegated of Hindu sacred texts. This work of over 14,000 Sanskrit verses ranks, along with the Ramayana and Mahabharata, as central to the contemporary Hindu corpus of sacred texts in the Sanskrit language. The Bhagavata has enjoyed considerable commentarial attention (with 81 extant commentaries), yet it has also permeated popular Hinduism, both in India and diaspora communities, through manifold interpretations in temple liturgy and architecture, ritual recitations, dance, drama, and more recently, film. All major vernacular languages of India have renditions of the Bhagavata, which often become regional classics in their own right. Because the Bhagavata has held such a central place in Indian thought and literature, a study of its highly developed discussion on suffering will prove useful to chaplains in understanding how Indian thinkers have approached this issue.

Before we turn to the Bhagavata's approach to suffering, it will be useful to see how the *Vedanta-sutra* has dealt with the problem. The *Vedanta-sutra* (250BCE–450CE) offers one of the earliest systematic discussions on the problem of suffering in Indian philosophy. Permeated as it is with key Vedantic terms and concepts, the Bhagavata is largely grounded in Vedanta discourse and is considered by certain North Indian Bhakti traditions to be a commentary on the *Vedanta-sutra* by its own author, Vyasa (also known as Badarayana). Thus, a brief outline of the *Vedanta-sutra*'s discussion on suffering will be especially useful in understanding the philosophical context of the Bhagavata's response to suffering.

The Problem of Evil in the *Vedanta-sutra*

The *Vedanta-sutra*'s resolution to the problem of evil is outlined in three sutras in the form of objections from opponents who hold that the world could not be the result of Brahman's (God's) creation, along with the replies of Vedanta philosophers (2.1.34-36).

An important concern for Vedantists is to maintain Brahman's creatorship of the universe without saddling him with blame for the world's problems.[2] The first *sutra* responds to the objection that if Brahman

---

2   A.L. Herman (1976) *The Problem of Evil and Indian Thought*, 1st ed. Delhi: Motilal Banarsidass, p.265.

is the cause of the world, then the presence of inequality and cruelty reflect a flaw in him. The *sūtra* asserts that the inequalities and suffering of the world are not the fault of Brahman, but are due to living beings' karma, their own actions. People suffer because of their deeds in this and previous lives and likewise enjoy due to their past good deeds. In their commentaries on this *sūtra*, Śaṅkara, Ramanuja, and Baladeva posit that although ultimately Brahman is the operative cause of the suffering and enjoyment of living beings, God always takes into account the karma of the soul (*jīva*).

In the second *sūtra*, the objector responds by saying that the karma explanation only pushes the problem a step back. The Upanishads state that "in the beginning there was Being alone, one only without a second" (Chandogya Upanishad, 6.2.1). Thus, the objector argues that since there were no *jīvas* in the beginning, there was no karma for God to take into account before the first creation. At some point God must have brought about imperfection, and therefore he is still to be blamed for the problems of the world.

The third sūtra, however, responds that this objection against the karma theory does not hold because karma and the souls are beginningless. Commentators on this *sūtra* justify the beginninglessness of creation and action by employing the seed-sprout paradox. They argue that action and creation have the relationship of a seed and a tree: a seed produces a tree and the tree produces another seed, and so on. In his commentary, Baladeva posits four categories that eternally coexist with Brahman: the *jīvas* (individual souls), *prakṛti* (substance), *kāla* (time), and karma (action).[3] It is important to note that Baladeva does not take karma as particular actions, which are changeable and therefore temporary, but rather as the flow of action that eternally accompanies the soul. According to his understanding, *jīvas* always remain active; and since *jīvas* are eternal, activity (karma) must be their everlasting characteristic, regardless of whether it is performed in the spiritual (*brahman*) or material (*prākṛt*) plane.

Thus, the *Vedanta-sūtra*, in a few brief statements, posits karma as the solution to the problem of suffering in the face of God's perfection; living beings suffer and enjoy only as a result of their free actions. In *The Origins of Evil in Hindu Mythology*, Wendy O'Flaherty raises an objection against the *karma* theory: "If God is under the sway of *karma*,

---

[3] B.D. Basu (trans.) (1934) *The Vedanta-Sutras of Badarayana with the Commentary of Baladeva*. Allahabad, India: L.M. Basu, Panini Office, p.269.

he is not omnipotent; if, as some theologians insist, God controls karma, then once again the blame is cast at his feet."[4] Various Vedantins have anticipated and responded to objections like these in their commentaries on the *sūtras*. Indeed, in an example offered by Francis Clooney, Vacaspati Misra points out that Brahman's deference to karma is a "freely chosen self-limitation," to allow for human free will and freedom.[5] God may simply choose not to control the free karma of living beings. "When a great king chooses to reward or punish his subjects based on their behavior, this restraint on his exercise of power does not diminish him. Arbitrariness, we would say, is not a necessary characteristic of omnipotence, nor is fairness a diminishment."[6] Baladeva also offers an explanation as to why the Lord, being all-powerful, wise and compassionate, might allow for karma:

> The Lord being perfectly independent, certainly could have created a world all full of joy, and with complete disregard to the karma of the *jīvas*. But then his actions, instead of being regulated by any law, would have been lawless, and it would not be a creditable attribute of the Lord. Therefore, His creation of a world with perfect regard to the karma of the *jīvas*, and to time and substance, does not detract from His omnipotence but shows forth His great wisdom and compassion. Although He can act against all the laws of matter, spirit and karma, yet He is not doing so. His allowing the *jīvas* to act in accordance with the tendencies generated by their beginningless karma, is a matter of His glory, and not an instance of His partiality.[7]

Baladeva argues that free action must exist. Freedom is necessary not just for love, but for life, for something that does not have freedom is not a person, but a mere puppet. The theory of karma allows for this freedom because it is based on the assumption that every person has a moral responsibility for his or her actions, and hence the freedom of moral choice.[8]

---

4   W. O'Flaherty (1980) *The Origins of Evil in Hindu Mythology*. Berkeley, CA: University of California Press, p.14.
5   F.X. Clooney (1989) "Evil, divine omnipotence, and human freedom: Vedanta's theology of karma." *The Journal of Religion* 69, 4, p.536.
6   Ibid., 536.
7   Basu (1934), p.270.
8   O'Flaherty (1980), p.19.

The Problem of Evil in the Bhagavata Purana

There is no doubt that the Bhagavata, like the *Vedanta-sūtra*, grants a significant place to the doctrine of beginningless karma. Both God and the *jīvas* are eternal, and activity, karma, is their everlasting characteristic. In its narrative of Purañjana, for example, the Bhagavata suggests that some souls, who are originally with God in the spiritual realm, fall and reincarnate in this world due to their own actions. When Purañjana reincarnates as Queen Vaidarbhi and is overwhelmed with grief due to her husband's death, Krishna approaches her in the guise of a *brāhmaṇa*. Krishna speaks of himself and the queen as friends who have wandered together, far from their original home: "Do you remember yourself as having a friend called *avijñāta* [your unknown friend] and that you, being given earthly pleasures, left me in search of some place?" (4.28.53). The Bhagavata here suggests that souls dwelt originally with God, with whom they enjoyed a relation of friendship, until some of them willfully gave up his company in order to enjoy the pleasures of this world. "O Friend! You…left me and with your heart set on carnal pleasures went down to the earth" (4.28.55). Commentators such as Viśvanātha Cakravartin have suggested that there is no reason for Purañjana's—the soul's—fall other than his own free will.[9] Śrīdhara Svāmi considers the soul's choice to be inexplicable: "The word, *yadṛcchayā*, 'all of a sudden, on its own,' indicates that it is extremely difficult to explain the union of these two [the soul and matter]."[10] Indeed, why Purañjana would exercise his free will in such a way is causeless and inexplicable, for the will's "freedom" must ultimately be defined in terms of causelessness and inexplicability.

Throughout the Bhagavata Purana one can find narratives such as this affirming the doctrine of karma. The Bhagavata contends that all the karma one performs, and the good and bad results of those actions add, in each lifetime, to the overall progress of the living being. "The mind is a storehouse of impressions unconsciously left by the good or bad actions in the past life; it…causes higher or lower forms of life in various kinds of physical bodies" (5.11.5). If living beings could remember their past lives, they would act righteously only out of fear. But on a subconscious

---

9   Viśvanātha Cakravartin's commentary on BhP 4.25.20 in B. Swami (trans.) (2004) *Sarartha Darsini: Tenth Canto Commentaries on Srimad Bhagavatam*. Mathura, India: Mahanidhi Swami.
10 Śrīdhara's commentary on BhP 4.25.20 in B. Dasa (2006) *Unveiling His Lotus Feet, a Detailed Overview of Srimad Bhagavatam, Cantos One-Four*. Vrindavan, India: Vrindavana Institute for Higher Education, p.896.

level, the living being learns by the impressions gathered in current and past lifetimes. Past impressions create certain dispositions and desires in this life, which propel the soul to its next body. In this way, the soul learns and progresses on its journey through the cycle of *saṁsāra*. "The Almighty Lord evolved the intellect, senses, mind and vital airs of all embodied beings, so that they could experience matter and take births [and deaths], and ultimately attain freedom [liberation]" (10.87.2).

Nevertheless, the Bhagavata does not see karma as an adequate solution to the problem of suffering. It admits that just as it is difficult or sometimes impossible to ascertain the cause of a forest fire, which may be due to lightning or the rubbing of sticks, so also "the cause of living beings' acquiring and losing physical bodies is difficult to understand" (10.1.51).

The Pandavas had undergone immense suffering. As children they lost their father and were harassed by their uncle and cousins. Their wife was humiliated, and they were banished to the forest for 14 years. In the end, they lost all their children, dear friends, relatives, and teachers in the battle. Their mother, Kunti, lost her husband at a young age and raised five children on her own.

Bhishma rejects the idea that the Pandavas' distress is a product of their past karma. Indeed, throughout the Bhagavata's narrative, the Pandavas' good character and spotless reputation are emphasized. Bhishma points out that although the Pandavas always lived righteously, they nevertheless had to undergo immense distress. How could such pure-hearted persons be afflicted by so much injustice? The doctrine of *karma* makes a person singularly responsible for his or her own fate. Bhishma, however, finds such a view of suffering to be unsatisfactory and proceeds to ponder other causes of suffering—the primary suspect being God himself.

Since Krishna, God, himself was always accompanying Yudhishthira, only He could be the ultimate cause of Yudhishthira's suffering. In verse 1.9.16, Bhishma implicitly implicates Krishna: "Oh King! No one can fully understand the intentions of this [Krishna]. As a matter of fact, even learned people who desire to fathom it become perplexed." Bhishma indicates that no matter how much one tries to understand the causes of suffering and the plan of God, who is supremely independent, it is impossible: "Even though great philosophers inquire exhaustively, they are bewildered" (1.9.16).

At this point in Bhishma's monologue, the commentator Viśvanātha raises a pertinent question: since Krishna was actually present before Bhishma and the Pandavas, why did they not simply ask the Lord about his plan? Viśvanātha answers his own question:

> Even if asked by Bhishma, the Lord will not speak, but instead will evade him... Even if he [the Lord] says something, he still bewilders everyone. Therefore his plan is to be followed, but is not subject to inquiry. (1.9.18)

Viśvanātha adds that Krishna confuses everyone, particularly by his oblique speech. In Book Eleven, Krishna announces that even the Vedas speak elusively and answer questions indirectly. "The Vedic seers and mantras deal in esoteric terms, and I am also pleased by such confidential descriptions" (11.21.35). Nevertheless, Viśvanātha admits that although "no one can understand or interfere with the plan of Krishna," one is still drawn to inquire (1.9.16).

> Inquiry is necessary. Does God want to give us suffering? Does he want to give us joy? Does he want to give us suffering and joy? It cannot be the first option, because his quality of being affectionate to his devotee would be canceled. It cannot be the second, because we have not seen any happiness. It cannot be the third option because that would be a contradiction to his kind nature. It is finally decided that no one can solve the problem by inquiry. (1.9.16)

Although no one can know the plan of the Lord, Bhishma urges one to accept that plan when it unfolds, because his plan "is perfect." "There never has been any change in his [Krishna's] mind or his actions, because he is the Soul of all, impartial, without a second, free from pride, and free from all sins" (1.9.21). Bhishma is confident that although the Lord may cause distress, he always acts for the benefit of all, and especially for the benefit of his pure-hearted devotees.

The Bhagavata contends that the Supreme Lord, being fully independent, uplifts his devotees in the way that is best for them. A devotee therefore understands that the happiness and distress he or she undergoes while performing *bhakti-yoga* (devotional actions) is the special mercy of the Lord. This point is made explicit in many passages: "Just as a father, out of his own accord, looks after the good of his child, you personally also do what is good for us" (4.20.31). Viśvanātha comments, "The Lord certainly knows what is best for me, even if I don't know. Karma and time have no effect on a devotee, so this is Krishna's personal arrangement for me. Out of His mercy, Krishna sometimes gives me happiness and sometimes gives me distress" (10.14.8). By giving temporary distress, Krishna frees his devotees from the actual cause of distress—namely their forgetfulness of God. Suffering drives a righteous person to remember and take refuge in God. That remembrance forever frees the devotee from repeated birth and death in this world (11.2.49).

The Bhagavata is so deeply convinced about the soteriological purpose of suffering that it even portrays devotees asking God for more suffering. After the Kurukṣetra battle, Queen Kunti, the mother of the Pandavas who witnessed the demise of her entire dynasty, asks Krishna for this rather unconventional benediction: "May calamities befall us at every step, O Teacher of the world, if in these calamities we are blessed with Your sight, which eliminates the possibility of our seeing another birth [and death]" (1.8.25). Calamity serves as a powerful aid in helping the Queen become free from temporary worldly attachments so she can constantly remember the Lord. "May my mind be continuously drawn in love to you and not be attached to any other object, just as the water of the Ganges forever flows into the sea" (1.8.42).

The Bhagavata often describes suffering as a burning (*tapa*) which purifies the soul: "Just as gold, when smelted by fire, gives up its impurity and again takes on its own form, similarly the soul, shaking off the contamination of karma by the practice of *bhakti-yoga*, attains Me [Krishna]" (11.14.25). The practice of *bhakti* burns off any remaining selfish desires (*kāma*) due to past karma and allows souls to experience the sweetness and beauty of Krishna and rejoin his eternal pastimes (*līlā*) in the spiritual realm (10.29.10). When the devotees' love for Krishna and other living beings is constant and selfless, they experience "limitless and unending happiness," and Bhagavan becomes controlled by their affection. He chooses to serve them, as he did in the case of the Pandavas. Viśvanātha states that Krishna's first expression of mercy "bears the fruit of tormenting pain." His second wave of mercy causes an "extraordinary shower of sweet *bhakti-rasa* to rain down" on his devotees, and Krishna promises that "I give mercy in the form of my very self" (10.88.9).

Conclusion

The Bhagavata does not tire of portraying the human condition as one dominated by suffering despite the best of intentions. In one such portrayal, the sage Śuka elaborates and explains an extended metaphor of a merchant caravan (5.14), in which a group of merchants, determined to make money by collecting wood to sell in the city venture into a dense forest full of tangled vines. There the merchants are attacked by rogues, thieves, and jackals, and before long a breeze makes some dry trees rub together and start a forest fire. As they flee in fear, they are scorched by the fire, their feet are pierced by thorns and pebbles, and they are faced with a very steep mountain pass.

Śuka explains that the merchants represent the souls (*jīvas*) who are originally with God. As the merchants leave their home to make money, so the *jīvas* leave God's kingdom to find pleasure in the temporal world. The forest's tangled creepers are likened to the *jīvas*' desire for profit, praise, and prestige. Intent on fulfilling their selfish desires, the *jīvas* traverse the path of *saṁsāra*, which is treacherous like a mountain pass. They burn in the forest fire of miseries, and like rogues and thieves, their uncontrolled senses constantly harass them. All the *jīvas*' endeavors are obstructed by numerous thorn-like difficulties, ultimately rendering them fruitless.

Śuka provides a happy ending to his parable: After experiencing immense tribulations, the *jīvas* finally betake themselves to the path of the Lord's devotees and resort to the lotus-like feet of Lord Hari (Krishna)— those "feet which pacify all the afflictions and agonies of *saṁsāra*" (5.14.1). And so it is that this caravan of merchants (humanity) "finally returns to the starting point of this journey (God) which, the sages say, is the terminus to the road of *saṁsāra*" (5.14.38).

Thus, the Bhagavata urges its readers to see that the soul's envelopment in matter is a temporal and temporary experience with a beginning and an end, which the soul undergoes only once. The Bhagavata argues that the souls' association with material nature is a necessary step in their spiritual evolution, and is therefore permitted, although not desired, by God. "Your *maya* [power] carries on the creation, preservation and destruction of the universe [for the progress of the *jīvas*], though not desired by You [for Your own sake]…" (5.18.38). When the soul remembers its eternal relationship with the Lord, and takes refuge in him, it gains the greatest freedom, even in suffering, and after death returns to its original home beyond matter.

For chaplains wrestling with questions concerning suffering and tragedy, the Bhagavata presents a message of hope—a message we find in the metaphor of the merchant caravan and in Kunti's prayers to Krishna: although calamities may befall living beings at any moment, "the sight of Krishna will occur, ending the repetition of worldly existence"(1.8.25).[11] Indeed, even after being shot with dozens of arrows, and seeing his entire

---

11 See also K.R. Valpey (2005) "The Bhagavatapurana as a Mahabharata Reflection." In P. Koskikallio and M. Jezic (2009) *Parallels and Comparisons: Proceedings of the Fourth Dubrovnik International Conference on the Sanskrit Epics and Puranas*, September 2005. Zagreb: Croatian Academy of Sciences and Arts, p. 276.

dynasty destroyed, the Bhagavata portrays Bhishma as being undeterred in his devotion and appreciation for Krishna. "Oh protector of the earth [Yudhishthira]! Look at his compassion on his staunch devotees that Krishna himself has appeared before me, when I am giving up my life" (1.9.22). Along the same lines, Bhishma encourages Yudhishthira to face and overcome all reverses in life by the strength of *bhakti* for Krishna. Thus Bhishma's sentiment is indicative of the Bhagavata's overall response to the problem of suffering, namely to celebrate "devotional heroism," the facing and conquering of unavoidable suffering through intensified devotion.[12] Implicit in this and other narratives of devotional heroism throughout the Bhagavata is that divine allowance of suffering are means by which devotees—*bhagavatas*—are understood to be elevated from already-existing greatness to eternal glory. As models for ordinary human beings, such conditions of adversity underscore the Bhagavata's message of hope, that all human beings, and indeed ultimately all living beings, may become exalted by imbibing the Bhagavata vision.

---

12 Ibid, p.275.

How Does the Goddess Help Us Handle Pain and Suffering?
A Shakta Theological Foundation for Hindu Chaplaincy

Rachel Fell McDermott

This chapter investigates how Hindu traditions focused on forms of the Goddess (or Shakta traditions) can provide succor for grieving devotees.[1] Before beginning, however, one must acknowledge that, as the other essays in this volume demonstrate, chaplains derive from very different backgrounds and likely apply an eclectic set of tools in their pastoral care practices. For instance, the first Hindu chaplain in the US was Swami Sarvaananda, who earned a degree in Chaplaincy Studies at the University of Virginia and then served as a chaplain there from 2001; she is a disciple of Swami Satchidananda, founder of Integral Yoga. Georgetown University's Hindu chaplain, Brahmachari V. Sharan, is a Vaishnava Hindu monk, a Hindu priest, and an adjunct Professor in Sanskrit at Georgetown's Department of Linguistics. Swami Tyagananda, volunteer Hindu chaplain at Harvard University, is from the Ramakrishna Vedanta Center, which is Vedantic and Shakta in orientation.

Another way of framing differences among Hindu chaplains is to think of different "levels" of approach: (1) some chaplains are drawn from formal religious or academic worlds but rarely have clinical training; (2) others, typically with theological and clinical training, are seen as promoting or representing one particular religious tradition in their ministries; and (3) others are clinicians with non-sectarian backgrounds who are

---

[1] This essay complements my earlier one on a related subject: "Evil, Motherhood, and the Hindu Goddess Kālī." In D.M. Eckel and B.L. Herling (eds) *Deliver Us From Evil*. New York: Continuum, 2008.

specialists in care and therapy.² In this chapter, we are operating mainly at the second level, since theological differences may determine approach. And yet, the extent to which chaplains—or the institutions that employ them—see their work along *sampradāyik* lines, with specific Vaishnava, Shakta, Śaiva, or Yogic teaching, is not at all clear. In a multicultural setting, even to employ one Hindu is a victory for most institutions.

The question of what a Shakta approach to chaplaincy might look like is further complicated by the lack of role models in India. Because of the government's secular stance, public institutions do not employ chaplains of any type, and private institutions (such as a Christian or sectarian Hindu hospital) tend to do so only if following a Western pattern.³ Instead, ill or grieving people consult gurus or adepts attached to their families, or temple priests if they have special relationships with them. Indeed, the very helpful *Guidelines for Health Care Providers Interacting with Patients of the Hindu Religion and Their Families*, published in Chicago in 2002, declares, describing all communities of Hindus, that there is "no expectation" that "Hindu clergy" will visit the sick at home or in hospital, although physicians or other healthcare providers who happen to be Hindu may be a resource.⁴ Even the newest pastoral care program I can find in India—Mrtyu Mrtyunjay, in Kolkata—is a trust with an 18-member governing board, drawn from academics, IT professionals, scientists, palliative care experts—and no sectarian religious leaders.⁵

"We rely on what we have been taught," said a cancer survivor to me in Kolkata in June 2018, "we do not expect religious teachers to visit us in hospital for counseling or support." When I asked her what she had been taught that she found helpful, she described common Hindu philosophical ideas of the imperishable *ātman*, or soul, which endures after the body is cast aside; the monistic, Upanishadic notion of Brahman, the imperishable, indescribable force that manifests as countless deities

---

2   See D.J. Lawrence, Secretary of the College of Pastoral Supervision and Psychotherapy (2018) "A new proposal: Three levels of chaplaincy and pastoral expertise." February 1. http://www.cpsp.org/pastoralreportarticles/5713636, accessed on August 29, 2018.
3   An exception is ISKCON's Bhaktivedanta Hospital in Mumbai, which is theologically driven. See R.C. Powell (2011) "Report from India: A pastoral care department that runs its own hospital." [American] College of Pastoral Supervision and Psychotherapy, July 18. www.cpsp.org/pastoralreportarticles/3778981, accessed on January 12, 2018.
4   Metropolitan Chicago Healthcare Council (2002) "Guidelines for Health Care Providers Interacting with Patients of the Hindu Religion and Their Families." www.advocatehealth.com/assets/documents/faith/cghindu.pdf, accessed on August 28, 2018, p.4.
5   "Forum to counsel terminally ill patients." Chakraborty, A. (2018). In *Sunday Times of India* (Kolkata), August 12, 2018.

to whom one can pray; the doctrine of karma and reincarnation; and, of course, the Bhagavad-Gita. This beloved text is a resource for all Hindus, irrespective of *sampradāya*, for it explains what happens after death in the context of God's love. The fact that "the Lord" in this case is Krishna is not a stumbling block for those who do not make Krishna their *iṣṭa-devatā*, or chosen deity, for Krishna himself claims to be one with all forms of the divine. Pratima Dharm, when working as a military chaplain to American soldiers in Iraq, made the Bhagavad-Gita her basis for counseling.[6] Swami Sarvaananda enumerates five resources of the Hindu tradition for helping alleviate suffering: the monism of the early tradition, karma, breathing practices, prayer, and the cultivation of inner stillness. None of these is "owned" by any Hindu community.[7] The Australian publication, *Health Care Providers' Handbook on Hindu Patients,* contains three parts, only one of which centers on "Hindu beliefs affecting health care."[8] Its Introduction states that because there are so many cultural and personal variations in the tradition, it is important that healthcare providers "consult the patient" about his or her level of religious observance and practice.[9] Nowhere is there any distinction between Shaktas and others.

It appears that in actual practice, up to the present, *sampradāyik* boundaries and guidelines seem not to be as important as we might think: there is a generic pool of pastoral resources, not all of which are defined by any Hindu sub-tradition. Perhaps equally important for our purposes here, Shaktas tend to be theologically liberal.[10] The Tantras and Puranas, as well as the devotional hymns often associated with the tradition, freely identify the Goddess with Krishna, claiming that ultimately there is no difference between them. Even the practice of chanting Krishna's name, "*Hari Nām*," can be comforting at death.

---

6   See N. Lakshman (2014) "Interview: 'Gita my basis for counselling hindus in the military.'" *The Hindu*, November 17. www.thehindu.com/opinion/interview/gita-my-basis-for-counselling-hindus-in-us-military/article6605265.ece, accessed on July 26, 2018.
7   S. Sarvaananda (2009) "The Hindu chaplain: Our faith's tolerant beliefs and powerful practices enable us to minster effectively to all in need." *Hinduism Today*, July/August/September. www.hinduismtoday.com/modules/sartsection/category.php?categoryid=386, accessed on July 26, 2018.
8   Queensland Government (2011) "Health care providers' handbook on Hindu patients." www.health.qld.gov.au/multicultural/health_workers/hbook-hindu, accessed on August 29, 2018.
9   Ibid., 5.
10 I have often been told in Bengal that Shaktas are more ritually conservative than Vaishnavas, in the sense that requirements for initiation are more stringent, whereas Vaishnavas are more theologically conservative, refusing to equate Krishna with any form of the Goddess.

Assuming, however, that one were to find a chaplain trained in Shakta approaches to the suffering and pain, what might he or she do, or counsel, or offer, from Shakta theology? This is the question to which the remainder of this essay now turns.

Shakta Theology as a Response to the Problem of Suffering

Shakta traditions refer to those forms of Hindu worship and devotionalism that are focused not just on a female deity, but on an independent, powerful goddess who is not subservient to a male god. For instance, Sita the consort of Rama, or Lakshmi the consort of Vishnu, are subsumed within worship accorded to their more powerful husbands, and devotees of Sita and/or Lakshmi would likely consider themselves Vaishnavas, not Shaktas. The latter label refers to worshippers of the goddess Durga in her various forms (Ambika, Jagaddhatri, Nanda Devi, Sheranvali, Vaishno Devi, Vindhyavasini, etc.), Kali and her more dread form Chamunda, Shitala the smallpox goddess, Manasa the snake goddess, and a host of potent, local "village goddesses," or *āmmans*, whose provenance is supreme over their own locales. Many of them are said to be married to Siva, but he is minor in relation to their autonomous volition. These goddesses are claimed to confer material benefits (*bhutki*), as well as spiritual liberation (*mukti*). Although a Hindu chaplain in the West is more likely to encounter a Durga- or Kali-worshipping devotee than one attached to a local goddess, the Shakta deities share in common a puissance and a fiercely maternal protection of their followers. They are also claimed as the feminine counterpart of the Upanishadic Brahman; as embodiments of Shakti, or female Energy, they pervade the universe in all its coincidences of opposites. They are one with, or cause, everything, whether weal or woe. The goddess traditions are frequently categorized as being Shaktadvaitic—in other words, based on a monism where all is reduced to Shakti.

The myths and iconography of the Shakta deities reinforce the philosophical claims of their coincidence and transcendence of opposites. Whether it is Durga or one of her multiforms riding a tiger or lion and striding into battle with demons, her hands wielding weapons while she smiles beatifically; or Kali, clad in dismembered body parts of her victims and yet showing "fear not" and boon-bestowing gestures with her hands; or Shitala, covered in small-pox pustules at the same time as she promises release from them, all are icons of the totality of life and death. The most famous Shakta Sanskrit text is the sixth century Devi-Mahatmya (Glorification of the Goddess), in which a sage narrates three stories of the greatness of the Goddess to two despondent listeners, a king named Suratha and a merchant named Samādhi. In all cases proper worship compels her rescue and mercy, and the recipient of the mercy pours forth hymns of praise, detailing her totality.[11] At the conclusion of the text, Durga promises that anyone in any danger, from forest fires, villains, death sentences, prison, shipwreck, or personal affliction, will be released by listening to the "Mahatmya" stories.[12]

As such, the classical "problem of evil" does not arise in a Shakta context, for goddesses are widely believed to test, or punish, or display their power, when such is called for, and there is nothing beyond their responsibility. Hence, they may not be "all good" any more than they are "all evil." And yet, if the Goddess is all-powerful, the devotee still yearns to know why She did not step in to save him or her in distress. This is powerfully depicted in the 1960 Bengali film *Devi*, directed by Satyajit Ray. In the story, a Kali-devotee named Kalikinkar Choudhuri is left at the end of the story a crushed man; having entrusted his sick grandson into Her care, he cannot fathom why She let him die, when She had healed so many other supplicants.

Devotees who can see through their pain to the unity of the Goddess find it easier to handle their suffering. The famed Bengali saint and devotee of Kali, Ramakrishna (1836–1886), suffered from throat cancer in the last two years of his life, dying slowly and extremely painfully:

> It was revealed to me in a vision that during my last days I should have to live on pudding. During my present illness my wife was one day feeding me with pudding. I burst into tears and said, "Is this my living on pudding near the end, and so painfully?"[13]

And yet, when asked by the future Swami Vivekananda to pray to the Goddess for his own recovery, Ramakrishna reported:

---

11 For examples of these hymns in English translation, see *Devi-Mahaymta* 1:45, 61–62, in T.B. Coburn (1991) *Encountering the Goddess: A Translation of the Devi-Mahaymta and a Study of Its Interpretation*. Albany, NY: State University of New York Press, p.37.
12 *Devi-Mahaymta* 12.23-29, in Ibid., p.81.
13 In a passage dated Wednesday, December 23, 1885, in M. *The Gospel of Sri Ramakrishna*, trans. Swami Nikhilananda, abridged edition (New York: Ramakrishna-Vivekananda Center of New York, 1942, 1948, 1958), p.471. Used by permission of the Ramakrishna-Vivekananda Center of New York.

I said to her, "Mother, I cannot swallow food because of my pain. Make it possible for me to eat a little." She pointed you all out to me and said, "What? You are eating through all those mouths. Isn't that so?" I was ashamed and could not utter another word.[14] He saw that Kali was all, a view consistent with a Shaktadvaita philosophy. During the rest of his illness he repeatedly spoke of his cancerous body, and the healthy bodies of his disciples, as pervaded by the same Shakti.

The idea that all, including suffering, grief, and loss, *is* the Goddess can therefore provide comfort and strength. But I suspect that a Hindu chaplain would need to tread carefully in putting this forward in a counseling session; for the concept is philosophical and not very personal. Not everyone has the strength of character of a Ramakrishna. The same, of course, is true of the karma "solution." It is one thing for a sufferer to claim that his illness is due to his own past karma, and quite another for a chaplain essentially to charge or blame him for his fate by bringing up the unknowable distant past from another life. Karma is an explanation that sufferers frequently have recourse to at a later period of reflection; it is not comforting in the moment of crisis.

Given the Goddess's potency, urging a devotee to pray to her for strength or healing may resonate with the resources of the Shakta tradition. Some ritually inclined devotees offer the Goddess vegetarian or non-vegetarian sacrifices, in the hopes that she will be pleased by the donation.[15] Chaplains could help facilitate such an offering at a goddess temple, if that were what the devotee felt the deity was requesting. In the same vein, others keep fasts or make vows (*vratas*) in the hope that, following the model of famed devotees who made promises and were rewarded, they too may be favored by relief from their suffering.[16] Other devotees take an approach closer to that of the Psalmist of the Hebrew and Christian Bibles, essentially chiding the Goddess for her negligence, especially given her renowned feats of power in the past. Or, they may plead with her for healing, or rescue, or mercy. The following is from the most famous composer of devotional poetry to Kali, Ramprasad Sen (1718–1775):

---

14   Ibid., p.110.
15   In the famed *Kālikā Purāṇa*, goat sacrifice is said to please the Goddess, guarantee prosperity (59.29), destroy the misfortune of the giver (55.7b–11a), and cause the death of one's enemies (sometimes understood as sins), which are being impersonated by the live animals (67.151). See D. Shastri (trans.) (1991) *Kālikā Purāṇa*. Delhi: Nag Publishers, 2:771–772, 849; 3:1025.
16   See A.M. Pearson (1996) *"Because it Gives Me Peace of Mind": Ritual Fasts in the Religious Lives of Hindu Women*. Albany, NY: State University of New York Press.

Supreme Savior of Sinners,
awarding the fruit of highest bliss,
grant the shade of Your feet
to this very wretched one,
    Wife of Śaṅkara.
In Your great goodness
be merciful to me
    Deliverer,
    Mā.
I've committed sins,
I've got no merit,
and as for prayer
I'm empty.
Take your form Tara
and rescue me
    Mother of the Universe.
Your feet are my boat;
they carry me over the sea of becoming.
Be gracious to Prasād,
    Bhava's housewife.[17]

Indeed, the Goddess is known for being a demon-killer, for putting things right. In the Bengali Ramayana she is said to have aided Rama in his battle with Ravana;[18] in the "Devi-Mahatmya" she restores Suratha's kingdom and gives liberation to the merchant Samādhi;[19] and, closer to our own times, she was adopted as a symbol of rebellion in the Indian Independence Movement from the 1920s on.[20] The "Father of Kali Studies" in North America, scholar David Kinsley (1939–2000), found the image of Durga slaying demons to be very helpful as he battled cancer cells in his body.

Chaplains may also partner with gurus or adepts already close to the suffering devotee. My Shakta mentor and friend Minati Kar, when dying from jaw cancer in 2014, traveled when she could from Kolkata

---

17 Rāmprasād Sen, "Patita pābanī parā," trans. R.F. McDermott, in *Singing to the Goddess: Poems to Kālī and Umā from Bengal*. New York: Oxford University Press, 2001, p.70. Reprinted by permission of Oxford University Press.
18 See H. Mukhopādhyāy (ed.) (1957) *Rāmāya (1957) ās Biracita*. Kolkata, India: Sāhitya Samsad, pp.384–385.
19 *Devi-mahatmya* 13.5-17, in Coburn (1991), pp.83–84.
20 For examples, see R.F. McDermott (2011) *Revelry, Rivalry, and Longing for the Goddesses of Bengal: The Fortunes of Hindu Festivals*. New York: Columbia University Press, pp.64–68.

into the countryside of Burdwan district, West Bengal, to seek blessing from a Tantric teacher named Mauni (Silent) Baba. After she ceased being able to travel, she wrote and spoke to him on the phone, and his words brought great comfort. He told her to pray to the goddess Kali, simply and sincerely. Before she died, he was tragically murdered for the jewels with which he adorned his image of the Goddess. Although this shocked and distressed Minati, she also found him to be a model of acceptance of pain and death.

While Shaktas do not have a concept of a Shakta heaven, like the Vaishnava Vaikuntha, to which devotees may hope to go after death—Shaktas veer away from the dualism implied in such a vision toward a more monistic view of the soul merging with the cosmic Sakti—and while they do not, like the Christian believer, have a suffering God on whom they can pattern their own anguished perseverance, they can lean upon the strong arm of the Goddess and rely upon the pioneers of their Shakta tradition who have shown how to love and accept the Goddess in all her paradoxical kindness. A sensitive Hindu chaplain, even if personally committed to a different Hindu *sampradāya*, can draw from this rich theological wellspring to offer comfort and aid to those facing pain and suffering.

Lessons from the Upanishads for the Spiritual Caregiver

Madhu Vedak Sharma[1]

The Upanishads are often celebrated as masterpieces of Hindu metaphysics. They form, along with the Bhagavad-Gita and the Vedanta Sutra, the canon for Vedanta—perhaps the most influential classical school of philosophy to arise out of Hinduism. And yet, at first glance they may appear to be vague, cryptic, and even inaccessible. What practical benefit can be drawn from these texts? What do they tell us about our lives in the here and now?

In this essay we suggest that the Upanishads do indeed provide guidance for living a life with purpose and thoughtfulness. We hope to demonstrate how lessons from the Upanishads can be of particular help to the spiritual caregiver. First, we discuss the Upanishads generally, framing them as texts that lend themselves to reflection and inspiration. We then turn to two of the most popular Upanishads: the Katha and the Isha. Not only are these two among the most beloved Upanishads in the Hindu community, but they are also texts that we both have found particularly useful in our work as college chaplains. We draw out a few key lessons from each of these Upanishads that a spiritual caregiver might find especially relevant.

The Upanishads

What are the Upanishads? A full exploration of that question is beyond the scope of this short essay, but suffice it to say that they are a body of

---

1   Thanks are due to Vineet Chander for his help in developing this essay.

writings that articulate the core of Hindu philosophical thought. The four Vedas, considered the ancient scriptural foundation of Hinduism, each have supplementary texts that seek to communicate the Vedas' essence by delving into deeper questions of philosophy and spirituality—these are the Upanishads. Tradition holds that there are 108 of these texts, although only nine are commonly studied or referenced. While these differ considerably in length, style, and content, the nine principal Upanishads share a common objective: to convey the cumulative experiences of various self-realized *rishis*, or seers of truth.

In the introduction to his popular translation of the Upanishads, Hindu scholar Eknath Easwaran argues that the message of these texts is "universal, as relevant to the world today as it was to India five thousand years ago."[2] Their relevance, he suggests, stems from the fact that these are not theoretical treatises on abstract concepts; rather, they are practical wisdom, designed to actually be applied in one's life. "Their purpose is not so much instruction as inspiration," Easwaran writes, adding that the Upanishads are tied to the notion of "personal experience."[3]

The word *upanishad* literally means "sitting down near." This most likely refers to the ancient practice of a student sitting down near his or her guru while receiving knowledge—that is, knowledge about the true self or about Brahman (*brahmavidya*). It also might suggest, more generally, that this knowledge is meant to be studied with another, and engaged with through dialogue, questioning, and reflection. A chaplain or spiritual caregiver, while not a "guru" in the classical sense, might certainly still be a resource for one to "sit down near" in this process of reflection in relationship. In this spirit, let us now turn to the lessons a caregiver might draw from two of the most popular Upanishads—the Isha and the Katha.

Balance and Devotion: The Isha Upanishad

The Isha Upanishad (also known as the Ishopanishad) is not the oldest, but is so beloved that an Indian tradition has developed to place it first in any Upanishad collection. Indeed, Mahatma Gandhi famously declared that, even if all other scriptures were reduced to ashes, Hinduism would last forever—if only the first verse in the Ishopanishad were left in the

---

2   E. Easwaran (trans.) (2007) *The Upanishads,* 2nd ed. Berkeley, CA: Nilgiri Press, p.19. Reprinted by permission of Nilgiri Press, www.bmcm.org.
3   Ibid., 20.

memory of the Hindus. Despite its small size—the entire Upanishad consists of 18 mantras and one invocation—it is densely packed with lessons for the aspirant.

The invocation and first three verses of the Isha offer us a paradigm of abundance. "When fullness is taken from fullness," the invocation mystically pronounces, "fullness still remains." The first and second mantras echo this idea by describing the mood of one who has this vision: such people see the divine in all, thus they neither covet nor fear. Rather, they are able to find joy while renouncing attachment. One with such a consciousness of abundance, the text teaches, experiences true freedom even while busy engaging with the world. On the other hand, those with a consciousness of paucity, limitation, or competition shroud themselves in darkness.

This idea of shifting our consciousness from a framework of insufficiency to one of fullness is profound and powerful, inviting introspection. How do we see the world and our relationship to it? Do we see a world of limited resources and possibilities, in which we must compete with others to carve out as much real estate as we can? Or do we see the same divinity expressing itself everywhere, reminding us to be grateful for whatever comes our way while celebrating the gains of others without envy or desire? A spiritual caregiver can draw from the Isha's paradigm of abundance to help others to take personal inventory and shift their way of thinking. The caregiver can encourage others to confront their own fears, anxieties, and insecurities—manifestations, perhaps, of the paradigm of insufficiency—and cultivate inner security and a healthy sense of non-attachment.

How does one develop the consciousness of abundance? The next three mantras offer the Isha's answer: by realizing the true self. This self is beyond the perception of the senses, the grasp of the mind, or even the reasoning of the intellect. It paradoxically defies categorization or binaries—far and near, outside and within, still and ever-moving—and is omnipresent. The wise, the Isha suggests, honor the unity in the apparent multiplicity, seeing themselves in all beings, and all beings in them.

Interestingly, the Isha seems intentionally ambiguous; its description of the true self may be applied to the individual self (*ātman*) or to Brahman, the cosmic totality of reality. Indeed, the text conflates these categories, suggesting a unity between the self and Brahman. Different theological schools interpret this unity in various ways. The Advaitins (radical non-dualists) argue that ultimately the self and Brahman are one and the same, while Visistadvaitins (qualified non-dualists) and Dvaitins (dualists) agree that *ātman* and Brahman are one in quality or nature, but remain ontologically distinct entities. All of these schools ground their position on their interpretation of the Upanishads generally, and the Isha in particular.

Spiritual caregivers need not get bogged down in theological differences. By suggesting a unity between the true self and Brahman on any level, the Isha gives us an opportunity to act on the basis of spiritual awareness. This awareness, the realization that all living beings are inherently one with Brahman and thus with each other, takes the idea of connectedness to the deepest level. Caregivers can help draw out the practical benefits of such an outlook: being nonjudgmental, treating everyone equally and with respect, honoring the inherent dignity and sanctity of all living beings.

The Isha's midsection (mantras nine through 14) is often regarded as the most challenging part of the text. One who dwells exclusively in the realm of the exterior material world is covered by darkness, the text poetically tells us, but one who dwells exclusively in the inner realm of spiritual knowledge is covered by even more darkness. One who worships the Lord as immanent and relative is covered by darkness; one who worships the Lord as wholly absolute and transcendent, however, is covered by even more darkness. This may strike us as surprising or paradoxical. Perhaps, the Isha is challenging our expectations and tendency toward "either/or" thinking. The truly wise, the Isha says, cultivate knowledge of the outer world *and* the inner world; they know God to be simultaneously immanent *and* transcendent. They thus "combine action and meditation" in a state of dynamic balance.[4]

A spiritual caregiver can help others to lean into the Isha's call for balance. This is especially relevant for those, such as college chaplains, who work with people in the process of forming their own faith identities. Chaplains can echo the Isha's challenging of the either/or approach and its advice to steer clear of extremes. They can offer synthesis and integration as a spiritual alternative, as the Isha does in this section.

The Isha's final mantras adopt a much more explicitly devotional tone. The unnamed narrator offers prayers to God, asking the Divine to reveal his "true face" to his devotee. Meditating on the body being reduced to ashes, evoking both the sacrificial fire and the cremation pyre, the narrator

---

4   Ibid., 58.

asks that his consciousness be absorbed in Brahman and begs his mind to remember his spiritual deeds.

It is hardly surprising that this section of the Isha has become an important part of the Hindu approach to death and dying. It is often recited to those about to pass away. Hindus assisting, formally or informally, with end-of-life care obviously find this a useful resource; those serving in other contexts, however, may also draw from this passage. The practice of "life review" is a powerful pastoral tool that caregivers in settings such as college chaplaincy or prison ministry might turn to, as well.

Fleeting Pleasure or Eternal Joy: The Katha Upanishad

The Katha is often held to be the favorite Upanishad of the collection. This may be due, in part, to its compelling and endearing narrative context: a teenage boy named Nachiketa approaches the personification of death, Yama, for instruction. When we first encounter our protagonist, he is observing his father Vajasravasa engage in ritual charity. The preternaturally wise Nachiketa senses hypocrisy—Vajasravasa makes a show of giving in charity, but in a miserly way he only donates cows that are too old to milk—and questions his father. Vajasravasa is annoyed and, in an angry outburst, tells Nachiketa that he will send him to the abode of death. Remarkably, Nachiketa remains calm and begins to reflect on a deeper meaning to his father's words. Reflecting on the inevitability and universality of death, he resolves to travel to Yama, the god of death, and learn from him.

By divine arrangement, Yama is away from his kingdom and Nachiketa must wait three days there for him to return. Embarrassed about this transgression, Yama offers Nachiketa three boons to atone for his lapse in hospitality. Nachiketa's first boon is that his father's anger be appeased and that the rift in their relationship be repaired. Yama immediately grants this. The second boon he asks is for Yama to teach him the ritual fire sacrifice that, according to Hindu mystic lore, allows one to experience the heavenly realm known as *svarga-loka*. Yama agrees, and not only does he teach the boy how to perform the sacrifice, but he also names the ritual after Nachiketa.

The third boon that Nachiketa requests forms the heart of this Upanishad: he asks Yama to reveal to him the secret of death. In marked contrast to the first two boons, Yama hesitates. Desiring to know if Nachiketa is a worthy student—and concerned that he understand the value of the wisdom he is asking about—the god of death tests the young seeker. He offers Nachiketa benedictions of good health and long life, wealth beyond comprehension, the delights of fine art and music, and pleasures of companionship with beautiful women. Nachiketa refuses all of these temptations, eloquently pointing out the futility of seeking happiness in the fleeting pleasures of the world. Now suitably convinced that Nachiketa is indeed a worthy student, Yama begins to teach him.

The secret of death, Yama explains, is essentially the secret of life: realization of the true self. The self—unlike the body it is temporarily cased in—is deathless. Like the passenger in the chariot of the physical body, the self is the witness. The senses, like wild horses hitched to the chariot, pull us down roads of desires for happiness. The undisciplined mind simply follows the dictate of the senses, like reins attached to the horses. But when an expert charioteer holds and guides the reins—that is, when the discriminating intellect (*buddhi*) trains the mind to direct the senses—the chariot safely brings its passenger to the destination. When we identify with the body and mind, we seek pleasure in the external treasures of this world; transient and fleeting, they are incapable of satisfying us.

Realizing the true self, however, we experience abiding joy that rises above the dualities of pleasure and pain and eternally satisfies our search for lasting happiness. Swami Nikhilananada explains it beautifully in his translation of this Upanishad:

> Ātman, the Self, is all-pervading Consciousness and the inner core of all things, great and small. Though dwelling in the body, It is bodiless; though associated with changing things, It is unchanging. When the mind becomes pure through devotion and righteous action, through self-control and contemplation, it then becomes serene and reflects the majesty of Ātman.[5]

Wisdom is that which brings us closer to the true self; ignorance further estranges us from it. Our senses cannot perceive the self, our minds cannot grasp it, and no amount of academic study can encapsulate it. But through meditation practice, the chanting of the sacred mantra *oṁ*, and directing the discriminating intellect towards the good rather than the merely pleasurable, we place ourselves in the best position to have the self reveal itself to us.

---

5 S. Nikhilananada (trans.) (1949, 1952, 1956, and 1959) *The Upanishads with Commentary*, vol. 1. New York: Ramakrishna-Vivekananda Center, p.111.

The Katha is rich with practical lessons for the practitioner. Here we will focus on two major ones. First, the Upanishad suggests that, in ignorance, we confuse the vehicle of the body with the self within, and fundamentally misidentify ourselves. It thus calls us to question how we see ourselves, and challenges us to re-orient our sense of self. This can be incredibly confronting. Spiritual caregivers can hold safe space within which to engage in this type of introspection and self-examination. For instance, a college chaplain might ask students to reflect upon ways in which they define themselves in terms of the externals—how they look, their academic engagement, their athletic prowess, their hobbies and talents, the money or resources they possess, the clubs or organizations they are a part of, and so on. These students often construct rigid identities that are tied to these external and transient factors. A chaplain can help students to push back against this tendency, and encourage them to identify more with the changeless self within.

The Katha's analogy of the chariot lays out a clear description of the self as distinct from the body, senses, mind, and intellect. Spiritual caregivers might take this framework to help those under their care reflect upon identity and direction for themselves. Are we sharpening the discriminating intellect to curb the restlessness of the mind and guide the senses with intention and purpose? Or do we allow the senses to be drawn to wherever the objects of the external world call them, and simply let the mind trail after them helplessly? A caregiver could draw on the Katha's analogy to help us ask these questions, to consider the possibility of separating ourselves from the layers of constructed identity, and to try to practice being a witness instead.

A second, and related, lesson that the Katha teaches us is one that Nachiketa demonstrates early in the story: choosing between the pleasurable and the good. The text encourages us to shift our priorities from the realm of the exterior to the more internal. When we choose that which is pleasing in the short run, we seek satisfaction in the objects of the external world. We chase after these things—not unlike the list of temptations presented by Yama—in the vain hope that they will make us feel fulfilled. In our quest for the pleasing, we turn our focus outwards. However, the Katha reminds us of the futility of identifying our happiness with the objects of this world and offers us an alternative. Rather than strive in the outer realm, we can turn our attention to the abiding joy that is found in the internal. The spiritual caregiver can be an invaluable helper and guide on this journey within.

Finally, although it is not the main point of the Upanishad, the earlier narrative section of the Katha is instructive, as well. Nachiketa has the best of intentions in questioning his father, and yet he is treated harshly in return. Rather than becoming vengeful or despondent, however, he draws out something positive—he sees the apparent curse as an opportunity to learn. He maintains his mood of wanting the best for others, and even uses his first boon to seek his father's welfare. Similarly, caregivers can encourage those facing challenges to see these situations as opportunities for spiritual growth and chances to express compassion and kindness.

Conclusion

In his translation of the Upanishads, Eknath Easwaran argues persuasively, that these texts are not meant to be studied theoretically; but, rather, are to be applied in one's life. Readers are meant to "not only listen to the words, but to *realize* them…to make their truths an integral part of character, conduct, and consciousness."[6] He goes as far as to suggest that the term philosophy, so often applied to these texts, falls short; instead, we should look at them as *darshana* (something seen).[7] The Upanishads offer us a refreshing, radically alternative lens through which to see ourselves, others, the world, and the Divine. Spiritual caregivers can benefit immensely from exploring this lens and can use it as an effective way of serving and facilitating others on their journeys.

---

6   Easwaran (2007), p.23.
7   Ibid., pp.22–23.

Part Two

CARE IN CONTEXT

Becoming Board-Certified
A Trail-Blazing Chaplain's Reflection

Swami Sarvaananda

I am a white, 76-year-old American woman who became a Hindu *swami* in 1977 and who, in 2001, became the first Hindu to receive Board Certification through the Association of Professional Chaplains. Perhaps my story will both instruct and inspire.

Setting the Stage

I was trained as an educator. During the 1960s, I earned Bachelor of Science and Master of Science degrees in Physical Education and Recreation from Springfield College in Springfield, Massachusetts, plus a sixth-year certificate for school administration in Connecticut. In 1980, I received a PhD in educational administration from the University of Connecticut. I held public-school teaching and school-administration positions in New York and Connecticut.

Religiously and spiritually, I was raised as a Protestant Christian in a farming area of Central New York. In 1975, I met my spiritual master, or guru, Swami Satchidananda, and began living at his Ashram in Putnam, Connecticut. With others, I developed the Integral Yoga School, which we structured as a South Indian Gurukulam. A formal school program for our children ages 3–14, it combined yoga practices with state primary and junior high curriculum studies. The teachers and students were together. All ages worked, playing and studying at each person's own academic and social level, with all studying and practicing the teachings of yoga. My PhD thesis was on the historical development of the Integral Yoga School, in the style of open education.

In 1977, while still pursuing my doctorate, I was able to take final vows of poverty, celibacy, obedience, and service in becoming a Hindu Sannyasi, or spiritual monastic. Having begun at the Connecticut Ashram, we moved as a group to land we purchased in Buckingham, Virginia in 1980. Our hope was to develop a self-sufficient community, so that we could eventually grow much of our own food, and to establish an interfaith temple, called LOTUS—Light of Truth Universal Shrine—with dedicated altars for major faiths and faiths yet unknown. Our teacher was one of the first *swamis* to come to North America, and Integral Yoga is among the founding paths of yoga study in the Western World. We moved some families down and started the next branch of the school at the new ashram. By about 1984, almost all of our activities had completely moved to the Virginia Ashram headquarters.

I was the principal and secondary head teacher in Virginia from 1980 to 1994; from 1994 to 1998 I served as the daily operations and resident services director of the Ashram. I also supervised health needs and developed a program for yoga students to learn in a one- or three-month internship. Our community was growing, so we had to keep building and expanding services; as a result, many of us changed roles and jobs to do the needful, seeing it all as part of the non-attached monastic ideal. In that spirit, in 1998, I was assigned to be the Ashram representative when the University of Virginia Health Center completed their interfaith hospital chapel. I accepted the assignment without much fanfare, unaware of the extent to which my life was about to change.

The Adventure Begins

My journey in becoming a Board-Certified Chaplain through the Association of Professional Chaplains thus began in May of 1998, when—as the Ashram's representative—I went to a lecture at University of Virginia Health Center. For the first time I heard of professional chaplains. Almost immediately, what was being described resonated deeply with me. I did not fully know what I wanted to do with it, but I felt a calling to move towards the idea of professional chaplaincy; I immediately filled out an application for the Summer Session through the Pastoral Counseling and Chaplaincy office. By the first week of June 1998, I was enrolled in the summer unit of Clinical Pastoral Education (CPE).

While in the program, I moved quickly to serving on the units, like "a duck to water." When I spoke to my spiritual teacher about my experience, he was positive and encouraging. He suggested that learning through CPE would be fulfilling to me and would be good for the Ashram. This confirmed what I had been feeling instinctively, and so I immediately applied for the first of two full years of CPE. What a wonderful experience and development of service skills as well as personal and professional growth! Near the end of the first year, we were informed that professional chaplains could seek certification from the Association of Professional Chaplains. We were given the materials to start the process, which is thorough and takes at least a year to complete. The second year CPE program included working on the professional essays and other materials necessary for the APC application.

Mentors and Unlikely Allies

As I soon discovered, the process of becoming a Board-Certified Chaplain through the Association of Professional Chaplains is quite a detailed one in general. Being from a non-Christian religion and having an atypical vocational background further complicated things. I realized that I would need help or guidance; I discovered that, at the time, there were no certified Hindu chaplains. Undaunted, I began to make contact with the national office of the Association of Professional Chaplains in 2000. Soon, I was assigned a mentor to aid me in the application: Ted Linquist, then the Certification Chairman. Ted was responsible for applications from candidates not from a Christian tradition. He was patient, encouraging, and helpful.

Ted encouraged me to participate in my first national APC conference in 2001. Through staff at UVA, I began to make national, regional, and state chaplaincy contacts. At that first conference, I also attended meetings with five Buddhists. Hindu and Buddhists have a lot of practices in common, but also have a history of rigorous philosophical debate. But at the conference, philosophical differences were far from our mind. Instead, we recognized each other as natural allies since we were all followers of Eastern religions seeking to serve as chaplains. With that in mind, I accepted their invitation to join the cohort of Buddhists who were brainstorming and assisted them by making suggestions on how the follower of Eastern religious traditions could pursue certification through APC. Those suggestions helped to form what is now called the "White Paper" on how to get to be a Certified Buddhist Chaplain through APC. We began that first year as a small group; over the years, that group has grown in size and impact. In fact, the APC has changed certification requirements for those following Eastern religious paths as a result of our work. One of the main changes was recognizing meditation as a legitimate practice and area of study within our traditions. Other changes affected the required hours of study to include a much larger area of "legitimate trainers" and eventually lead to changing a lot of the wording of the entire process necessary for board certification to include more universal religious and spiritual backgrounds.

At that first conference, I also met another group of people who were really unlikely allies—Christian pastors of Indian, and in some cases Hindu, heritage. At first glance, one might think that our meeting would be awkward or tension-filled. A white-skinned Christian woman who "converted" to Hinduism meeting a group of devout Christians who had converted (or whose parents or grandparents had converted) from Hinduism! Remarkably, however, we all immediately bonded. Perhaps we could see, in one another, the same East/West mix and hybridity. Whatever it was, we connected on a deep level. We even began holding an informal worship service together that drew from both Hindu and Christian sources, honoring their Hindu heritage as well as their chosen faith traditions. The conference also helped me to get my "toe in the water"—I was asked to serve on some national committees. Since then, I attend whatever conferences I can afford, mainly on the East Coast, and have presented workshops and led interfaith services at many.

An Uphill Climb

As I started to seriously pursue certification, I found that it was an incredibly challenging task. A major hurdle seemed to be my lack of formal pastoral training as the APC defined it; although I had my PhD, I did not have a Master of Divinity degree and had never studied in a typical seminary context. So my application hinged on arguing that the APC recognize my Graduate Education Equivalency as equal to the amount of spiritual study and instruction found in a traditional Master of Divinity program. As challenging as this seemed, I was graced with blessings that made it easier.

First, my mentor was very helpful. He helped me to better articulate my experiences as a Hindu monastic in terms that carried over to what the APC was looking for. He also began aiding me in finding ways to document and catalog my Equivalency.

Second, my many years working and serving in various organizational roles at the Ashram gave me a clearer picture of how to document my study and practice there. Monasteries are not usually known for being very organized with records or bookkeeping, but mine was something of the exception in this regard. I was able to research things like records of talks that were given by our teacher and many special guests, or workshops and courses taught, over the course of many years. That helped immeasurably; I was arguing that my years at the monastery were analogous to seminary experience, and so I needed to document this in detail. I began gathering and xeroxing documentation, building up my application, while also working on the two big papers and two case studies.

I also had the support of colleagues. Those of us seeking certification formed a group to study, discuss, and work with our instructors—Dick Haines, Joan Murray, and Mildred Best—in order to produce the best materials we could muster. Later in the year, we also met with state-wide candidates to share going over our materials and to finalize our applications.

If I had to put together a guide for applying for APC certification in 2001, it might look something like this: gather up copies of transcripts, certificates, diplomas, workshops, CPE unit evaluations, and anything else you think may aid or support your application. If you do not have a Master of Divinity degree, complete the documentation and explanation of your equivalency courses. This is the most difficult part for many practitioners from Eastern religious traditions. Mine included documenting 1,100 hours of theological study, equaling 11 college credits, having a Master of Science in Education degree, and nine units equaling 15 credits of CPE. In addition to that, find three chaplaincy references. (Your CPE supervisor provides an additional reference, as does a spiritual advisor at your temple or monastery.) Have a letter of recommendation from your faith tradition in broader terms. (Ask all making recommendations to send you a copy and/or tell you when their letter was submitted to APC.) Apart from all of that, you must write two case studies. I submitted one illustrating a hospital visit and another describing a home visit, with plenty of background as well as the almost verbatim commentary. Finally, address each of the APC's 29 competencies for chaplains, item by item, detailing your personal, pastoral, and professional skills in relation to them. Finally, share your continuing education and future peer review plans.

The process has changed since then, due in no small part to some of our efforts. Meditation, yoga practice, and studying under many teachers from many faiths are all accepted methods of pursuing spiritual study now. In addition, the APC's 29 Common Standards (competencies) for Professional Chaplains has been revised. They now include competencies in Theory of Pastoral Care (5), Identity and Conduct (9), Pastoral (9), and Professional (6) competencies. Candidates now meet with a regional board or at a national convention. This group sends their recommendation to the Certification Committee at APC.

In any case, I finally sent my application in April 2001. It felt momentous! I was accepted as a Board-Certified Chaplain at the March 2002 national convention. I became the first Certified Hindu Chaplain in the APC and, as far as anyone could tell, the first professionally Certified Hindu Chaplain in North America.

The Journey Continues
Committees and Communities

I must confess that when my guru encouraged me to make CPE a priority, suggesting that it would be good for me and good for our Ashram, I didn't realize how prescient he was. In the years since I became certified, I have come to realize how meaningful and inspiring serving in this way can be.

Since that first conference, I've developed quite a taste for serving on national, state, and local committees, and being a part of educational initiatives within the community of chaplains. Through APC, I have served on the National Graduate Education Review Committee that reviews application process for those seeking equivalency for the Masters of Divinity requirement. I have also helped to coordinate interfaith services, instruction, and committees at all three levels. I was part of the 2009 Conference Organizers Committee; this included hands-on work like inviting local clergy for the interfaith worship service, adding a meditation room to the conference, and offering classes in *haṭha yoga* and meditation in the mornings.

Something of which I am especially proud began in January 1999, when I was just starting my journey to board certification. The UVA Health Center started the first (then) Lee-King day celebration. This moved quickly to a Martin Luther King Day celebration at the University, which finally broadened out to a celebration celebrating African Americans at the university and in Charlottesville, throughout the month of February. I was very pleased to be part of this change in celebrations and to raise a voice of support as a practitioner of a minority religious faith.

I continue to teach at the UVA CPE program, especially on Hinduism, interfaith services, on being a hospice chaplain, and other topics. I also serve on their UVA Hospital Pastoral and Chaplaincy Department advisory board. When possible, I attend local, state, and national events and conferences on chaplaincy topics. This includes a group of chaplains in Central Virginia that meets monthly to discuss timely issues in the field.

Raising Awareness in Hindu Spaces

One of the unexpected blessings of my journey has been the opportunity to become an advocate for, and educator of, chaplaincy in the broader Hindu community. In 2009, I wrote a long article for *Hinduism Today* on the subject of chaplaincy.[1] I have also published in the *Integral Yoga Magazine* on the topic.[2] I have produced many papers on death, dying, grief, loss, and recovery that I use at workshops at our Ashram, at other Hindu temples, and occasionally to the local public.

I have also been a part of developing a Hindu/Eastern Studies chaplaincy program for Hindu University of America, a non-accredited institution located in Florida, which I have served as Dean of Spiritual Studies. This includes training chaplaincy volunteers for use in temples and health facilities, a two-year Chaplaincy Master's program, and for a few students, a doctorate in spiritual studies. I have now trained others to work with these programs and still act as an advisor.

I am called on, throughout the year, to speak at Hindu temples on services they want to develop or provide to meet their members' needs in their temple and local communities. I have been able to observe an increased interest in using chaplaincy skills to serve the needs of the communities. There are issues that arise from multi-generational and cultural tensions. Chaplaincy skills can be helpful in curbing feelings of frustration and anxiety that many Hindus experience while adjusting to western life and dealing daily with different generational needs within families. And as a hospice-trained chaplain I also do community

---

1 S. Sarvaananda (2009) "The Hindu chaplain: Our faith's tolerant beliefs and powerful practices enable us to minister effectively to all in need." *Hinduism Today*, July/August/September. www.hinduismtoday.com/modules/smartsection/item.php?itemid=3088, accessed on November 25, 2018.

2 See, for example, S. Sarvaananda (2016) "What is real life? What is real death?" and "Yogic preparation for death." *Integral Yoga Magazine*, Winter. www.integralyogamagazine.org/winter-2016-integral-yoga-magazine, accessed on November 25, 2018.

workshops and meet with individuals about finding housing for sick seniors, dealing with death and dying, grief, and recovery.

Of course, I continue to teach at the Ashram and at other Integral Yoga Centers on topics related to this professional background. At the Ashram I am usually the person to coordinate healthcare when someone is dying or dealing with a death event. I develop and conduct memorial services and special religious ceremonies for death; coordinate the disposing of ashes; and facilitate grief and loss trainings.

Lessons Learned Along the Way

In closing, let me point out three lessons from my journey that I have found particularly meaningful. First, I have been humbled and amazed to encounter the divine in my interactions with the religious "other." From my Christian and Jewish mentors to other faith practitioners—like the Buddhists or the Indian Christian pastors I worked with—I have learned so much and have deepened my own faith. My guru was an interfaith visionary. His motto was "Truth is One, Paths are Many." Chaplaincy has allowed me to experience and understand that like almost nothing else I have done.

Second, my experience pursuing certification was a reminder to be both humble and bold. It is humbling to see how far my tradition has to go to develop the type of infrastructures and formal programs that I encounter in other faiths. At the same time, the experience taught me to be bold and advocate for myself and my faith. Rather than simply accept the way chaplaincy was being defined, thus conclude that I did not have what was required, I was able to argue that my experiences of meditation, yoga, and other Hindu practices should also be recognized and given equal weight. I learned how to respectfully challenge the existing criteria and frameworks and help the APC to broaden the way they look at chaplaincy.

Finally, my journey has taught me to try to see the bigger picture. We might think of chaplaincy as a very small, niche field. And Hindu chaplaincy is even smaller. But what I have learned is that a chaplain can impact others in a number of ways. Becoming a Board-Certified Chaplain has opened many doors for me. It has allowed me to be an educator, a writer, an advocate, and so much more. In short, becoming an APC Board-Certified Hindu Chaplain has been, for me, a blessing beyond words.

Oṃ Tat Sat
Oṃ Shanthi, Shanthi, Shanthi

The Hospital Chaplain at Work
A Hindu Perspective

Shamā Mehtā

Hospital chaplains are spiritual care professionals who, regardless of their personal beliefs, seek to immerse themselves in the spiritual worldview of the patient or the patient's family and also to be a resource to the staff of the hospital's various units. This is a stressful environment in which to work. A trained professional chaplain can take up the supportive role when someone experiences life-altering crisis. Spiritual care, especially in a healthcare setting, encompasses not just the individual care recipient but everyone who is identified as family by the care recipient. A professionally trained chaplain is skilled in assessing spiritual needs and offering nonjudgmental presence and active listening as well as spiritual reflection. Sometimes we engage in happy events such as the blessing of a newborn, but often our work is with those who are critically ill or dying. This presents a challenge not only in meeting the needs of the patient and their family, but also in maintaining one's own spiritual and emotional health.

The variety of faiths represented by both patients and staff leads to some interesting discussions of beliefs and practices that are helpful when one of us is faced with a patient from a different spiritual group. It has also permitted us to share our theological standpoints and come to a clearer understanding of where we find common ground one with the other.

When one enters a room the thing that a patient or their family member needs most is simply to have their story heard, to share their fears, and to receive comforting words of faith. This is where the skill of listening is valuable. The patient will let you know what it is that they need from you if you take the time to listen instead of making assumptions about what to do. The challenge here is to be able to enter the patient's spiritual belief system and offer support within that system even if it differs from your own; especially if it differs from your own. Thus, anyone thinking of being a hospital chaplain would do well to study the beliefs about illness, death, and dying from many different religions.

Personally, I follow the Advaita Vedanta philosophy—vehemently promoted by Shankaracharya—which states that God (traditionally referred to as Brahman) is the totality of all existence. The path of non-duality (Advaita) is based on constant pursuit of knowledge or realization of the ultimate reality of oneself. The foundation for my work as a chaplain of the Hindu faith, my theology of spiritual care, is the notion of *dharma*, which in a general sense, is living and acting in accordance with the moral order as prescribed in the Upanishads. The underlying belief is that by living in accordance with *dharma* an individual gains benefits either in this life or in the next birth, with respect to the individual's karma (actions). The goal of the religion is to achieve *moksha*, that is liberation from the cycle of rebirth, either through self-transformation via realized knowledge, or through the grace of a merciful and loving Ishwara (God).

I believe human suffering is the direct consequence of forgetting the reality of who humans are: inherently divine. Suffering is due to the ignorance of this true nature. Suffering then in its many manifestations offers opportunities to learn about myself. The chaplain's role is then to provide safe presence and reminder to reflect upon one's real Self, while taking assistance of Hindu scriptures. Knowing that every form of being is inherently Divine, I seek to serve in a capacity of a nonjudgmental, compassionate presence to whichever form the Divine takes in the patient's room. These beliefs inform my theory of spiritual care practice. One patient encounter in which these beliefs came alive occurred with an elderly Hindu patient who made a decision to sign up for hospice services as a result of his declining health condition.

During our conversations, this patient spoke regularly about going from wholeness to wholeness as he reflected upon his life so far and the phase coming up next. He spoke about his conviction, quoting frequently what the Isha Upanishad has to say about *wholeness*, in the ultimate reality of one's self. His demeanor, as he lived out his final days, reflected a sense of peace that comes with acceptance of death as a transition into the next incarnation. This was immensely powerful for me. The doctrine of karma teaches that one's present embodiment and psychology are a direct result of actions, including words and thoughts, performed in a previous life.

Hinduism teaches that every action performed is preceded by a particular state of consciousness, such as compassion preceding an act of kindness, or hatred preceding an act of violence. This state of consciousness then subtly reshapes the individual identity, so that action performed shapes the nature of future existence. Psychological dimension within the Hindu context therefore focuses on relief from suffering through spiritual means, turning the individual to the ultimate purpose of life through practice (*abhyāsa*) and healthy detachment (*vairāgya*).

This was evident in an encounter with an elderly patient who had a requested a chaplain visit. Upon my arrival, the patient expressed being pleasantly surprised to see a younger woman chaplain compared to the patient's preconceived impression of what the chaplain would typically look like. Further conversation in the visit led to the patient sharing her story about growing up questioning why only men held power in her particular denomination. There was a bond formed with the patient as my presence encouraged the patient to share her beliefs and convictions. The patient was able to reflect through different phases in her upbringing and share her personal experiences that tilted her spiritual scale towards her current faith denomination. She was able to visualize herself as a woman minister who struggled to earn leadership within her place of worship.

The fact was that she herself made history when she became the first female pastor of her church. This reflected not only in her professional life but in the way she was also able to take more control of her personal life. Our conversation became an opening through which she allowed herself to fully accept her own reality: being the whole person she is now. While this particular patient encounter was with an adult woman, there are also aspects of human development that impact people across the age spectrum. I had an encounter with a preteen girl who had attempted suicide for the third time. When I met with the patient, she had surrounded herself with dolls and was busy brushing the dolls' hair. When I asked this patient about her love for dolls, she began to adopt me as a friend. Having noticed my nail polish, she explained her own love for different hair colors and nail paints. She told me about her struggle with her mother who, according to her, does not address her needs that revolve around looking pretty according to middle school standards. I recognized that her emotions were directly impacted by a sense of self-esteem of a preteen that is in turn dependent on her acceptance by her fellow classmates. When she felt discouraged by her mother, she began to feel inferior. Her suicide attempts appeared to be her cry for attention from her mother. This preteen's spirituality was directly dependent on her sense of belonging. During our interaction, I was able to take on the role of a peer and modeled acceptance that allowed her to enter into an honest dialogue with me.

Among the various encounters with patients and families, the words said to the patient give hints and help me understand the family dynamics. I received a page from a medical doctor in the Intensive Care Unit looking for a chaplain to visit with a family as the patient was being weaned off machines. He asked me to speak with a family member who identified herself as the daughter of the patient. The patient's daughter asked for someone non-Catholic to visit with them. Once I arrived on the unit, I quickly checked in at the nurses' station and was told that the patient's death was imminent. I entered the patient room and introduced myself to about ten family members present. The older daughter I had spoken with on the phone informed me that they would like me to pray for her mother who was a "good Christian woman." I invited the family members to say their final goodbyes. There were stories and memories shared and there were tears. The first daughter, the lead of the family, spoke briefly but touched on a few words that led me to think that she was a lesbian and that this had been an issue between the patient and her relationship with the daughter and the family. I took this cue and ensured that every family member present had a chance to say what they needed to say to the patient.

It helped to be able to realize the dynamics within the family and to choose my words even more appropriately when I prayed with them. This visit reminded me to pay attention to my gut instinct and to listen for words that may or may not confirm my initial instinct. I believe I empowered the oldest daughter to do the talking instead of her feeling as though she could not tell other family members what her mother, the patient, would have wanted. In the words of the family, a knot had been undone in their hearts with respect to their personal relationships. This helped the oldest daughter and comforted her as she called the nurse in to extubate the patient.

The above example is just one instance of the diversity that exists within the patient population I serve as a chaplain. Due to my undergraduate background in Health Administration, it has become a learned skill to recognize and address diversity within a healthcare setting. One of my patient encounters was with a male Muslim patient who was hospitalized to undergo bypass surgery. He initiated the visit by having the nurse page the chaplain. I received the page and arrived at the bedside to meet with the patient and noticed that there was a woman sitting by his bedside. I acknowledged her and introduced myself to both of them. The patient began to share in English his health concerns and how he wanted someone to help him comfort his wife and for her to keep the faith that his surgery would go well and that he would be okay.

I initially spoke to both the patient and his wife in English; but it was not until the patient began to ask about my cultural background that I realized that his wife spoke limited English. The patient asked me whether I spoke Arabic, Urdu, or Punjabi—the languages that his wife understood. I said I could speak Hindi (which is close to Urdu) and got his approval to talk to his wife in that language. The wife now became involved in the conversation with me and the patient. I, too, was glad to be able to speak in one of my native languages and being able to express myself differently and clearly so the wife could understand. We spoke about the wife's concerns and also expressed her concerns to the patient's nurse when the nurse briefly entered during the visit. The patient and his wife—especially—were happy that I had come by and had spoken with them in their language. It did not matter that I was not the same faith or even the same nationality; but it became clear to them that I understood their culture and respected it. As I wrapped up the visit, the wife gave me a hug and verbalized her gratitude. During my first unit of clinical training, we had been taught about the spiritual needs that are part of being human. One of the spiritual needs is the need to belong—the sense of belonging to something, to someone, to a community, to a nation, to the universe. Belonging—what it looks or feels like—is different for each individual.

As clinical training is geared towards exposing oneself to one's own self, I underwent the journey to explore my own sense of belonging. What makes me feel that I belong? How does this translate to caregiving as a hospital chaplain? Certainly, a patient's native language is important. The language brings with it a sense of our-ness, a familiarity, and a sense of belonging. This helps me understand the limited talk with a patient whose first language is not English and the unlimited conversations with a patient who speaks a mutual language. It shows how much a language impacts perception. For example, the anger and rude behavior from some English speakers towards people conversing in their native language amongst themselves is probably due to a heightened sense of not belonging, not knowing. And "not knowing" is scary. It reminds me how important and vast the need is for native languages speakers, especially as it relates to the larger South Asian community who predominantly speak Hindu/Urdu, Gujarati, Punjabi, Tamil, Bengali, and other major languages spoken in the Indian subcontinent. My professional practice has made me aware for the need of language-appropriate resources to ensure that caregiving can be thorough. This realization enabled me to take the training and become a Qualified Bilingual Medical Interpreter.

As part of the interdisciplinary team, I have the privilege to serve patients who are nearing the end of their life. One such encounter provided me the chance to serve a Hindu patient who was being taken care of under inpatient hospice services. His family mentioned that he took great comfort in listening and reciting Hindu chants. So, to the patient's room I brought a CD player and some CDs of Hindu chants for the family to play softly in the background. I also photocopied the particular chapters from the Hindu scripture, the Bhagavad-Gita, in two different languages, so as to allow for the multi-generational family to recite the scriptures together as they kept vigil at the patient's bedside. The patient's family was grateful for the gesture and support.

An important aspect of professional growth is also recognizing one's own strengths and limitations. Being an Indian Hindu chaplain functioning in a hospital with diverse patients and staff, my strength lies in being able to acknowledge and accept diverse belief systems. Through my personal experience of living in different countries, I have developed an understanding of the spiritual need to belong, and to be able to find meaning and purpose in life events. My strength also lies in the ability to recognize that there are cultural, linguistic needs that form an important part of caring for the patient. The limitations come up in terms of being able to cater to nuances of other faiths. For instance, in an encounter with the parents of a stillborn baby who have requested a Christian blessing of the baby, it is imperative that the parents be informed that, as a non-Christian, I am not able to provide such a blessing.

I remind myself daily of the Hindu notion of *vasudhaiva kutumbakam*, the world is one whole family. My experience of living in three different countries allows me to appreciate multiple realities of parallel life experiences that are equally valid and to realize that friendships across faith traditions are real. Patient encounters remind me that one's assumptions about others are transient.

As a chaplain, I see my role as being an advocate for the patient, the family, and the hospital staff. For example, there was a patient on the critical care floor who had been hospitalized due to heart complications. I visited the patient as she was on the consult list requesting prayer. When I arrived to visit with the patient, I noticed the patient sitting up on the chair by the bedside. After introducing myself, the patient looked up at me and asked me to sit across from her. She tearfully began talking about her concerns about her heart health and, in an effort to comfort the patient, I moved my chair closer and extended my hand to slightly touch her hands. She immediately held my hand tightly and began crying heavily.

As I sat by her, she spoke about how she is HIV positive and that in the five years since being tested positive, her husband and family had abandoned her. She cried as she shared that no one had held her hand to comfort her in all these years. She spoke about feeling isolated and lonely. I was saddened to hear her story. After concluding the visit, I approached the patient's nurse and informed the nurse regarding the patient's concern. I also reached out to a social worker to help find support groups for HIV patients close to where that patient lives. Both the nurse and the social worker followed up on the request. The patient was grateful as she recognized that someone had listened, cared, and advocated for her wellbeing.

It is important that, as a chaplain, I continually try to ensure ethical decision-making and care of the patient and families I serve. I encourage patients to articulate and express their concerns to the medical staff and also to critically think through their medical experience. Through my active participation in the interfaith work, I have developed solid professional relationships with area clergy as well as diverse faith group leaders.

Thus, it can be seen that healthcare chaplaincy for Hindus brings forth a new dimension of lay Hindu leadership. With proper training and clinical experience, hospital chaplaincy presents itself as a potential profession for Hindus—a profession that is not only gaining importance in the healthcare field, but that also provides a sense of self-contentment and positive contribution to the wellbeing of others.

Connecting to the Energy of Grace

End-of-Life Care

Joseph Ghanashyam Caruso

A call came in at 2:00am. I shot out of bed and reached for the phone. "We need an Orthodox priest immediately!" a nurse said urgently. "The patient is actively dying." I fumbled for a referral slip and explained, "I am the only chaplain here on-site overnight, and I'm a Hindu priest. We don't have an Orthodox priest on staff, but I'll try calling an Orthodox volunteer who left us his phone number. It's probably unlikely that he'll be able to come at this hour." The nurse was silent, waiting for more. I added, "I'll come immediately after I make this call and see if there is some way I can support the patient and family." "Okay, thank you…" she said. "And please come quickly."

I called the Orthodox volunteer and—as I had expected—there was no answer. I headed over to a sink and splashed water on my face three times, changed my clothes quickly, and called the volunteer one more time before leaving. Again, no answer. I rushed to the Intensive Care Unit to find a middle-aged woman standing at the bedside of her 66-year-old husband. He lay there unresponsive, eyes closed. He was intubated and breathing slowly with long intervals between each breath. The daughter and son were sitting in chairs near the rear of the bed. Their faces looked tired from lack of sleep and hours of crying. And yet the atmosphere was calm and quiet. A sad and deep acceptance of what was happening pervaded the room. Mira (pseudonym), the wife of the patient, grabbed my hand and thanked me for coming. She said, "My husband may pass away at any time now. He's a spiritual person and we wanted spiritual support."

"I understand," I replied.

With tears in her eyes she told me, "We've had a remarkable life together." The word "remarkable" caught my attention. "Can you tell me something of your shared life together?" Without hesitating, Mira told me the story of how they first met as immigrants in the late 1960s in New York City's Lower East Side. They married young, worked hard, and raised two children. They always respected and supported each other through life's many highs and lows. The daughter and son listened quietly, sometimes smiling at one another or adding a few words or details to the story. I attentively listened, said little, and simply appreciated their openness to share their lives with me.

The nurse came and assessed that the patient was very close to passing, perhaps just minutes or so. The room fell silent. Suddenly, the daughter spoke up and looked to me. "So you're a Orthodox priest?"

"Oh no, I am not," I said. "I'm actually a Hindu priest, but…" The daughter shouted, "A Hindu priest! Mom, did you hear that? He's a Hindu priest!" I thought to myself, *Oh no. Is this not good?*

Mira looked at me in disbelief. "Are you serious? You're a Hindu priest?"

"Yes I am," I said.

"That's so perfect," Mira exclaimed. I was relieved but very confused.

The daughter explained, "My father prides himself on having friends from all of the different religions. He has a Muslim friend and he had a Hindu friend who would come to our apartment on occasion. My father always insists on being inclusive and accepting of the various faiths. That's who he is at his core. It's very befitting that you're here with us and I know my father is glad."

Mira grabbed my hand again and pleaded, "We don't know what Hindus do when someone is dying, but I give you permission to do it for him now. I only have one request: Whatever it is, please do it with your full heart."

I felt deeply moved by Mira's request. I explained to the family that their desire to create a sacred atmosphere for their loved one was in perfect accordance with the teachings of the Bhagavad-Gita, which speak of the crucial importance and precious opportunity at the time of death. I briefly shared with them the idea and power of mantra, and how Hindus believe that chanting and hearing the holy name of God at the time of death is the most auspicious way of departure. Mira expressed her sincere desire to participate and offer this to her husband. I taught them the

Hare Krishna mantra, which, to my surprise, they vaguely remembered hearing from their father many years before. We sang together for about ten minutes. With Mira holding her husband's hand, and the children tenderly touching their father's arm, we chanted in unison as the patient's breathing pattern began to slow. His vital signs indicated that the end was approaching. The nurses came into the room and stood off to the side, respectfully observing and listening to our chant. Our singing became more focused and heartfelt and we all watched the patient as he released one final breath and let go. His body was motionless, his face peaceful.

Afterwards, Mira and her children told me that they could never have imagined such a blessed departure at an intensive care unit in a hospital. She said it was one of the saddest and yet also one of the most beautiful experiences of her life. She requested that I come to speak at the funeral a few days later. When I arrived, I asked what she would like for me to speak about. She simply said, "Just describe everything exactly as it happened that night. None of us could have planned it any better. God arranged it."

As a Hindu chaplain, I used to think that providing care to non-Hindus might pose some unexpected challenges. I've learned, however, that this has rarely been a barrier to connection and support. In fact, when we're willing, these very differences can cause us to seek and find a higher ground to unite on. Differences can separate, or they can encourage us to go deeper and connect with what is universal and most essential. Mira wasn't daunted by her unfamiliarity with the Sanskrit words or the particularities of the ritual. She accepted the *intention* and the essence behind the external form, and through the chanting, offered blessings and love for the benefit of her husband.

Hinduism teaches that "The Truth is One; the Seers have expressed it in many ways;" "He is that single Fire that burns on many altars." These two quotes taken from the ancient hymns of the Rg Veda point to the One God, described differently, and approached in various ways according to differences in time, place, circumstance, and people. Embracing this idea has allowed me not only to tolerate the differences in the religions, but to see them as natural and necessary expressions and facets of a complete whole. The languages and the forms of the Religions will naturally differ, just as they do within different cultures throughout the world. But behind the form is the substance, and on this basis, we can comprehend and value the essential unity of religions.

Besides the diversity of the spiritual traditions, each individual is on a unique and personal journey through life which may or may not include adherence to a particular tradition. I find that Hindu principles align well with this truth and encourage me to trust that each person is where they are for a good reason. My service as a true friend is to, as Jalaluddin Rumi put it, "walk one another back home." "Back home" aptly conveys the experience of arriving or returning to ourselves, to comfort, to health, to peace, to God.

Even for people within the same religion and family, spiritual journeys can be intensely unique. I believe that recognizing these differences and responding compassionately is the challenge and the mark of a good chaplain or caregiver. I recall my experiences with a Hindu man from Queens, New York, named Rama (pseudonym) who was relatively young—only 30 years old. He was suffering and dying from lymphoma and acute kidney failure. His mother, who almost never left his side, was devastated and requested a Hindu chaplain to provide support throughout this terribly difficult time.

Rama's room was often full of people: siblings, friends, and his temple community from Queens. On one rare occasion I found him alone in the room and asked how he was feeling.

"I feel so lonely," he said.

At first, I was surprised and thought, *but you are constantly with your mother and your brother; so many visitors come to see you each day; you have such an amazing supportive community.* I discovered that a common tendency I sometimes have is to stop, block, or change what another person is feeling. I may do this for a variety of reasons, but my instinctive reactions, especially to suffering and death, are often more about me and my fears, and less about others and what they may need in the moment. In the name of supporting another person, I may involve myself in a sort of subtle competition, seeking, with all good intentions, to steer them in what I imagine to be a better direction. Many patients, especially in trying situations, simply seek to be acknowledged, accepted, and understood. To serve others in this way requires presence, the effort of empathy, and deep, conscious listening.

Instead of challenging Rama's loneliness, I recalled a time in my own life when I had felt profoundly alone and isolated. I allowed the pain from the past to seep into my heart, and at last I spoke simply and spontaneously, "Loneliness can really sting."

Immediately, tears poured from Rama's eyes and he released an upwelling of emotion that had accumulated from the reality of his impending death. I just sat with him for about 15 minutes as he wept.

His crying became softer and drifted away until finally it ceased. "Sleep after toil, port after stormy seas." Rama became calm and peaceful. He thanked me for being there and understanding him, and he fell asleep.

I marveled at how I had only tuned in to what Rama had been feeling and spoken four words. Through that simple act of empathy, he had then felt accepted and unafraid to show himself. He had developed trust in me. This trust proved to be important and powerful in the weeks to come as we talked about his life, his relationship with God, and what he wanted from friends and family.

Rama's mother's struggles and challenges were, of course, quite different from her son's. Unlike Rama, she considered herself to be very religious, and her mind was preoccupied with a tension between her deep emotions of anguish and, as she expressed it, the "proper Hindu perspective." In addition to her overwhelming sadness, she felt guilty that these very feelings seemed to indicate an "un-Hindu" or "un-spiritual" attitude of attachment. I acknowledged and understood her point. The Hindu or Vedic scriptures often venerate the quality of equanimity in the face of happiness and distress (*sama-duhkha-sukham dhiram*). From our previous conversations I knew she responded best to, and, in fact, only considered my views valid when they were supported by, scriptural references. My goals, therefore, were to acknowledge her conflict and help her to be aligned with true Hindu teaching, and at the same time, give her permission to feel her pain without condemning herself.

One day I shared the story and relationship between Arjuna and Krishna. During the battle of Kuruksetra, Arjuna, the great devotee and friend of Krishna, came to learn of the unjust killing and death of his son Abhimanyu. Arjuna, at first outraged, soon became despondent and downcast. With natural fatherly affection, Arjuna wept and grieved the loss of his son, and by doing so, he acknowledged and honored Abhimanyu as most dear to him. Yet, with a soft and also strong heart, Arjuna continued on with his duties as a warrior in the battle, always seeking the guidance and shelter of Krishna, his Lord and friend.

This story of Krishna and Arjuna soothed Rama's mother's heart, if only for an hour or so. It helped assure her that her pain and grief were acceptable and natural. After all, the great warrior and devotee Arjuna had wept for his son. This led to an ongoing conversation about healthy and natural affection versus unhealthy or even harming affection. I witnessed how our discussions assisted and comforted her three weeks later when Rama passed away. She seemed surer of herself.

Her grief gradually shifted from a conflicted and *hard* pain to a healing, vulnerable, and *soft* pain.

To move through and cope with the dying of her son, Rama's mother sometimes needed time alone and away from the hospital. When she wanted to speak with me, she appreciated discussing Hindu teachings. She sought scriptural guidance and affirmations in making certain decisions and she received solace and comfort in discussing the stories and lessons found in her loved Hindu spirituality.

This was much less of a need for Rama, who wanted from me someone who could share in the seriousness of his situation and all that he was experiencing. At other times Rama valued talking and telling me about his life, which allowed him to feel less isolated in his pain. He wanted his friends and siblings around him as much as possible and felt comfortable when his room was full.

Recognizing and honoring differences is the essence of powerful caregiving, as it shows people that their lives are uniquely valuable. There is no "right thing to say" to a dying Hindu man or his grieving Hindu mother because each man and each mother will undoubtedly differ in countless ways. The caregiver's duty is to learn patiently from each patient his or her needs.

This leads to a question that I'm frequently asked in a variety of ways: Isn't it draining or exhausting to involve yourself with so many people in this way? Don't you get depleted or burnt out by dealing with so many people's emotions? How do you enter in to each person's unique world, while remaining securely in your own?

The word *compassion* comes from roots that mean literally to "suffer with." According to Hindu teaching, an ideal devotee of God is *para dukkha dukkhi*. He or she feels the suffering of others as one's own. Having dissolved the illusory walls of *separateness* between themselves and others by awakening their love for God, a devotee suffers in communion with every living being. Yet, by their practice or state of *śaraṇāgati* or "surrender and dependence on God," which keeps them always in contact with God, they're able to *come down* and feel the suffering of others without losing sight of the higher perspective or losing touch with the reality of God. Therefore, the suffering they share in union with others never has the sting of hopelessness or meaninglessness and they gratefully dedicate themselves to compassionate service.

The Bhagavad-Gita culminates in Krishna's appeal to Arjuna: "Just Surrender unto Me. Do not fear." Through three years and eight units of clinical pastoral education I've learned how to apply various helping skills and spiritual assessment models to determine the strengths and needs of a patient. Alongside this valuable training, I've recognized how puzzling, complex, and overwhelming end-of-life care and circumstances can be. I find myself returning often to this Hindu practice and mindset of *śaraṇāgati*, or surrender and dependence on God, in order to remain energized and inspired in my work with patients. Ironically, this surrender helps me feel *more* secure and stable by trusting that I have access to a power within and beyond myself that is greater and more resourceful than my own. All is not dependent on me. This grounds me in the reality of my own limitations and opens me to guidance and prayer: "Please give me the compassion, intelligence, and energy to serve this person in the best possible way." This is my simple and continuous prayer to God, especially while I'm with patients at the end of their lives. I believe it's based on the solid idea that intuitive intelligence, compassion, and energy will come from the sincere desire to serve another person and surrender to God. This practice helps me to feel balanced and more prepared to handle the stresses and complexities of end-of-life caregiving.

A personal and important realization I've come to in my work as a Hindu chaplain is that illness, suffering, and dying are not *interruptions* in my life, but natural and important aspects of my life to be lived through fully. In the heart of this world lies the principle of duality: happiness and distress; joy and sorrow; love and hate; peace and war; health and disease; and finally, the fundamental duality of life and death. The mistake I often make, which keeps me fearfully caught in this continuous interplay of opposites, is that I *seek the one side* with all my power, and I try to *avoid its opposite*. But by facing and accommodating *both* poles I can develop the capacity to stand firmly in the center of the opposites without being overwhelmed. The "negative" side of the duality is not an interruption or something to be avoided. It's an *opportunity* to become more comfortable with what is uncomfortable and thereby achieve balance and freedom.

In the twelfth chapter of the Bhagavad-Gita, Krishna repeatedly refers to such a poised devotee as being "very dear" to Him. This is so because from this steady platform of consciousness one can then be *free to serve* others without being tossed or shaken by the inevitable and incessant changes of life. To the degree I face suffering with acceptance and integrity in my own life, I'll be able to stand with and support others in their suffering.

I believe that while pain and sorrow are deep and real, another reality lies still deeper: The unassailable reality of Divine Grace. This power penetrates and flows through all of life on the subtlest plane. When we're able to connect to this energy of grace through the doors of surrender and sincerity, we're blessed with a trust, eternal and absolute, which knows no fear and heals from within. This conviction and experience has been the cornerstone and heart of my Hindu chaplaincy.

Hindu Chaplaincy as Karma Yoga in the Tradition of Sri Ramakrishna and Swami Vivekananda

An Interview with Swami Tyagananda

Jeffery D. Long

Hindu Chaplaincy and the Vedanta of Sri Ramakrishna and Swami Vivekananda

Is the contemporary Vedanta tradition that is rooted in the experiences and teachings of the nineteenth century Bengali saint and sage, Sri Ramakrishna Paramahansa (1836–1886), and which was transmitted to the West by Ramakrishna's pre-eminent disciple, Swami Vivekananda (1863–1902), particularly conducive to the idea of a Hindu chaplaincy? What issues are involved in the practice of Hindu chaplaincy from the perspective of this particular school of thought? This essay will focus upon Hindu chaplaincy as it is lived by one of its most prominent practitioners, Swami Tyagananda, who serves as a Hindu chaplain at not only one, but two major American universities, and who is an ordained monk in the Ramakrishna Order.

Chaplaincy, as such, is a fairly new concept and practice for Hindu traditions. The services typically provided by chaplains have been dispersed across a variety of roles in traditional Hindu societies. Thus, ritual services, for example, have tended to be the province of the *phapla*, or temple priest, while healing and counseling have more often been carried out by a variety of local religious healers,[1] and spiritual teaching has more often been the domain of ascetic renouncers, or *sannyāsīs*, also known as *sādhus* or *swāmīs*. The idea of a *minister*, who provides all these services, has arisen in a Christian context, and seems to have no traditional Hindu parallel, in terms of a singular, all-purpose religious role. Additionally, some of the services provided by chaplains are very specific to the modern world. They involve the idea of there being secular spaces into which a religious representative is invited to provide some sense of the spiritual in an inclusive and non-sectarian fashion, while retaining some sense of a connection with a particular tradition, provided by the fact that the representative does inhabit some specific religious organization. An example might be a non-sectarian prayer—potentially led by a priest, rabbi, minister, *swāmī*, or imam—at a secular event, involving people of many faiths, like a college graduation, or an opening session of the US House of Representatives.

One could argue that the Vedanta tradition of Sri Ramakrishna and Swami Vivekananda is particularly conducive to the idea of Hindu chaplaincy (though this would not be to claim that it is *uniquely* or *exclusively* so). The basis of this claim is that, when Swami Vivekananda established the Ramakrishna Order, he did so specifically with the idea that the monks of this order would go beyond the traditional *sadhu's* roles of teaching and practicing solitary meditation. The monks of the Ramakrishna Order were to go forth and serve society in tangible, this-worldly senses, as well as in the more traditional fashion of teaching and of being living exemplars of renunciation. This mission is well captured in the motto, *ātmano mokṣārthaṃ jagaddhitāya ca*: "For the liberation of the Self and the welfare of the world."

Given their charge, the monks of this Order have been in the forefront of providing services such as education and poverty relief in India, starting schools, orphanages, and hospitals, and doing the day-to-day work of running them.[2]

What justifies and grounds this transformation of the role of the Hindu monk is the idea of karma yoga proclaimed by Swami Vivekananda as a path to God-realization no less valid than the more traditional paths of knowledge (*jproc*), meditation (*dhymed*), and devotion (*bhakti*). The practice of karma yoga, as Vivekananda defines it, is the practice of *sevā*,

---

1   See J.B. Flueckiger (2015) *Everyday Hinduism*. Oxford: Wiley Blackwell, pp.193–219.
2   See S. Gambhirananda (1957) *History of the Ramakrishna Math and Mission*. Kolkata: Advaita Ashrama.

or selfless service. In other words, one does good, not based on a vain, ego-based belief that one is in a position to help others, but rather in a spirit of selfless service: seeing God as manifested in the form of the poor and suffering person who has given one the opportunity to serve in this way. One thus comes ever closer to perfection by purifying the ego through the practice of service. As Vivekananda has said:

> [T]he desire to do good is the highest motive power we have, *if we know all the time that it is a privilege to help others*. Do not stand on a pedestal and take five cents in your hand and say, "Here, my poor man," but be grateful that the poor man is there so that by making a gift to him you are able to help yourself. It is not the receiver that is blessed, but it is the giver. Be thankful that you are allowed to exercise your power of benevolence and mercy in the world, and thus become pure and perfect… Be grateful to the man you help, think of him as God.[3]

Swami Tyagananda and the Practice of Hindu Chaplaincy at Harvard and MIT

Though, again, it is still a relatively new concept, Hindu chaplaincy has been practiced in Boston, at the Massachusetts Institute of Technology (MIT), for over 60 years (as of this writing). The idea of karma yoga propounded by Vivekananda through the Ramakrishna Order and Ramakrishna Mission in India, and through the Vedanta Societies in the US, has made this tradition very open to participation in chaplaincy as an appropriate extension of the work of the monks of the Order. Swami Tyagananda currently serves as the Hindu chaplain at both MIT and at Harvard University, as well as running Boston's Ramakrishna Vedanta Society. As he has explained: "The Ramakrishna Vedanta Society is associated with the chaplaincy program at MIT from its inception in the early 1950s."[4] As he further elaborates on the history of Hindu chaplaincy at MIT:

> In fact, Swami Akhilananda was one of the founder-members of the program [the chaplaincy program at MIT]. When it started, he was chaplain not only for Hindus but also for Buddhists and Muslims.

---

3 S. Vivekananda (1979) *Complete Works*, Vol. 1. Kolkata: Advaita Ashrama, pp.76, 77; emphasis mine.
4 Swami Tyagananda, personal communication, July 2018. (This also applies to the remainder of the quotations of Swami Tyagananda in this essay.)

Eventually the Buddhist and Muslim communities were able to find chaplains of their own. Akhilananda was succeeded by Swami Sarvagatananda, and I, in turn, succeeded him in 1999.

Swami Vivekananda's direct disciple, Swami Paramananda, founded the Order's branch in Boston in 1909. Swami Akhilananda, who arrived in 1926 as his assistant and founded the branch in Providence, Rhode Island, took charge of the Boston work as well after Swami Paramananda's passing in 1940.[5] He was succeeded by Swami Sarvagatananda in 1962 as head of the Ramakrishna Vedanta Society and as MIT Hindu chaplain. Swami Tyagananda, prior to his move to Boston, was serving as editor of *The Vedanta Kesari*, a journal of the Ramakrishna Order based in Chennai.

How is it that Hindu chaplaincy first came to be instituted, not only at MIT, but at Harvard University as well? As Swami Tyagananda explains:

Until the 1970s Harvard's chaplaincy program was limited to a handful of [Protestant] ministers whose churches were in and around Harvard Square, and Catholic and Jewish representatives. Sometime in the early 80s they wanted to have a larger representation to reflect the diversity on campus. Swami Sarvagatananda was invited to be a Hindu chaplain and I succeeded him in 1999.

As one can see from the account of Swami Tyagananda, the institution of Hindu chaplaincy is part of the larger trend of American society becoming more diverse and more inclusive through the course of last century. As he mentions, Swami Akhilananda served as the chaplain at MIT not only for Hindu students, but for Buddhist and Muslim students as well: in short, for all students who were members of faith communities from outside the "Judeo-Christian" tradition predominant in American religious life. It was only later, presumably as larger numbers of students with diverse religious backgrounds became part of MIT's student body, and as the institution came to realize that this diversity merited a chaplaincy reflecting it, that Buddhist and Muslim students came to have their own chaplains. Similarly, Swami Tyagananda mentions that Harvard University also instituted its Hindu chaplaincy and invited Swami Sarvagatananda to serve in this role when the Harvard administration "wanted to have a larger representation to reflect the diversity on campus."

What are the duties of a Hindu chaplain at Harvard and at MIT? What are some typical activities and interactions that Swami Tyagananda has

---

5 Information supplied by Swami Tyagananda in personal communication, July 2018.

in this role at these two institutions? As he explains, the arrangements at both institutions are relatively informal, allowing for a good deal of autonomy amongst a religiously diverse group of chaplains. This enables each chaplain to pursue his or her chaplaincy work in a way that is appropriate to his or her tradition:

> There are no "duties" per se, since on both campuses the chaplains are not employees of the schools. They are technically "volunteers" supported by their respective denominations and are part of the chaplain bodies on invitation. They are given the school IDs and have certain privileges (such as the ability to book spaces on campus for their activities and are provided with email IDs of students who have specifically requested information about the programs of their respective chaplaincies). Since Hindus don't have a specific day in a week for worship, I generally choose the late afternoon of a day of the week that works for most in the Hindu student groups that I advise and lead.
>
> Typically, the weekly program comprises of a short prayer and meditation, and study of a specific text (such as the Gita or an Upanishad) followed by informal discussion. There are in addition celebrations of major Hindu festivals. I attend when I can—when the timings don't conflict with my engagements at the Vedanta Society. Also, many of the student led programs (which tend to be quasi-religious and mostly sociocultural) begin around 9:00pm and sometimes last past midnight. I don't participate in these because of my own schedule at the monastery.

The relatively informal and decentralized character of Hindu traditions enables a situation in which neither Swami Tyagananda nor the students are bound by a rigid set of requirements that shape their interactions. The engagement of each with the other is based on their respective needs and desires and the demands of their respective schedules.

How do the teachings of Vedanta, and in particular, of Sri Ramakrishna, the Holy Mother Sarada Devi (the wife and spiritual companion of Sri Ramakrishna, and a sacred figure in her own right), and Swami Vivekananda inform Swami Tyagananda's practice of Hindu chaplaincy?

> The practice of acceptance (instead of merely "toleration"), the conviction that there is a deeper unity underlying the stupendous diversity, and the pragmatic approach learnt from the lives and teachings of Thakur [Sri Ramakrishna], Holy Mother and Swamiji [Swami Vivekananda] have been especially helpful in my work... The teachings give me the freedom

to interact with the campus community in an open, transparent way, even with those whose ideas are diametrically opposite to mine. Students find this open-mindedness refreshing, especially since many of them have a stereotypical view of religious people as being dogmatic and narrow-minded. I have good friends among those who self-identify as atheists and humanists. They are often surprised to know that I too don't believe in (the kind of) "God" whom they find problematic.

It is important to note that, as a Hindu chaplain, Swami Tyagananda does not see his service as being only to Hindu students. Like chaplains in many secular contexts, he also serves as a living embodiment of his tradition, representing it to the outside world. As he notes, the open-minded approach enjoined in the Vedanta tradition often surprises those who identify religiosity with more narrow and dogmatic attitudes. A university being a place where critical thinking is engendered, it is unsurprising that a Hindu chaplain in a university setting would encounter students, as well as faculty and staff members, with a skeptical bent of mind toward religion. By exhibiting the values of the Vedanta tradition in the way that he does, Swami Tyagananda provides educational service not only to Hindu students—those who would be most likely, for example, to come to one of his Gita classes—but to the wider public, by showing a face of Hinduism and of religion generally with which most Americans are likely unfamiliar.

Because chaplaincy is a new concept to the Hindu tradition, does Swami Tyagananda find that there is some awkwardness in adapting, as a Hindu, to the role of the chaplain? Or does his practice of chaplaincy flow naturally from certain Vedantic teachings and ideals, such as the ideal of karma yoga already discussed?

> I am not a trained chaplain, in the sense that I don't have an academic degree specializing in chaplaincy work. To my knowledge, no such program exists at present for Hindu chaplains. It will be good to have one and hopefully some program may evolve in the future. I use my monastic training and study of Vedanta scriptures to do the best I can. I see myself primarily as a resource person to provide a Vedanta perspective on issues that students might bring to me and to provide opportunities for students to know the basics of Vedanta, the philosophical foundation from which the various traditions within Hinduism have evolved.

For Swami Tyagananda, then, Hindu chaplaincy is essentially an extension of the work he already does as a monk in the Ramakrishna Order: to teach

Vedantic principles to those who are interested, both by embodying them, and also by bringing these principles to bear on student issues and also creating spaces in which students can learn these principles.

What kinds of adaptation are involved to Swami Tyagananda's traditional role as a *swami* in fulfilling the duties of a Hindu chaplain? Does he ever find himself having to negotiate between his duties as a *swami* and chaplaincy work, or do these flow together relatively seamlessly?

> One of the things that chaplains are often called upon to do is officiate at religious ceremonies. In Hinduism, the priestly duties and monastic duties are distinct and different. Monastics are primarily spiritual teachers and don't officiate at weddings, funerals, etc. Whenever I am approached for help at weddings and funerals, I direct the students to other resources or to Hindu priests who may be able to help them. I do, however, visit the sick in hospitals and spend time with students who are passing through difficulties and need advice and help.

The traditional Hindu distinctions noted earlier, which distribute the duties carried out by a chaplain in the Western world to various types of Hindu religious specialist, are foregrounded in this response by Swami Tyagananda. There are both philosophical and practical reasons that a *swami* does not officiate at events like weddings and funerals. As a *sannyāsī*, Swami Tyagananda has stepped out of the traditional set of stages and transitions that mark the life of a householder, and that are sanctified by the *saṃskāras*, or Hindu sacraments. In terms of the traditional *ashrams*, or stages of life, as described in Hindu sacred texts, he is in the fourth, renouncer stage, having, in effect, stepped out of the series of steps defined by the student, householder, and retirement stages which define the lives of most Hindus. It is therefore inappropriate for him to participate in the rituals associated with lay life. Practically speaking, also, the correct performance of these rituals is not part of his training (precisely for the reason that it is not appropriate for his role). We see here, then, an instance in which the practice of chaplaincy as traditionally conceived in the West needs to be adapted to the realities of Hindu life. To be sure, householders can (and do) serve in the role of Hindu chaplain in varied settings in the US. If they have the requisite training, it would be perfectly appropriate for these householder chaplains to engage in the more traditional chaplain's activity of officiating at events like weddings and funerals. In a case, though, in which the chaplain is, like Swami Tyagananda, a renouncer, the appropriate Hindu officiant—a *pūjārī*, *purohit*, or *paṇḍit* —would need to be brought in to perform these activities. We can see that Swami Tyagananda navigates the differences between the demands of chaplaincy and the requirements of Hindu practice by adhering to a role appropriate to his training and his station in life as a monk.

In terms of the particular challenges involved in being a Hindu chaplain, the main concern that Swami Tyagananda expresses is that this job, if it is to be done well, involves a good deal of responsibility and a time commitment that most Hindu chaplains are not able to sustain, due to the voluntary nature of this work:

> Many students don't know who chaplains are or what they do. Among those who think they know, the popular idea seems to be that a chaplain should be approached only in times of distress or difficulty. Or when someone needs a priest to do something. My idea of a chaplain is one who is primarily a friend who can provide me, in good times as well as difficult times, with a perspective from whatever tradition he or she represents. In order for this to happen, the chaplain needs to spend longer time on campus to win the trust of the students. Ideally, therefore, it should be a full-time job. Most Hindu chaplains (there aren't many at present in North America) at present do their work alongside other duties and jobs that they have. For instance, I have the responsibility of managing the Boston branch of the Ramakrishna Order in addition to being a Hindu chaplain at two premier schools in the country. So the time I am able to spend with students is necessarily limited.

Conclusion

For a monk in the Ramakrishna Order, the work of Hindu chaplaincy—providing teaching and guidance to all who request it—flows quite naturally from the ideal of karma yoga proclaimed by Swami Vivekananda. When asked specifically if he sees his work as a chaplain as a form of karma yoga, Swami Tyagananda answers promptly and without hesitation: "Yes, I do. In all the work I do, at the Vedanta Society or outside, I make an effort to do it as a form of karma yoga." There is thus a seamless connection, philosophically speaking, between his duties as a monk and as a chaplain.

At the same time, challenges remain, as the adaptation of the ideal of chaplaincy to a more multi-religious and multi-cultural environment—in this case, to the needs of Hindu students in a university setting—is still an incomplete process. The average person expects a chaplain to perform life rituals, like weddings and funerals, that are inappropriate for a Hindu monk to perform. And not all institutions are fully aware of the need for, or are not yet ready to make the commitment of resources that would be involved in creating, full-time positions to support the work of a Hindu chaplain if it is to be carried out properly.[6] Swami Tyagananda nevertheless perseveres, carrying out the task of serving students at two major institutions and meeting the needs of the local Vedanta community, in the spirit of Swami Vivekananda's famous injunction, to "Arise! Awake! and stop not until the goal is reached!"[7]

---

6   Anecdotally, I have heard even Christian chaplains make similar comments about institutional comprehension of and support for their work.
7   Vivekananda, *Complete Works*, Vol. 1, p.351.

A Hindu Chaplain at a Jesuit Catholic University

Brahmachari V. Sharan

A few years ago, I walked along the northern bank of the Potomac with the spires of Georgetown University punctuating the skyline in the distance, pondering the enormity of the task ahead of me. Life had kindly taken me through decades of training and experience, but to be given the burden of being the first Hindu priest and monk in history to be employed by a Catholic institution and then be asked to construct a Hindu chaplaincy from the ground up in the oldest Jesuit Institution of Higher Education in the country within the month before the students returned to campus for a new year—this was a little disquieting.

Hindu Priests and Gurus: The Standard

For at least four millennia, sacerdotal training has been the main focus of Hindu religious instruction, producing Hindu priests (*paṇḍita/purohita*) who memorise one of the four Vedas, along with their auxiliary literature (Vedangas) and Upanishads belonging to their specific recension, plus the sacramental and life-cycle rituals particular to their specific soteriological *dharma* (religion) within Hinduism (Vaisnavism, Shaivism, Shaktism, or Smartism).[1] This 12-year schooling is undertaken at a Veda-Pathashala

---

[1] Here I am following Gavin Flood's assertion of the appropriateness of applying the western term "religion" to the Vaishnava and Shaiva theistic traditions and am expanding it to include Shaktism and Smartism. (See G. Flood (1996) *An Introduction to Hinduism.* Cambridge: Cambridge University Press, p.117.) It should be noted that soteriological *dharma* is distinct from "communal religion": the widely known *varṇāśrama dharma*—or religious duties and practices that ought to be performed by a person in accordance with their membership of a certain class (*varṇa*) or stage of life (*āśrama*).

(Vedic "seminary") after which proficient students graduate as *Shastrins* (Bachelor's-degree equivalent), or *Ācāryas* (Master's-degree equivalent). Yet, they are not given any preparation for pastoral care, due to the fact that every Hindu household, in theory at least, should be initiated into one of the Hindu *dharma*s through a *saṁnyāsin* (renunciate) guru of the religion in question. *Saṁnyāsin*s are extensively regulated, facing the toughest rules of any social order.[2] Their dedication to prescribed regulations and their embodiment of scriptural tenets qualifies them to become initiating gurus (spiritual preceptors) when their own guru deems them competent. The guru who possesses both sacerdotal knowledge and experience of the practical application of the philosophies of their *dharma* is considered capable to counsel and guide initiates not only in spiritual and religious matters, but also worldly and mundane. The role of the Hindu chaplain apparently has no formal location in the scriptures as a separate category of religious leadership.

Hindu Chaplaincy in the US

In the US, Hindu chaplaincy is in its relative infancy regardless of the setting. While the experience I gained at the University of Edinburgh as the Honorary Hindu Chaplain was purely pastoral, in taking on the task at Georgetown University I researched scholarly literature on Hindu chaplaincy in higher educational institutions—only to find a limited number of studies, most of which subsumed Hinduism within discussions of chaplaincy provision for students of "other religions" after the three so-called "monotheist" religions.[3] Vineet Chander, a pioneer in the field, succinctly assesses this and other approaches adopted by universities with regards to including provisions for their Hindu students:

> The first is to attempt a sort of translation process that seeks equivalence by way of analogy to Christianity and encourages students to "defend, re-define and create [a version of] Hinduism on the model of Christianity"… A second response seems to take the exact opposite approach. Hinduism is viewed as inexorably and irrevocably different from and outside of the other faiths in its midst and thus no meaningful discourse, comparison, or translation is truly possible. Hindus are ostensibly

---

2   See, for example, the *Yatidharmasamuccaya* of Yāmunācārya.
3   "So-called"—as I find the moniker to be an alarmingly supremacist and overly simplistic self-designation when contextualized against, for example, the historicity of Indo-Iranian religious traditions, and, in fact, the actual trajectory of development of the *theos* of the Abrahamic faiths.

"honoured" by being excused from participating in shared discourse... Both [approaches] implicitly accept a particular faith or group of faiths... as the measuring stick by which Hinduism should be dealt with. And both envisage administrators as the benevolent gatekeepers of religious legitimacy, doling out *space* and *time* to Hindu students who function as passive recipients.[4]

From this overview of the rather frail contemporary situation of Hindu chaplaincy, Chander proceeds to perspicaciously outline the role of a Hindu chaplain in terms of current discourse given the recent trend towards inclusivity.[5] His recommendations, I venture, delineate a reliable standard for those training in Hindu chaplaincy in the US. In her essay entitled *A New Kind of Dharma Leadership*, Rita Sherma even suggests a chaplain might be a better interface for Hinduism than a traditional priest within interfaith settings, corroborating my initial assessment.[6] Comparing both Chander and Sherma's observations to the traditional role of the Hindu priest (*purohita/paṇḍita*), the difference between the role and character of a Hindu priest and Hindu chaplain is stark.

Enthusiasm born of possibility is, reassuringly, pervasive in the Hindu diaspora when it comes to faith representation. We do, however, ignore the calls of our *dharma* to thorough, rigorous training and measured, carefully supervised practice at our peril.[7] For Hindus, the ultimate authority (*āptatama-śabda-pramāṇa*) is scripture. It is from scriptural precedent that qualified, erudite Hindu gurus deliberate on even contemporary matters, substantiating any deviations through reference to wider scripture and scientific evidence (which has always featured as an essential part of *dharmic* philosophy). While the behavioral

---

4   V. Chander (2013) "A Room with a View: Accommodating Hindu religious practice on a college campus." *The Journal of College and Character*, May, 107.
5   Ibid., p.108.
6   R. Sherma (2013) "A new kind of dharma leadership: The necessity of a Hindu American chaplaincy." *The Interfaith Observer Journal,* September. https://interfaith-observer.squarespace.com/journal-articles/2013/9/6/the-necessity-of-a-hindu-american-chaplaincy.html, accessed on October 8, 2018.
7   As "Hinduism" was leveraged by politicians to unify Indians for independence in the late nineteenth and early twentieth centuries, the role of the actual religions (Vaisnavism, Shaivism, Shaktism, and Smartism) were downplayed. One of the myriad problems with this is that their millennia-old training rigors and regulatory bodies were deemed no longer necessary should one desire to become a guru—one simply had to adopt the garb and trappings to gain a following. No need for 12-year intensive trainings and seemingly impossible rules. The recent years have seen numerous Hindu "godmen" (a sensationalized translation of guru) in the news for various crimes and calls for regulation have landed on the shoulders of the Indian government in the absence of the traditional regulatory bodies.

and educational prerequisites of a guru and a *purohita* are very clearly delineated in the scriptures, the role and training of a Hindu chaplain in higher education must be distilled from between the lines. I focussed my search on the Ramayana of Valmiki (c. fifth–fourth century BCE) because of a certain chaplain-esque figure therein documented: Vashishtha.

The Ramayana on Hindu Chaplains

Vashishtha is renowned before the Ramayana as one of the seven great Vedic seers.[8] However, in the Ramayana, the reader is introduced to Vashishtha (in this episode of history at least) as the *rāja-purohita*[9] to the Ikṣvāku Solar dynasty and its King Dasharatha. He is the chief of eight royal priests who are consulted repeatedly to assure that the orders of the king align with religious and spiritual principles. Yet, at the beginning of the epic, Vashishtha, knower of all Vedic wisdom, is seemingly subordinated in two occasions.

The first instance occurs during the performance of a ritual to seek the birth of a son (*putrakāmeṣṭi*) for the hitherto childless Dasharatha. Sumantra, one of the king's ministers and personal charioteer, informs him that there is a powerful seer by the name of Rishyashringa who brought an end, by dint of the powers generated through perfected celibacy, to the famine that ravaged the kingdom of Dasharatha's ally, King Romapada. Sumantra suggests to Dasharatha that Rishyashringa should be put in charge of performance of the *putrakāmeṣṭi*. Dasharatha follows the advice of his charioteer and seeks the consent of Vashishtha to have Rishyashringa preside, which Vashishtha magnanimously grants.[10] I use magnanimous because Rishyashringa was afforded a regal welcome by the citizens, greeted with trumpets and drums to a city that was specially decorated just for him;[11] the King and his queens offered him the lavish ritual honors that were customary and then entertained him (and his

---

8   See J. Brereton and S. Jamison (2014) *The Ṛgveda*, Vol. 3. Oxford: Oxford University Press, pp.1681–1684.
9   Patrick Olivelle translates *purohita* as "chaplain" in his translation of the *Manusmṛti* (see his *Manu's Code of Law: A Critical Edition and Translation of the Mānava-Dharmaśāstra* (Oxford: Oxford University Press, 2005), pp.158, 232), though it generally has the sense of "family priest" (see M. Monier-Williams (1899) *A Sanskrit-English Dictionary*. Oxford: Clarendon Press, p.635). As described in the *Manusmṛti* (7.78–79), the function of the Royal Chaplain is not too dissimilar to that of the mediaeval Christian iteration.
10 Ramayana 1.11.13.
11 Ibid., 1.11.26–27.

new wife) in the royal apartments until spring.[12] Vashishtha is content renouncing these instances of fame and fortune and giving them instead to Rishyashringa, even though, ritually speaking, as a composer of the Vedic hymns himself, Vashishtha is clearly senior. Dasharatha goes on to laud Vashishtha, saying "you are my loving friend; the greatest and best spiritual guide—the burden of preparations and performance of the ritual that has been undertaken shall be yours alone." Even though he has not received any of the customary regard, he graciously accepts the King's request.[13] Accordingly, Vashishtha discharges the "burden" of being public relations supervisor, royal emissary, logistics coordinator, hospitality provider, resource and personnel manager, and then consultant senior priest of the mammoth undertaking.[14]

If one were to disassociate the pre-eminence of Vashishtha from the role of royal chaplain he takes in this episode, it is clear that there is helpful guidance that is transferrable to a Hindu chaplain in higher education. First, the ability to perform sacerdotal duties is a desideratum but not as important as having a solid understanding of their import and utility. Especially as diasporic Veda-Pathashalas remain desiderata, the chaplain should be able to develop a network of vetted, qualified *purohitas/paṇḍitas* in the vicinity that can be consulted to preside over major rituals at festivals or for life-cycle rites. Where a linguistic and sometimes cultural disconnect becomes counterproductive for the needs of the university audience, the chaplain should be able to step in to enable smooth interfacing. As with the case of Vashishtha, this is not sidelining the training of the Hindu chaplain to that of the priest. Rather, it is an opportunity to highlight the obvious necessity of both roles—one that demands lengthy, specialist ritual training that is simply not available nor possible for the majority of Hindu chaplains, and the other that entails academic and professional training that would be quite unnecessary for a trained Hindu priest to serve in their specific role, usually as the priest of a Mandir.

While the above should suffice for most colleges, Georgetown University adds a unique nuance to the discussion. The university is home not only to a Jesuit Community, a vast Department of Theology, and the Berkeley Center for Religion, Peace and World Affairs, but has

---

12 Ibid., 1.11.29–30.
13 bhavān snigdhas suhrin mahyaṁ guruś ca paramo mahān | oḍhavyo bhavatā caiva bhāro yajñasya codyataḥ || Ramayana 1.13.4.
14 The full list of duties Vashishtha undertook is detailed in the Ramayana of Valmiki, 1.13-9-35.

one of the most dynamic private college campus ministries in the US. The sheer number of interfaith engagements, organized by both students and the department, requires a depth of research that sometimes exceeds the training of a Mandir priest, but the vastness of the traditional knowledge could not be brought to bear without it. Furthermore, in a faith-based private institution of higher learning such as Georgetown, it is vital that the ordained representatives of a religion maintain scholarly erudition in order to serve as resources worthy of consultation by the broader university community. The management of the Office of Mission and Ministry's insistence that the Hindu chaplain be able to assist Hindu students to deepen their spiritual formation meant the convergence of priest, chaplain, and academic training would be the only way that Georgetown could hire a Hindu chaplain.

Beyond interfaith engagements, a chaplain will receive all manner of requests—from students, staff, faculty, management, the wider community, local and national organizations, and even civic or government bodies. I knew that at a university such as Georgetown, these duties would devour the lion's share of my time, but I was initially blindsided by the sheer number of hours spent shopping or ordering for festivals and weekly meetings, reconciling receipts with the budget, staying current with electronic correspondences, ensuring compliance with university directives and regulations, and other types of "back-of-the-house" activity. Even researching caterers that would both adhere to the strict *sāttvika* dietary standards of Hinduism while possessing the variety of certification to enable food from their establishment to be served to students on campus (and the ability to deliver to our "remote" hilltop location) became a time-intensive affair.[15] Vashishtha's example was thus very reassuring—I was doing exactly what a Hindu chaplain should be doing, even if that was not an immediately apparent facet of the role. The facilitator "hat" of a chaplain is thus scripturally mandated.

---

15 Chander's notes on the complex issues arising when attempting to situate *sāttvika* diet-compliant items during hospitality-heavy, explicitly interfaith events is similarly pronounced, especially when the rebuttal comes from the Bible, Acts 10: 9–15, 1 Timothy 4, and Mark 7:15. See: Chander (2013), p.110.

Vashishtha and the Nature of Hindu Chaplaincy in Higher Education

As a Hindu develops spiritually, it is necessary to become connected with one of the traditions within the established *dharma*s in order to progress. This is all the more urgent at a university, for after a mere four years, a student will need to be connected to pathways to continue their spiritual growth beyond the reach of the university Hindu chaplain. So, a major focus of the chaplain beyond those attendant on the religious calendar should be to assist students to begin to discern their spiritual path. Can the chaplain simply provide their own spirituality and connections as *the* path for continuing spiritual development? That is one option; however, the second episode of Vashishtha provides a scriptural precedent.

After the *putrakāmeṣṭi*, Dasharatha was blessed with four sons: Sri Rama, Lakshmana, Bharata, and Śatrughna—incarnations of the *catur-vyūha* (four emanations) of Vāsudeva-Nārāyaṇa (the monotheist Supreme Lord of Vaisnavism).[16] They studied the Vedic sciences under Vashishtha. Towards the middle of their student life, another seer, Vishvamitra, arrives at the palace. Vishvamitra is another of the seven seers, but is also known to have transitioned from the royal class to a scholar (*brāhmaṇa*), and then to a *brahmarṣi* (seer) by the grace of Vashishtha himself.[17] He requests that Dasharatha give him the young Sri Rama for ten days to dispatch two miscreants that were impeding the successful completion of an important ritual. This would be the first time that Sri Rama would be involved in battle—supernatural at that—and Dasharatha was understandably perplexed. He could not refuse the request of this eminent seer, but was unable to entertain the thought of being separated from his dearest 15-year-old son.[18] He refused, but before calamity struck, Vashishtha counseled the king, saying that Vishvamitra was not only supremely capable, but a knower of all manner of supernatural weaponry and able even to create new ones. Not only would no harm come to Sri Rama, he would attain mastery of such weapons, too.[19] The prospect of losing regular contact with his best student did not for one moment delay the mind of Vashishtha, nor did any concerns about retaining the title

---

16 Ramayana 1.15.30.
17 W.J. Wilkins (2003) *Hindu Mythology*. New Delhi: D.K. Printworld, pp.380–382; Ramayana 1.65.24.
18 Ramayana 1.20.1-2.
19 Ramayana 1.27 details the various weapons and martial training given to Sri Rama by Vishvamitra.

of the sole instructor of Sri Rama. Vashishtha was eminently capable of teaching the arts of warfare and weaponry to the sons of Dasharatha—indeed, Vashishtha's effortless defeat of the entirety of Vishvamitra's army prompted Vishvamitra to seek spiritual progress in the first place. Vashishtha thus happily handed his prized student over to the tutelage of Vishvamitra.

This seemingly benign fable yields great insight for the design of a Hindu chaplaincy; however, for those unfamiliar with the conundrum that requires traversing before one can even contemplate designs on student spiritual formation and direction, I'll attempt a brief sketch.

Hinduism, as we know, is a broad designator plastered upon the four autonomous, ancient religions of Shaktism, Shaivism, Vaisnavism, and Smartism. It also is expanded (thereby superficially allotting equal levels of legitimacy) to include various regional orthopraxies, dynastic religiosities, and the cults of non-affiliated charismatic leaders, of which there are thousands. In approximation, Hinduism would be akin to a term such as Abrahamism wherein Judaism, Christianity, and Islam are rough equivalents to the four Hindu Dharmic religions. Then one must add to the mix the nineteenth century politician-created "Hinduism," which claims to be the religion of Indians and the diaspora without regard for the ancient religions. The number of denominations and sub-denominations of Christianity, for instance, might be an indication of the diversity of *sampradāya*s (lineages) within Vaisnavism—let alone the "totality" of Hinduism.

At Georgetown, there are Methodist, Baptist, and Presbyterian clergy that comprise the university's Protestant chaplaincy, with numerous affiliated ministries of nearly every major US Protestant denomination. Instead of a similar system, the singular Hindu chaplain must provide for Hindus of all manner of Dharmic religions (even including students of Jain, Buddhist, and Sikh background), with historical familial affiliations to denominations that will most likely be unbeknown to the student and sometimes even their parents, but will nevertheless affect the degree of familiarity with "Hinduism" that they will feel at a Hindu chaplaincy-organized worship service, for example.

Of course, it would be easier if the Hindu chaplaincy reflected the Hindu religion and denomination that is best known to the chaplain (i.e., one's own). However, following Vashishtha, each individual's spiritual "flavor" should be sought out—whether by acknowledging familial or personal membership of a denomination, or through divining such allegiance through gentle curiosity. In the absence of a firm spiritual identity, it is the chaplain who takes the lead from Vashishtha that retains the most integrity.

The Vashishtha model, if you will, urges us to recognize which of the valid pathways within the Hindu *dharma*s best aligns with the student's proclivities—an enormously demanding task, not the least because it may involve putting the student in contact with authentic denominations which one may have previously discarded during one's own spiritual voyage in favour of the one within which they are ordained. Developing an in-depth knowledge of the variety of Hindu religions, their major and sub-denominations, their US-based membership and leadership, and maintaining networks with them is a task that seems impossible, though, I contend, is absolutely unavoidable, lest one become a missionary rather than a chaplain. Indeed, an effort to understand the spectrum of religious tastes of our students led to the crystallization of one of our most successful programmes, entitled *Decoding Dharma*—regularly attended by a number of Hindu students who do not attend our worship services. All of this must be factored into the design of the chaplaincy's four-year arc of student engagement.

Concluding Thoughts

In the absence of definite scriptural guidance, a few Hindus have taken up the challenge to provide spiritual sustenance to college students. From curating an interfaith event on *śaraṇāgati*, or self-surrender, as envisioned by Sri Vedanta Deshika and St. Francis de Sales, to teaching a theology elective entitled *Religion without God*; from making trays of mango cheesecake with a good friend (who happened to be a Muslim Resident Minister) for Sunday *aarti*, to shining a light on the dark history of the Goa Inquisition for this year's Jesuit Heritage Week; and everything in between—nothing in my training as a priest, instructor of priests, nor even as a senior *brahmacārin*[20] could have prepared me directly for any of this. Yet, as is ubiquitously experienced in the Hindu *dharma*s, the seeds to the answers were sown long ago when the great epics[21] such as the Ramayana

---

20 As opposed to the general undergraduate *brahmacārin*, this category refers to those monks who have completed all monastic training but for whom the final vows of renunciation remain to be taken.

21 *Itihāsa*s (great histories or epics) and Purāṇas (ancient histories) are further categories of Hindu scriptures. The Ramayana and the Mahabharata are the most famous epics of Ancient India.

were taught to us by our elders. The foregoing, I hope, reflects the fact that even in the most confounding of circumstances, the methodology for Hindu chaplains in higher education lies in final admonishment of the Lord in the Bhagavad-Gita: "Having duly deliberated on the totality of [relevant scriptural] wisdom, do as you [a practitioner of *dharma* with integrity] see fit" (18.63).[22]

---

22 A context-sensitive eisegetical translation of a line that literally runs "deliberating on this knowledge thoroughly, do as you wish" (*vimṛśyaitad aśeṣeṇa yathecchasi tathā kuru*).

Space for Spiritual Care

Asha Shipman

The Hindu Prayer Room at Yale University sits nestled in a basement corner of a freshman dormitory on the campus. On one side is an elevator shaft and on the other is a classroom. Down the hallway is the unmistakable clanking of laundry machines and whiff of dryer sheets. Its plain wooden classroom door suggests the standard interior marked by "Yale White" painted walls and gray carpeting. Yet, to cross the threshold of the Hindu Prayer Room is to enter a space where the din of washing machines, lecture halls, laboratories, and city streets recede. Inside the door, just beyond the shoe racks, a temple bell hangs from the ceiling. Further in, a circle of plump square cushions in sea green, pale blue, and vibrant orange hues lie on a low-pile carpet. Walls painted yellow-gold and saffron bathe the room in warmth and showcase framed posters of Hindu deities and inspirational quotes. A tall metal statue of Nataraja (Shiva as the Lord of the Cosmic Dance) tops a bookcase housing a small library and bins filled with silk garlands, colorful altar sheets, and floor coverings. Ritual materials—bells, incense sticks, ash, *haldi*, *kumkum*, metal cups, bowls, and plates—and smaller statues of Hindu deities reside within a painted wooden cabinet. The whiteboard announces upcoming events: worship services, study circles, festival observances, and socials. Even empty, for Hindus the room radiates comfort and quietude. When populated it offers the opportunity for communal spiritual elevation and a reminder of home by way of the familiar sacred syllables and images, the tang of Asian flavors, and poly-linguistic chatter. This Prayer Room, set on a university campus, is not a consecrated Hindu temple and the colorful walls cannot quite mask its earlier incarnation as a college classroom. Yet for those familiar with Hinduism and Hindu worship the combination of the room's use and physical landscape psychologically align the Hindu

Prayer Room with a Hindu temple, rendering it a space that holds an intangible essence—a spiritual vibe so to speak—in support of ritual practices and spiritual care.

Hindus believe in Creator—an immanent and transcendent supreme being who has no form, no beginning, and no end. This entity represents the highest truth in the universe; everything else is said to be a reflection, like moonlight. The gods and goddesses in the Hindu pantheon represent less abstract notions that are easier to grasp and connect with. However, each deity is a representative of the Divine. Hindus also believe that our bodies house the Divine deep within us in a place Aubrey Menon refers to as "the space within the heart."[1] Connecting with that space requires an elevation of the consciousness, possible through meditation, yoga, controlled breathing (*pranayama*), and participating in *yagnas*. *Yagnas* are complex fire-based rituals codified in ancient sacred Hindu texts designed to invoke, honor, and petition aspects of the Divine and help ease the burdens associated with human existence.[2]

The Sanskrit word for a Hindu temple is *devasthanam* which translates as "abode of God." These carefully designed spaces are focal points of spiritual energy where Hindus believe they may come into direct contact with the Divine. Some temple complexes stretch out for acres and include terraced water tanks, flower gardens, and winding walkways leading devotees towards the entryway to the temple. One or more carved towers crown the temple and are bedecked with elaborately carved stone human, animal, floral, and divine forms, re-enacting mythic stories and the patterns of life. Stretching skyward, they mimic the mythic Mount Meru, a central axis around which the cosmos itself revolves. Most devotees arrive already bathed and dressed in fresh clothing; but, prior to entering the temple, they remove their shoes and sometimes take a dip in the tank or traverse a small stream to purify themselves. Once within, they enter a space built according to rules set out in the *Vastu Shastra*, an architectural treatise with ancient origins that dictates the construction of sacred as well as secular dwellings. The geometry of a temple layout is based on a grid formation that takes into consideration the cardinal directions and their relationship with the Hindu pantheon and humankind in its conception and design. Gods and goddesses are associated with specific directions; for example, Surya the Sun god is assigned the eastern part of the temple and the presiding deity always faces east. Metaphorically laid

---

1   A. Menen (1970) *The Space Within the Heart*. New York: McGraw-Hill, p.177.
2   A.V. Srinivasan (2014) *Yaksha Prashna*. Glastonbury, CT: Periplus Line.

over the grid in diagonal fashion is the form of a human with the head placed in the northeast. Set at the navel point, beneath the primary tower, resides that presiding aspect of the Divine. Access to this central sanctum in some large temples involves traversing a series of inwardly coiling halls which house smaller sanctums for other divine forms, each elaborately carved, gleaming in colorful silk clothes and fine jewelry and illumined by lit brass oil lamps. As they head towards the innermost sanctum, often crowded together in the company of family and friends, devotees hear sacred chanting, the ringing of temple bells, and the shuffle of bare feet while they inhale the scents of incense, flowers, fruit, and oils. At popular pilgrimage sites worshippers gain only a few glances at the primary deity, long enough to proffer a plate of fruits and flowers to the priest, bow down with hands folded in prayer, and then receive a dab of crimson or ash powder on the forehead and a handful of blessed food (*prasadam*) and water (*tirtham*). In contrast, at a local temple the ceremonies—particularly for the major religious festivals—may last for hours while devotees sit in congregation in front of the deity chanting prayers, singing hymns, and ringing bells while the priests chant, light oil lamps and incense, and make offerings to God. Later devotees sit together and partake in the blessed food. After taking *darshan* (literally, seeing God) at the temple, whether the experience lasts moments or hours, devotees leave with a feeling of relief, inner peace, and spiritual upliftment.

As is clear from the above passage, the entire temple environ, attendant to physical and metaphysical relationships, is designed to spark the senses and elevate the consciousness of the individual when walking through the space. The eyes are drawn to the carved designs depicting sacred stories, the sanctums housing exquisitely dressed deities, and the golden glow of oil lamps and natural light. The sounds of bells and chanting fill the air with the intention of pushing away negative vibrations and thoughts. As the devotee's senses attune, they internally reverberate with the holy space.

These experiences in houses of God, whether milestone pilgrimages to famous shrines or weekly services at a local one, evoke such powerfully positive emotional reactions because of the special setting and the physical activities associated with being in that space. As Shampa Mazumdar and Sanjoy Mazumdar observe, a religion differentiates a space as sacred through specific symbolic referents as well as geographic and architectural elements that "have the capacity to…foster attachment, devotion, spirituality and a certain 'disposition,' 'ethos,' and 'worldview' in its believers, and in some instances in others as well."[3] These responses are deeply internalized and naturally develop as an individual matures within their natal setting. Childhood memories of the sights, sounds, smells, tastes, and textures related to religion lay the groundwork for neuro-physiological responses to the rituals and the space. Listening to stories narrated by elders from the scriptures, legends, and myths, learning to sing the hymns and participate in the rituals, exploring the key philosophical tenets linking individual soul to the world's souls, the cosmos and the Divine create further networks of emotional and physiological responses to the religion and its artifacts. In a lecture on "The Science of Worship" (2009), Swami Mahayogananda comments that ritual worship has a certain salience because it "engages our senses, our bodies, our minds, our speech in a prescribed set of actions all connected with the Divine, engaging the whole personality in god-oriented thought and action." He further notes "The very act of simple worship performed regularly leads gradually to an awakening of devotion, a deepening of devotion."[4] Even the domestic rites, though simpler than those conducted in a temple, are considered authentic in their ability to guide a devotee along the path of the inner *yagna*.

Rigorous scientific studies of religiosity and its effect on health, dating back over a century, offer substantial empirical evidence of a positive correlation between religious practices and improved mental and physical health.[5] For example, numerous studies find that people who participate in weekly religious services experience neuro-physiological responses (e.g., changes in heart rate, blood pressure, and hormone levels) and that ritual participation is positively associated with alleviation of stress, bolstering of the immune system, and an overall increase in health and longevity.[6] This is particularly relevant for college students who in the

---

[3] S. Mazumdar and S. Mazumdar (2004) "Religion and place attachment: A study of sacred spaces." *Journal of Environmental Psychology* 24, 385–397. See also, C. Geertz (1966) "Religion as a cultural system." In M. Banton (ed.) *Anthropological Approaches to the Study of Religion*. London: Tavistock Publications.

[4] S. Mahayogananda (2009) "The Science of Worship." Vedanta Center of Greater Washington D.C. published lectures, May 24. www.vedantadc.org/the-science-of-worship-swami-mahayogananda, accessed on April 4, 2019.

[5] See J. Levin (2017) "'For they knew not what it was': Rethinking the tacit narrative history of religion and health research." *Journal of Religion and Health* 56, 28–46.

[6] This point is made in C.S. Alcorta and R. Sosis (2005) "Ritual emotion and sacred symbols." *Human Nature* 16, 4, 323–359.

face of academic and social pressure often experience great anxiety, depression, and loneliness.[7]

Like all incoming first year students, Hindu students quickly form a family away from home in order to feel secure and comfortable. Ideally, as students work towards acculturating into the campus milieu, they rely on their personal value system as they navigate this new terrain. This often includes retaining their spiritual practices and cultural ties. While many will create worship altars in their dorm rooms or find a quiet space to meditate for their daily practice, they often miss the colors and flavors of home and the joy of congregational worship—particularly that which is associated with the religious holy days. The core of my work as the Hindu chaplain at Yale University has been to build and nurture a vibrant Hindu campus community. The Hindu Life programming is designed to be spiritually and mentally uplifting and to connect students and post-graduates with like-minded individuals who share their beliefs, values, cultural and ethnic traditions, and cuisine. The Hindu Prayer Room is central to that mission. It is host to many different activities and unsurprisingly attendance is greatest for the worship services celebrating major religious holy days and festivals.

In recognition of our collegiate space and mission, we mark the beginning and end of each semester with a service to Maha Saraswati, the Goddess of speech, music and learning. We also celebrate Krishna Janmashtami, Ganesh Chaturti, Navaratri, Shivaratri, Ramanavami, and Hanuman Jayanti. Diwali and Holi celebrations require much larger spaces. But for the services conducted in the Prayer Room, just like at home and in their local temples, students sit together side by side on the floor prepared to worship the Divine. They hear the ringing bells, see the lit lamps (tea lights, in our case), inhale the fragrances of incense, fruit, and flowers, chant the prayers, and sing the hymns. The entire service and the catered Indian dinner afterwards feed the mind, body, and soul—with the goal of supporting the inner *yagna*.

Even when students come for smaller events, the room effects a visible change in them. They may walk in with the burdens of the secular student day—anxious, hunched, tired, and pressed for time. Surrounded by people of a similar religious and cultural background, bathed in the warm colors

---

[7] See A. Novotney (2014) "Students under pressure." *Monitor on Psychology,* online magazine of the American Psychological Association 45, 8, 36. Also, F. Bruni (2017) "The real campus scourge." *New York Times online,* September 2. www.nytimes.com/2017/09/02/opinion/sunday/college-freshman-mental-health.html, accessed on Julu 30, 2018.

and soft sounds, they visibly straighten, their faces brighten, and worry lines fade as they embark on a shared inquiry into themselves and their faith. The need for a special space devoted to spiritual practices was made very clear by Swami Vivekananda, a Hindu monk who introduced modern Hinduism to American culture. Though he wrote on the benefits of creating specifically a meditation space, the idea can be broadened to include a space like that of the Hindu Prayer Room at Yale University. Swami Vivekananda advised:

> Those of you who can afford it will do better to have a room for this practice alone. Do not sleep in that room, it must be kept holy. You must not enter the room until you have bathed and are perfectly clean in body and mind. Place flowers in that room always; they are the best surroundings for a yogi. Also, pictures that are pleasing. Burn incense morning and evening. Have no quarreling nor anger nor unholy thought in that room. Only allow those persons to enter it who are of the same thought as you. Then, gradually, there will be an atmosphere of holiness in the room so that when you are miserable, sorrowful, doubtful, or your mind is disturbed, the very fact of entering that room will make you calm. This was the idea of the temple and the church and in some temples and churches you will find it even now. The idea is that by keeping holy vibrations there the place becomes and remains illumined.[8]

The Hindu Prayer Room at Yale University aspires to emulate such a holy atmosphere and is accessible for students for private worship, reading, and meditation. Sometimes first year Hindu students who live in the dormitory use the room to perform their daily morning prayers. Yet the space has a communal role as well, so it must be a bit more flexible. We hold welcome dinners for first year students, philosophical discussions, lectures, and cultural activities—all with the goal of nurturing hearts and minds along with souls.

Spiritual care can occur in various, sometimes unexpected, forms. One of the most popular events I coordinate is *Mehendi* Night, an evening devoted to celebrating this ancient South Asian body art tradition. Though *mehendi* is most typically associated with pre-wedding rituals in South Asia, it is now popular in the US for parties and even at fairs. I recruit students skilled at applying the henna paste and, for those who prefer a more ephemeral version, I supply gold and red toned temporary tattoos

---

8   S. Vivekananda (1915) *The Complete Works of Swami Vivekananda,* Vol. 1, 2nd ed. Mayavati, India: Gauranga Press, p.165.

that require little skill to apply. I also provide pens and coloring pages with *mehendi* designs. Often the event is co-sponsored by our Hindu and Muslim student groups and includes creamy mango lassi (a popular Indian yoghurt drink).

Applying *mehendi* paste literally requires holding someone's hand, sometimes for about an hour. Even applying the temporary tattoos involves touching a hand or arm. Coloring in these delicate patterns—whether on the hand or on paper—requires some focus and the gentle physical contact can be very comforting. This absorption into the designs and the companionship offer a welcome diversion from their student workload. During the evening, students sit side by side, sharing materials, drawing, peering at design concepts, telling stories, drinking lassi, and laughing together. Students talk about their families, visits to India, weddings they have attended, and other social topics. These are usually very heart-warming, delightful evenings that leave everyone uplifted. They are also opportunities for engaging with students who may benefit from some amount of individual pastoral counseling. In the course of conversation, they may need a chance to vent or may seek advice about navigating social dynamics, balancing work and extra-curricular activities, choosing a major, negotiating parental expectations, their own lived experiences, and other challenges presented by campus life or life in general. Peers may chime in with advice and sometimes students will set an appointment to see me to talk in private.

Whether it is via *mehendi*, meditation, scripture study, ritual worship, or a free-wheeling discussion that anchors Hinduism with contemporary issues, participation in events held in the Hindu Prayer Room validates the relevance of students' spiritual and cultural traditions and reinforces their sense of belonging—thus rendering them happier, less stressed, and better able to focus and thrive on campus.

Spirituality in the University

Community and Diversity

Tahil Sharma

Spiritual care in American academic institutions has traditionally always been a space for chaplaincy governed by Christian theology. This norm is being challenged by the changing landscape and demographics of the average student body that is now in need of support from religious leaders coming from various religious, spiritual, and ethical backgrounds that fulfill the need for guidance and community. A setting like Los Angeles is unique in this case as it contains one of the most populous and religiously diverse cities in the country, where pluralism between communities is a social norm. Hindu students at the University of Southern California (USC) have a space for spiritual care that requires them to engage with this diversity head on and impact the way the students learn to create a sanctuary for themselves and their fellow Hindus. To understand this, it is useful to explore the roots and formation of USC and the way it has developed as an institution which values diversity and the identity of the individual.

USC was established in 1879 after Judge Robert Maclay Widney secured 308 lots of land from a few affluent community members: Ozro W. Childs, a Protestant horticulturalist; former California governor John G. Downey, an Irish-Catholic pharmacist and businessman; and Isaias W. Hellman, a German-Jewish banker and philanthropist.[1] As such, coupled with the financial support of the Methodist community in the region, USC's very origins had already set it apart. It was destined to continue that legacy of diversity on its campus.

---

[1] USC Communications (n.d.) "The era of the founders." www.about.usc.edu/history/founders, accessed on July 19, 2019.

Minority leadership at academic institutions continues to be lacking. As the College and University Professional Association for Human Resources reported in 2017, approximately 14 percent of positions such as deans and department heads across colleges in the US were filled by people from communities of color.[2] If the ethnic representation of the administrative or faculty body does not reflect that of the student body, imagine the impact it can have on religious minorities who may not have the platform to voice their concerns to senior colleagues and mentors.

Hundreds of students, mainly from India, who are hoping to earn a Master's degree, make up a large percentage of the Hindu population on the USC campus. They can usually be seen en masse during the celebrations of Diwali and Holi, saying their prayers and taking part in the festivities of food, song, and dance that can be found at such gatherings. What makes USC so unique in its ability to host and carry out such festivities is the fact that its Dean of Religious Life is the first practicing Hindu to hold such a position.[3]

The impact Soni and Laemmle have in the lives of students goes beyond being an administrator at an academic institution. When students have mentors or leaders who share their own background or worldview, it affects their ability to see progress and to fill higher positions of power themselves. As he explained in an interview, Soni regards his selection as dean as an "anomaly." Several concurrent circumstances, including the 2008 US General Elections, made it the right time to call him towards this leadership position: "If it were not for the structure, the particular committee on that search committee, the particular political moment in time I don't think it would've been possible."

Furthermore, Soni says, while his hire was not surprising in a landscape like Los Angeles, it did not spark a trend toward similar hires. In the past decade—with the exceptions of rabbis at Dartmouth College and Wesleyan University and a Buddhist at Emerson College—universities have continued to prefer to hire deans of religious life who are Christian.[4] So, it was of great significance that, in 2017, USC hired Vanessa Gomez

---

2   R. Seltzer (2017) "Racial gap among senior administrators widens." *Inside Higher Education*, March 2. www.insidehighered.com/news/2017/03/02/racial-gap-among-senior-administrators-widens, accessed on July 19, 2019..
3   Dean Soni is not, however, the first non-Christian to serve as USC's Dean of Religious Life. Rabbi Susan Laemmle was appointed to that office in 1996.
4   R. Xia (2017) "Most college head chaplains are Christian. At USC, a Hindu leads the way." *LA Now, Los Angeles Times*, April 3. www.latimes.com/local/lanow/la-me-usc-chaplain-20170403-story.html, accessed on July 19, 2019.

Brake, making her the first Secular Humanist chaplain in the US to be selected as a university's Associate Dean of Religious Life.[5] In its selection of Soni and Gomez-Brake, USC has taken steps to address the urgent need for leadership that displays minority community affiliation and puts minority skills to work in multicultural and religiously pluralistic spaces.

Administrative factors are only one side of the "Rubik's Cube" that describes the identity formation of undergraduate and graduate students. A major aspect of Hindu spiritual care is the ability to form a community, encompassed generally by the idea of *vasudhaiva kutumbakam*—a phrase from the Maha Upanishad meaning that the entire universe is one big family. In a diverse setting like Los Angeles, seeking community among diversity—acting on the urge to build community with those who can be an ethnic, cultural, linguistic, or spiritual counterpart—can be a bit of a challenge. To this end, the Hindu Student Organization (HSO) has, for more than a decade, provided a means for students of diverse Hindu perspectives to dedicate their time to share culture, theology, and traditions.

The HSO precedes the tenure of Dean Soni; but as he noted when I interviewed him, the organization has taken on different forms as time has passed. Leadership has transitioned between undergraduate and graduate students from a spectrum of Hindu denominations, which makes any HSO activity a unique setting for dialogue and intra-religious understanding. Students also have the opportunity to share religious and cultural celebrations with the community at large through services, meals, temple visits, and occasional service projects. Much of the HSO's work has included collaborating with students and organizations of various worldviews, both on campus and off.

While the HSO is completely student-led, it is supported by a board of six Religious Directors who help students with various conversations, religious ceremonies, and events that promote understanding among students and the wider community about the diversity that exists in Vedic philosophy. The Directors come from various parts of the world and represent various schools of thought, including the Vedanta Society community that follows in the footsteps of Swami Vivekananda and the Ramakrishna Mission, the International Society for Krishna

---

5   A.H. Silverman (2017) "At the University of Southern California, a humanist chaplain takes the lead." *The Humanist*, September 5. https://thehumanist.com/features/interviews/university-southern-california-humanist-chaplain-takes-lead, accessed on July 19, 2019.

Consciousness (ISKCON), the Chinmaya Mission, and a few advocacy-based organizations. Students benefit immensely from these resources as they endeavor to explore their faith in more depth, while also gaining insight that will be useful in promoting religious literacy throughout the USC community. This approach to representation is definitely unique to USC. Other campuses have done differently.

Regardless, Hindus have had to face a challenge familiar to other campus religious communities: must the leader of a campus faith-based group be a member of an ecclesiastical body? In the case of Hindu representation on college campuses, Soni and numerous other leaders around the country have proven that one does not have to assume the role of Hindu clergy to support a Hindu student body. Asha Shipman, Director of Hindu Life and Hindu Chaplain for Yale University, has noted that "Hindu chaplaincy" can take numerous forms. In her experience at Yale, she offers: "spiritual support and work with Hindu students to host events on campus surrounding Hinduism and Indian culture." Rather than assuming the role of a guru, or a spiritual teacher, she serves as an adviser who facilitates conversations and mentors students to lead the way in raising awareness about Hindu religious traditions, cultures, and customs. Although no Hindu Life program looks the same on any campus around the country, Shipman argues that: "Consistent among us, however, is the belief that our presence serves a vital need for the Hindu populations we support while at the same time enhancing the wider campus community."[6]

Another facet of Hindu spiritual care is the established space in which adherents are able to practice their faith in privacy and in union with others. Although devotion takes on a variety of different manifestations in the Hindu diaspora, one common aspect of prayer, or *bhakti*, is expressed through community chanting, recitation, and song. At USC, the second floor of the University Religious Center (URC) is home to a dedicated Hindu Prayer Space, where a *puja sthal* (traditional altar) can be found filled with images and statues of various Hindu gods, goddesses, and reincarnations. The provision of a dedicated Prayer Space and numerous supporting staff members allows Hindu students to gather in more intimate ways during times of prayer and situations that may require

---

6   A. Shipman (2017) "Hindu chaplaincy." *Convergence* blog, October 4, 2017. https:// onvergenceoncampus.org/hindu-chaplaincy-asha-shipman, accessed on August 15, 2019.

solidarity and solace. Weekly *aartis* (prayer ceremonies) are usually attended by a dozen people at most. The space cannot accommodate the exponentially larger numbers that attend ceremonies for major holidays. Other meetings spaces in the URC, including the Fishbowl Chapel, are made accessible for Hindu gatherings on a larger scale—if need be, for upwards of 1,000 people.

During the 2018–2019 academic year, most of the leaders of the HSO were from various parts of India; however, Eesen Sivapalan, its president, was of Sri Lankan heritage. Sivapalan reports that he found sanctuary with the HSO as he pursued his studies in business administration. "I was raised in a religious household and Hinduism was a big part of my life," he told me. "When I came to USC, it was the first time that I would be away from home. I joined HSO so that I could have a community and a place to feel at home, even when I was away from home." In fact, many of the students who were involved with HSO as an organization or through an event that the HSO hosted found a place that really helped them feel that they were with their own family.

Sivapalan felt that his ability to interact with fellow Hindus connected him across geopolitical borders with students coming from other countries to study. He recognized that this not only had a personal benefit for spiritual growth, it also had the hidden benefit of professional growth. As he explained to me: "Communicating with people from a variety of countries made my experience all the more interesting and I certainly grew from the interactions I had with all of them. As we live in a multicultural country, I greatly benefited from joining HSO even from a professional standpoint. As someone who studies business in school, I know that it is essential for me to understand or at least acknowledge and be aware of cultural differences."[7]

Neha Koul, who received her Master's degree from USC's School of Computer Science Engineering in 2017, was introduced to HSO almost immediately upon arriving on campus from the state of Jammu and Kashmir in India. She eventually became a board member. The HSO thus was a deep part of her USC experience that she'd remember for the rest of her life.[8] Upon reflecting on time spent with her fellow Hindus on campus, Koul recognized that her own exploration of faith, especially coming from an area in India famous for numerous pilgrimages, was deepened by the

---

7   Author conversation with Eesen Sivapalan, July 23, 2018.
8   Author conversation with Neha Koul, July 27, 2018.

interactions she had with her fellow religious counterparts: "Even earlier I was a religious person, but HSO made me understand and learn what Hinduism truly is, what historical significance our [Hindu] culture has, and, most importantly, what's brought me in touch with a more diverse group of people to learn how Hinduism is practiced and the different festivals that are celebrated in many different forms, with different rituals across the country."[9]

Both Neha Koul and Eesen Sivapalan express a deep gratitude for the availability of HSO because it filled a gap in their heart for deep thoughts and new relationships that had not been explored. However, both these aspects reached a new level when they learned that those values applied to the same "universal family" that their faith taught them about. First, they both explicitly mentioned that their interaction with folks from various religious, spiritual, and secular traditions made them appreciate and made them more introspect about their own tradition; through learning about others they grew stronger in their own faith and spirituality. And second, the spiritual care that came with "creating a family" with other members of the HSO has now become a sustained tradition that goes with them beyond their academic careers.

Interfaith cooperation as a university commitment has been a newer part of the University's legacy in the past decade, with formations of an Interfaith Student Council and a renewed commitment to student accommodations throughout the campus community. This call for pluralism between the dozens of student groups on campus is, of course, a two-way street. The HSO was one of those groups that was always interested in working with different religious groups with the desire to learn about their views on life and discovering the shared values and experiences that bring people together.

One example of these efforts is the HSO's effort in hosting a yearly free meal for the community, also known as a *langar*, that is either prepared or organized between HSO board members, student volunteers, and members of the USC and Los Angeles communities. When this yearly meal was first hosted in 2017, over 20 Hindu students came from the university campus, bought materials, cooked, and served food to over 300 members of the Sikh and Los Angeles communities at the Vermont Gurdwara of Los Angeles. Although the service of these students was invaluable, the content of their conversations was even richer. For many

---

9   Koul interview.

people, generalizations are usually made about the level of pluralism between South Asian religious communities in the US. But for many folks in countries such as India, Pakistan, Bangladesh, Nepal, and Sri Lanka, your strategic location truly defines your exposure to religious diversity and engagement.

Some students were accustomed to a visit to the Sikh gurdwara, or temple, while others had never been exposed to a Sikh place of worship. Several linguistic barriers between Punjabi, Hindi, Tamil, Telugu, and Malayalam brought students and staff together to strategize bridge-building skills for translation. And the ability to reflect on one's individual journeys through life and comprehending much of what is beyond our comprehension made for new friends made on the common ground of service towards those in need. Students who participated in these projects, past and present, still speak about how much they enjoyed taking part and how they hope to continue participating in similar projects when they go back home. The aspect of sustaining a mind for interfaith work extends beyond the borders of a school or a city; it goes along with any person capable and willing to engage diversity in dialogue and action.

Another way of engaging diversity has been through the weekly discussions that follow *aarti*. Swami Atmavidyananda, the leading Religious Director of the HSO, hosts weekly topics of discussion for students to discuss a plethora of topics that may relate to or intersect with one's Hindu identity. Sometimes, the topics have required critical thinking between students and the *swami* or among the students themselves. Those dialogues produce deep, relevant, and sometimes heated conversations that prove to be laboratories for progress. Topics discussed can be controversial and relevant to international student experiences in a setting like Los Angeles or the US. While students may arrive on campus with the stereotypes and generalizations, their attitudes do change over time from these opportunities for exposure to, and engagement with, the numerous ethnic, cultural, and religious communities around the USC campus.

Many long-term participants in USC's HSO describe it as a family. Neha Koul explains this emotional and spiritual connection best: "The best part of being part of HSO is that even after leaving the university, you have another home for the rest of your life. Once you become part of HSO, it gets built into you and you carry the lessons with you always. Today when I talk about my beliefs, I can see the difference in me as now I carry the entire HSO experience with me through India!" The sense of belonging and desire for responsibility that arises from taking part in HSO activities makes others want to become involved. The value that members accord each other builds a sense of character and self-esteem that influences individuals to accept leadership roles. Says Dean Varun Soni, this sense of "interdependence" that USC's Hindu Students Organization encourages is what turns engaged students into engaged alumni.

Military Service and Spiritual Care by and for Hindus

Vineet Chander and Lucinda Mosher

Why, the reader might ask, should the pair of us be offering our thoughts on interrelationships between military service and Hindu spiritual care? After all, neither of us has ever been (or has plans to be) a member of any armed forces. That said, one of us is the Hindu chaplain at a major US university—thus is entirely likely to have eventual or former military personnel under his care. Indeed, he has published previously on the provision and receipt of spiritual care by Hindus in the military.[1] The other, an educator and consultant on spiritual care in multifaith contexts, grew up in a military family. In recent years, she has played a role in the formation of several Hindu chaplains, plus a significant list of US military chaplains (albeit none of them Hindu). Thus, we both are aware that personnel who identify as Hindu are a small segment of America's armed forces.[2] Even so, their need for spiritual care—while

---

1 This essay is profoundly informed by the material on the topic of military chaplaincy penned by Vineet Chander for inclusion in *Hindu Chaplaincy* by N. Sutton, V. Chander, and S. R. Das (Oxford, UK: Oxford Centre for Hindu Studies, 2017). See particularly 57–65; 78; 133–137 in that volume.
2 It has been asserted that, in July 2015, Indian-Americans on active duty in the US military numbered 1,031 in the Army, 764 in the Navy, 614 in the Marine Corps, and 190 in the Air Force. In addition, 294 were serving in the Army National Guard, 727 in the Army Reserve, 205 in the Navy Reserve, 133 in the Marine Corps Reserve, 99 in the Air National Guard, and 55 in the Air Force Reserve. That said, it must be remembered that not all Indian-Americans are Hindu; thus, even though it is conceivable that some Hindus in the US military are not of Indian origin, their actual numbers almost certainly are fewer than implied by these statistics. See E. Dutt (2016) "Remembering our patriots." *Desi Talk* website, July 8. http://epaper.desitalk.com/2016_07_08/files/assets/basic-html/page12.html, accessed on July 2, 2019.

on active duty, while home on leave, after discharge or retirement—is nonetheless significant. This chapter reflects on several overlapping issues: Hindus as military chaplains; the need for chaplains by Hindu military personnel; spiritual needs of present and former Hindu members of the armed services; and Hindu notions that could be of use to spiritual caregivers (Hindu or not) who have reason to care for Hindus who are or have been in the military.

Chaplains for the Military

On July 29, 1775, the Second Continental Congress—by order of George Washington—established the chaplain corps as an integral part of the US Amy, making this branch second only to the Infantry in age.[3] The Continental Navy followed suit on November 28, 1775. The importance of the military chaplain to the religious, moral, and spiritual health of American soldiers, airmen, sailors, and marines has been valued since the era of the War of Independence itself. US military chaplains are commissioned officers whose task is to support the spiritual and moral wellbeing of service members and their families—regardless of their own or the service member's religious affiliation. They are stationed on US bases at home and abroad—and accompany service personnel to combat environments.

Essentially, to become a US military chaplain, one must hold a Bachelor's degree, have the requisite theological and ministerial training (i.e., a Master of Divinity degree or its equivalent), further experience as a religious leader, plus the recommendation of an endorsing agency approved by the Department of Defense.[4] (Currently, Chinmaya Mission West is the recognized endorsing agency for Hindus.) To date, only Pratima Dharm has been commissioned as a Hindu chaplain in the

---

[3] See R. Murray (2009) "Army Chaplains Corps: Serving 'God and country' for 234 years with 25,000 chaplains." *US Army* website blog, July 9. www.army.mil/article/24086/army_chaplains_corps_serving_god_and_country_for_234_years_with_25000_chaplains, accessed on December 1, 2018.

[4] For a basic outline of requirements, see: www.goarmy.com/chaplain/become-an-army-chaplain/requirements.html, accessed on July 19, 2019.

US military—and she is no longer serving.⁵ So, in almost every case, Hindus in the US military—especially those on deployment—will be getting their spiritual care from non-Hindus.

To the extent that their particular religious affiliation allows, military chaplains perform religious rites and officiate at worship. They also provide confidential counseling. Wherever they cannot perform or provide, it is their duty to facilitate: to do their best to find someone who can.⁶ Thus, a Hindu military chaplain would never be expected to perform a Christian baptism or conduct a service of Holy Communion— nor would s/he ever be expected to lead Muslims in *salat*—but would be expected to help make such things possible. Military chaplains may also develop, conduct, or administer religious education courses or retreats; help personnel deal with grief, substance abuse, financial difficulties, deployment concerns, marriage and family matters, combat stress; or advise other officers on religious or ethical matters. Therefore, a Hindu member of the US military can expect to be provided such spiritual care.

---

5   Pratima Dharm served in the US Army as battalion chaplain for the Special Troops Battalion, Fort Stewart (3ID), GA, September 2006–July 2007. From August 2007 to August 2008, she was deployed as a battalion chaplain for more than 3,000 soldiers in Q-West, Iraq. From October 2008 to May 2009, she was a Wounded Warrior Battalion Chaplain serving some 500 soldiers at Fort Stewart, GA. She was Chaplain Resident at the Eisenhower Army Medical Center, Fort Gordon, GA, June 2009–June 2010; and was Chaplain Clinician at Walter Reed National Military Medical Center, Bethesda, MD, August 2010–June 2013. From August 2013 until March 2015, she worked in Integrative Health Services at Walter Reed National Military Medical Center with patients and service members with combat stress and PTSD.

   Dharm began her military service as a Christian, since—as she herself notes—there was no avenue at the time by which to gain the necessary training or commissioning as a Hindu. When, in 2011, the Department of Defense recognized Chinmaya Mission West as a Hindu chaplain-endorsing agency, Dharm received its endorsement, thus becoming the US military's first Hindu chaplain. She retired from the Army in March 2013, having attained the rank of Captain and having earned a Bronze Star for the ten humanitarian missions she ran. After additional education, she was ordained a Unitarian-Universalist minister in March 2017 and now serves as such. See L. Melwani (2016) "She was the US Army's first Hindu chaplain." *Lassi with Lavinia* blog, November 11. www.lassiwithlavina.com/features/people/meet-the-us-armys-first-hindu-chaplain/html; also, P. Dharm (2018), "Biography". http://montevistauu.org/wp-content/uploads/2018/06/Biography-Rev-Dharm.pdf; and "About Me"(2018). http://montevistauu.org/wp-content/uploads/2018/06/About-Me-Rev-Dharm.pdf accessed on December 12, 2018.

6   For a summary of duties, see Military OneSource (2018) "The Unit chaplain: Roles and responsibilities." November 28. www.militaryonesource.mil/family-relationships/spouse/getting-married-in-the-military/the-unit-chaplain-roles-and-responsibilities, accessed on December 12, 2018.

   See also "Careers and jobs: Chaplain." *US Army* website. www.goarmy.com/careers-and-jobs/browse-career-and-job-categories/administrative-support/chaplain.html, accessed on December 12, 2018.

How often is "Hinduism-specific" care offered? Probably not often enough; but when it is, the result can be quite wonderful. In an essay for *Huffpost,* Ravi Chaudary—then an officer and pilot in the US Air Force—recounts the occasion, in 2012, when a ceremony honoring the birthday of Sri Ganesha (the "Remover of Obstacles" in the Hindu pantheon) was held in the iconic Air Force Academy Chapel for the first time ever. To welcome such a Hindu ceremony, Chaudhary argues, is in line with the US Air Force Academy's intrinsic nature:

> For it is cross-cultural engagements like this that make the Academy a crucible for creativity and innovation—innovation that fuels the most technologically advanced organization in the world, the United States Air Force. Through his spiritual life force, Lord Ganesh encourages the development of wisdom in the arts and sciences, exactly what the Academy is designed to produce.[7]

In short, accommodation of a Hindu holiday and ceremony was of benefit to all cadets, faculty, and staff at the Academy at the time.

What Care Might Non-Hindu Chaplains Offer?

Some years ago, West Point graduate Rajiv Srinivasan, then a Lieutenant in the US Army, wrote an online essay about the complexity of his successful effort to integrate his Hindu-American and military identities. "The army challenged my most extreme patriotic influences against my peaceful Hindu beliefs," he notes. Yet, ultimately, he asserts, "no other endeavor has ever given me [more] professional and spiritual fulfillment than the experience of military service." Recalling Krishna's counsel to Arjuna in the Bhagavad-Gita, Srinivasan asserts that, "when peaceful attempts to reconcile fail, we must be prepared to defend the values in which we so whole-heartedly believe."[8]

Whatever their own religion, chaplains can help Hindus in the military reconcile the inherent violence of military service with the tenets of their Hindu faith. In fact, the place of violence in a Hindu worldview

---

7 Chaudhary, R. (2012, updated 2017) "For Air Force academy cadets, faith traditions spark innovation." *Huffpost,* October 17, 2012, updated December 6, 2017. www.huffingtonpost.com/ravi-chaudhary/for-air-force-academy-cadets-faith-traditions-spark-innovation_b_1965800.html, accessed on April 24, 2019.

8 Srinivasan, R. (n.d., prior to July 2009) "My battle within: The identity crisis of a Hindu soldier in the US Army." Hindu American Foundation blog. www.hafsite.org/media/pr/rajiv-srinivasan, accessed on April 24, 2019.

is complex. On the one hand, *ahimsa* (non-harming) is often noted as a dominant characteristic of *sanatana-dharma*. On the other hand, major (and highly revered) Hindu texts are full of violence and warfare. The great epics, the Mahabharata and the Ramayana, seem to champion military action against the forces of that do not accord with *dharma*. A battlefield is the setting of the much-loved Bhagavad-Gita; in it, Krishna urges Arjuna to fight, even as he extols the virtue of non-violence!

Among the many Hindu teachers and leaders who have attempted to resolve this obvious paradox, probably the best-known is Mahatma Gandhi. He contends that desire and anger are foundational to violent behavior—a notion that both history and present observation seem to validate. For Gandhi, *ahimsa* (non-harming) is both the means and the essential mark of spiritual progress. The ancient texts often equate *dharma* with *ahimsa*; without doubt, non-violence is a vital aspect of the Hindu revelation. Gandhi thus argues that the Bhagavad-Gita's battlefield is to be taken metaphorically rather than literally: it is to be seen as the site of conflict between the lower and higher forms of consciousness that exist in every person. He asserts that, since violent acts usually result from anger or desire, the desireless person will be non-violent naturally. Therefore, the Gita's point is that we are to abandon selfish desire, acting only out of duty and in service to others. Gandhi's absolute pacifism was informed profoundly by the teachings of Jainism—another great Indian religious tradition. The ancient Hindu texts are, however, less absolute. The Ramayana and the Puranas depict (and seem to endorse) violence. Moreover, none of the classical commentaries suggest that these texts or the Mahabharata are to be read allegorically.

Simply put, Gandhi's approach, while attractive, does not resolve the fact that the Mahabharata—a massive epic tale of which the Gita is a portion—is laden with political intrigue and explicit recognition of the role of the military. It explores the tension between the pure virtue of non-violence and the necessity of using violence in considerable detail, with significant arguments coming from both sides. Thus, in the Book 5, Chapter 70, we hear—on the one hand—the peace-loving Yudhishthira argue firmly and passionately that violence is never the answer. Yet, on the other hand, the Mahabharata also advocates *kshatriya-dharma*— the insistence that it is the religious duty of kings and warriors to use their martial prowess in the protection of the weak. The Bhagavad-Gita extolls such *kshatriyan* characteristics as vigor, resolve, heroism, and staying the course in battle (BG 18.43). Yet, it also expresses Hinduism's ambivalence toward violence and warfare. Witness the advice Krishna gives to Arjuna! Yes: Arjuna must take up arms and fight in the battle; he is, after all, a *kshatriya*. It is, therefore, his *dharma*—his duty—to stop the wrongdoers militarily. However, as Krishna makes clear, military action is to be performed, not out of desire for wealth and power, but only for society's welfare.

The Mahabharata has much more to say about *kshatriya-dharma*, particularly in Book 12. Repeatedly, it stresses that, without the *kshatriyas*, society will collapse into a state of chaos. It also stipulates that those whose *dharma* is military action must be highly trained—not just in the science of warfare, but also in ethics and morality—so that they take seriously their responsibility and do not abuse their power. In short, the Hindu tradition fully accepts the need for a class of highly trained and qualified personnel who can and will implement measured, reasonable violence when necessary.

Thus, it should be obvious that—while they acknowledge that violence is a sometimes-necessary recourse for the safeguarding of society's wellbeing—Hindu teachings also issue important caveats. Whosoever be designated to take military action must be a person of impeccable character who will never abuse that power and training, nor use it with selfish intent. Moreover, motive is everything!

Indeed, the Mahabharata—the Bhagavad-Gita in particular—teaches that a military profession can be undertaken in a manner that accords with the values of compassion and non-harming. In this epic, on the battlefield at Kurukshetra, Arjuna wages war against Duryodhana—a king who shows scant respect for the values of dharma, interpreting it as bald self-interest. These two warriors undertake a similar course of action, Yet, the text ultimately reveals Arjuna to be a practitioner of karma yoga, and a man of dharma; Arjuna fights to protect the innocent from the aggression of wrongdoers; he fights out of compassion for the weak, and so that they do not suffer any further harm; he fights in a mood of detachment, without selfish desire, because he adheres to the edicts of karma yoga. Duryodhana is presented as just the opposite. The difference is motivation rather than behavior.

Following in the footsteps of Arjuna, those who serve in the military and related professions can regard their actions as a service to society, protecting the weak from aggression and belligerence. The vital point of Hindu ethics is that action of this type must be undertaken only out of a sense of duty and service to others, to preserve the wellbeing of others.

Hindu ethics is, therefore, not so much a set of rules and regulations as it is a mindset. Once again, the demand is for intelligence and integrity in order to properly establish the correct course of action that is pursuant of the ideal of *dharma*. Violence is in many ways the antithesis of *dharma*, but at the same time absolute pacifism seems an implausible doctrine to apply to the world as we find it. The challenge is to establish when the use of violent means is genuinely in accordance with *dharma*, and to understand how Hindus in the military may participate in acts of violence yet sustain their sense of integrity.

Just as we have seen Hindu texts exhibit a degree of ambivalence about the role of state-sponsored violence, Hindu servicemen and women may also struggle to reconcile their faith with the violent nature of military service. Many might experience doubt—in themselves, in the correctness of their actions, or in their religious beliefs themselves. Some may express their ensuing discomfort outwardly as rage, vengeance, and a lack of self-control. Others may become emotionally withdrawn and apathetic—thinking this to be a faithful embrace of Hinduism's teachings on eschewal of attachment. In every case, a chaplain, in the process of offering spiritual care and empathy, might issue a reminder of the ideal of *kshatriya-dharma*—military engagement out of a sense of duty and in pursuance of the good of others, free from desire for gain or vengeance.

Knowledge of the intrinsically paradoxical nature of the message of Hindu sacred writings can be helpful to spiritual caregivers (Hindu or not) to Hindus in the military. However, an active soldier or veteran may even resent being compared constantly to Arjuna. The spiritual caregiver to Hindu military personnel might remember and teach that *kshatriya-dharma* is something toward which to aspire rather than something one must have in the present moment. The military chaplain might remind Hindus in his or her care that Hindu texts present these ideals as something to strive toward through regular spiritual practices. While scripture-study and theological discussion groups may be helpful for some, others may now find the Bhagavad-Gita off-putting. For them, simple meditation and yoga practices or meditation sessions may be more useful in addressing the dissonance between one's beliefs as a Hindu and one's experience in warfare, in dealing with strong feelings of guilt, inadequacy, and frustration. In the military, as elsewhere, chaplains must be active listeners, sensitive to the needs of the individual, flexible in the given situation.

Relatedly, chaplains may also help Hindu in the military by emphasizing the need for self-care. The culture of the military tends to favor the collective over the individual. The needs of the nation, one's branch of the military, or one's unit come before one's own. In this respect, military life bears some similarity to traditional Hindu culture, where the benefit to the larger group—the extended family, the temple group, the caste community—takes precedence over one's personal needs. These can be noble ideals. At the same time, meeting individual needs is vital to the survival of the individual and the larger group. Here, chaplains can remind military personnel that, in order to serve others effectively, they must be physically, emotionally, and spiritually healthy. Balance, moderation, and sustainability are key principles. They can remind the Hindus in their care that the Bhagavad-Gita endorses this, teaching that, to be truly caring toward others, one must be a yogi; and yogis, says the Bhagavad-Gita, are measured and balanced in their diet, rest, and recreation. The chaplain can point to such teachings to help Hindus in the military see their service to others, their own health and wellbeing, and their own spiritual and religious commitments as interrelated.

Hindus in the military in the West are a tiny minority, so they may feel awkward about requesting religious accommodation or expressing their needs.[9] Military chaplains can be proactive. They could, have copies of Hindu texts—the Bhagavad-Gita, at the least—on hand. They can advocate on behalf of Hindus and others who wish to maintain a vegetarian diet. Hindus themselves can be proactive. The recent emergence of "interfaith/interreligious studies" as an academic discipline is simultaneously acknowledging and facilitating the expansion of programs through which Hindus, Sikhs, Jains, and others may earn graduate degrees that will enable them to become credentialed as chaplains alongside Jews, Buddhists, Muslims, and Humanists. The US Department of Defense has had, since 2011, a protocol by which Hindus may become military chaplains. For Hindus who believe it is their *dharma* to provide spiritual caregiving in that paradoxical milieu, opportunity beckons!

---

9   None of the US military chaplains we interviewed for this essay could recall having someone in their care who identified as Hindu.

Tough Love

Prisons, Hinduism, and Spiritual Care

Ramdas Lamb

The Call, My Call

In 1993, I received a phone call from the chaplain at the main prison—a medium and high security facility—on the island of Oahu, Hawai'i, where I live and teach. He told me of an inmate who self-identified as Hindu and wanted to meet with a Hindu teacher or counselor if possible. Someone had recommended that the chaplain reach out to me, which was why he called. After speaking about the inmate briefly, he requested that I consider visiting prison to meet with him and then with the inmate, if after learning something about him, I chose to do so. At the time, I had no chaplain training, nor any formal training as a religious counselor. However, I had performed religious counseling on many occasions during the nearly ten years I had been a Hindu monk prior to entering academia and becoming a religion professor. Thus, when I received the phone call, I knew I was unprepared, yet I considered the situation as both a challenge as well as an opportunity given me by Ramji (God) to aid in my own spiritual growth while helping another. I therefore agreed and set up both meetings.

The inmate, whom I'll call Jason, was a young male with a variety of psychological problems. Today, he would probably be said to be on the autism spectrum; but at the time, he had not been diagnosed in that way. Although he was a very intelligent and at times a very perceptive person, his psychological difficulties led him to several run-ins with the law, and he eventually ended up in prison. In our initial conversation, he told me that he had met a Hindu teacher where he had lived previously who had helped him begin to learn about himself. After his move to Hawai'i,

Jason lost contact with that man, but never lost the feeling that a Hindu teacher had been one of the only people who had understood him and his problems. It was for this reason that Jason had asked to speak with a Hindu teacher now. After a few preliminary conversations with Jason, I began to see him on a regular basis, approximately two to three times a month, until he was released from the facility nearly two years later.

Several months into the process with Jason, I was asked to attend volunteer counselor training. I learned important information about the prison facility and gained valuable insight on interacting with inmates. This helped me to feel more comfortable being involved there. At the time, I assumed my visits would be limited to Jason, and possibly other inmates with an interest in the Hindu tradition. However, a few months before Jason was released from the prison, Mr Taketa (a pseudonym), the official who oversaw volunteer services, contacted me to ask if I would be willing to counsel another inmate. Part of the job of that official was to evaluate the efficacy of the various inmate services. He had been told by several of the Adult Correction Officers (ACOs) that they noticed significant progress with Jason, which they felt was due, at least in part, to my efforts with him. The official explained to me that another inmate with whom he wanted me to speak was not Hindu, but Jewish. This inmate felt uncomfortable with the other counselors available, all of whom were Christian. Two of his previous counselors had wanted him to attend church services; he felt pressured to convert as a part of, or in exchange for, their counseling. I agreed to meet with him—sporadically, at first. After Jason's departure, my visits with him became regular.

Within a few months, Taketa called me again—this time to discuss some issues regarding a Native American inmate. Because of my knowledge and understanding of world religions, the overseers asked me to help him decide on the validity of the inmate's religious requests and claims. He gave me a copy of the federal statutes dealing with inmate religious rights and asked if I could help him understand them. We met together several times to determine the best way to deal, both ethically and legally, with the new inmate's requests. By this time, since the chaplain apparently preferred to focus on his work with Christian volunteer counselors—of which there were many, Taketa was bypassing the chaplain and contacting me either directly or through someone I'll call Mr Goodman, one of the assistants to the warden. Gradually, one or the other would call me whenever an issue dealing with non-mainstream Christian religious beliefs, practices, or requests came up with an inmate.

Although Taketa was an evangelical Christian and Goodman was a practicing Jew, both were extremely open to the ideas and evolving methods I discussed with them and had begun incorporating into my counseling. The three of us came to understand that we all had the same essential goal, which was to address and fulfill to whatever extent possible the spiritual needs and requests of the inmates, especially the ones who were being funneled to me. We became partners in the process. Over the years, as we got closer, these officers would call me to ask my perspective on various problematic situations, or simply to ask my thoughts on dealing with certain dynamics within the Christian world. Their faith in and respect for my efforts was incredibly touching.

While most of the inmates I worked with were non-Christian, some claimed affiliation with Christian denominations that Taketa had never heard of. Since none of the other religious counselors were knowledgeable about the religious organizations or groups that such inmates identified with, it often fell to me to research the legitimacy of their claims, and then become their counselor as well. In the course of a relatively short time, I had come to be regarded by Taketa as the "go to" counselor for inmates not connected with a mainstream Christian denomination—as well as some of the latter. All the inmates with whom I spoke had spiritual needs or questions but did not want to work with any of the available Christian spiritual counselors.

Thus, during my 17 years of counseling at the prison, I came to know and learn about many religious denominations and movements about which I had been previously unaware, and this exposure influenced what I was teaching at the university as well. Altogether, my "clients" at the correctional facility included not only Polynesian, Native American, Buddhist, Hindu, Jewish, and several mainstream Christian inmates, but also persons who were connected with a variety of obscure Christian religious denominations, and some who had no formal religious affiliation, yet sought spiritual counseling. The diversity for me was not at all problematic, because I saw little ultimate distinction between counseling Hindus and non-Hindus. Whatever inmates' religious or cultural labels were—or even if there was none with which they identified—this had little or no relevance because they all seemed to have similar basic needs. A primary one was simply the need to talk on a personal level with someone who was willing to listen, not look down at them, and not force them into adopting a sectarian belief system. Because I made it clear to each of them at the outset that I was not there to proselytize or condemn, but simply to listen to them and give input if they wanted it, this fact in itself seemed to relax them and help them begin to find a place of calm within—at least while we were together. For the vast majority, I felt that if I could do nothing more than just be a vehicle in some way for them to feel some inner peace and a closer connection with whatever concept of divinity they believed in, then that was an important step. Of course, to me, helping them in this way is itself a Hindu approach. Early on in my life as a Hindu monk, my teacher had taught me not to identify myself with narrow labels that constrict more than guide and to be hesitant about identifying others with labels as well. Focusing on practice that gets us closer to God should be the primary focus, irrespective of labels.

Tools and Methods

Even though I worked with only two Hindu inmates during my years of prison counseling, the methods I developed clearly came out of my Hindu training and learning. I adapted them to meet the needs of whomever I counseled. In addition to the general techniques and methods I learned through the training I received, I also began to draw from my Hindu study and practice in communicating with inmates. For instance, because I was usually told ahead of time what crime had caused the inmate to be there and the approximate length of sentence they had been given, I would simply ask them to tell me about themselves and their views about their current situation. This would usually lead us to a point where I could speak with them about the doctrine of karma, although not always using that term, and the need to take responsibility for whatever they did that had led them to prison.

I would ask them to think about their choices and their actions, and how the repercussions of those choices inevitably come back to them. I would remind them that for everything in life there is a balance; for every action, an equal and opposite reaction. Once we could start delving deeper into a reflection on choices and actions, I would usually get to the point of being able to say to them something rather bluntly like, "You need to accept the reality that you are here because of what you did." Since many tried to live in denial that they should be incarcerated, some would become defensive or angry in response to such comments. Nevertheless, I would usually persist. "There is no one else to blame. You have to take responsibility, and you will never grow spiritually or emotionally until you own up to your own choices." I would remind them that they could not ultimately avoid the repercussions. Even if they could do so on a legal level, it would come back to them in some way that may be even worse.

I would also remind these inmates that I was there, meeting with them, because they had asked me to come; and that I could not help them if they insisted on denying any responsibility for their current situation. Most of the inmates would eventually come to be able to see that my point was not to browbeat them or to get into the nitty gritty of their cases on a legal level, but to communicate to them and help them. However, any help would ultimately be connected with first accepting responsibility, then seeing their situations as opportunities rather than simply punishment and something to resent or resist. At that point, I might say, "You are here because God created an opportunity for you to learn and to grow and to work through the karma that you created."

I would also touch on related concepts such as empathy and respect. This was especially helpful in working with non-Hindu inmates who may have no familiarity with the concept of karma. I would encourage them to reflect by stepping outside of themselves and into the shoes of others. I learned that a powerful way of doing this was to zero in on the things and people that mattered to them. Most of the men I counseled had children. "Okay, you did something," I would say. "You hurt someone. Now think about your own child. What if someone had done that to your kid? How would you feel?" Often, I could see them getting quite agitated and upset. Even the *thought* of somebody harming their child or loved ones would be hard for them to think about. I would encourage them to talk about that, and to reflect on what they had done in that light. I would also say to them that if they believe in the divine as our collective parent, then we are actually all connected in a larger human family and they, in fact, were hurting members of their own larger family. "The way you are feeling thinking about that, it is what you may have caused to others. Do you want to go around sewing those kinds of seeds in the world? Do you want that negative destructive energy coming back to you or your family members?" Again, I would introduce karma as a framework to understand this.

Pacific Islanders made up a significant percentage of the overall prison population with which I dealt; and among them, Samoan was one of the dominant ethnicities. A significant number of ACOs were also Samoan. Thus, in many ways the inmates and guards came from similar cultural, familial, and socio-economic backgrounds. They had grown up in the same neighborhoods—or at least under similar circumstances. Some of their families actually knew one another—which was, at times, difficult for both.

When inmates would use the excuse of their upbringing as the reason they ended up in prison, I would ask them to reflect on the guards, volunteers, and corrections officials there who came from similar backgrounds. I would challenge them, asking, "What is the difference between you and them? You have chosen to hurt people to get ahead, while they have chosen to help straighten people like you out so you can have a productive, rather than destructive, life. It all comes down to choices." Eventually, I could get some of them to start seeing the guards and others who worked at the facility as people much like them, but who had chosen a better path in life. Next, I would try to get the inmates to see their victims or people hurt by their actions as members of families much like their own, as well. For those who could begin to see their victims in this way and reflect on what they did, many would feel a sense of sorrow and even cry about it.

A significant number of the inmates I counseled were gang members. I would tell them about tribal identity in many parts of the world and how, on one hand, it can help one gain a sense of self but, on the other hand, can also cause one to discount the humanity of those not in one's own tribe, similar to the way gang members view those belonging to other gangs. I would speak with them about moving beyond such identity to something deeper, something greater and more fulfilling. I would ask them again to reflect on respect. Who did they have respect for, and why? Why should they expect others to respect them? What is real respect and how is it earned?

In a similar way, I would ask the inmates to think about strength. In the world of prison culture, strength was often seen as the most important thing. I would ask them to identify their strengths. Invariably, many of them would begin by speaking about physical prowess—lifting weights or being able to win a fight. Some would talk about the cleverness in being able to get away with many crimes before ever being caught. I would push them to go deeper, reminding them that physical strength comes and goes, and if they were really clever, they would not have ended up in prison. I would talk to them about strength as a freedom from dependency or the power of something over us. I challenged them to see their tendency to react to things—another inmate crosses you and you react by becoming violent, for instance—as signs of being controlled by anger and fear, and ultimately as weakness. Drug and alcohol addiction is also rampant in prisons. We would speak about this in relation to strength. I would tell them, "Real strength is living your own life, without being controlled by your desires or fears, cravings, or addictions." I would paraphrase Mahatma Gandhi: "The greatest strength is renunciation, because nobody can buy you, nobody can threaten you." I would use this as an opportunity to share the *dharmic* ideals of becoming free of cravings and attachments.

"Where is your real strength?" I would ask. "It is not in your muscles. Muscles can be developed and can go away. It is not in being able to intimidate someone else. You can intimidate someone, but how about when someone bigger or more powerful intimidates you? I don't want you to have strength that only lasts you until the next inmate comes and beats you up. I don't want you to be weak, and I don't think you want to be weak. Let us start working on getting you strong. Let's work on a strength that will last, a strength that you can find so that you can walk through this prison as strong as anyone and can walk out of this prison as strong as anyone on the outside."

I would start teaching them simple practices. For those who identified with physical strength, I would analogize to lifting weights. I would ask them to think about what they needed to do to grow spiritually; you have to struggle to grow, keep increasing the weight, increasing the resistance. With some, I talked to them about taking vows, or making lifestyle changes. Sometimes, I would teach them concentration techniques or simple breathing methods that would help them to slow their minds down and bring them some sense of calm. I would remind them that there was a place of real security, and peace, and strength inside themselves, and that I was willing to help them find it.

Being Hindu, Counseling Christians

As my chaplaincy practice developed, Christian inmates would occasionally ask to see me as well, and I counseled several during my time at the prison. Because of both my personal and academic backgrounds, I found this easy to do, and became quite comfortable in that role. I recall one inmate who had been seeing a Christian counselor regularly, but then fell away from his Christian practices once that particular counselor relocated. Perhaps he could not connect with the other Christian counselors. In any case, he asked to see me, and I began to work with him. I had been counseling him for six months or so, when one day he looked at me with tears in his eyes and said, "Getting arrested was the best thing that happened to me. If I had not gotten arrested, I'd probably be dead now." We talked about gratitude. He started to see his whole prison experience in a whole new light. My talks with him addressed psychological issues as well as spiritual ones. Throughout, I encouraged him to stay on a Christian track, because I felt that it was the path with which he had the closest connection. I knew there probably would not be a readily available non-Christian religious or spiritual community that could help him and foster his continuing growth once he left prison, but there would likely be a Christian one. I knew there would also be gangs, and I wanted him to opt for the community near him that would best help follow a life of goodness over crime. I saw my role as encouraging him in that walk.

Interacting with some of the Christian co-workers and administrators was a bit trickier, however. While it was easy to have a comfortable relationship with most, there were those in the system who viewed me with suspicion or questioned if what I was doing there was really religious counseling at all. Some might have thought that rather than God's work, I was doing the Devil's work! Fortunately, those officials with whom I worked most closely—Taketa and Goodman—consistently supported my efforts and offered me backing and guidance. Because Goodman was also a non-Christian, he was able to draw on his own experiences at the facility and offered me a lot of practical advice. He helped me to get to know the administrators and guards who could more easily transcend the religious divide. "These are the people you can really work with," he would tell me; "these are the people who will help you to do the kind of work you want to do." Of course, he would also help me to identify those who could not—so that I could maintain my distance and not waste a lot of energy on potential clashes with them. Together, he and Taketa encouraged me in so many ways. We came to value each others' friendship, insights, and feedback.

One situation with a group of ACOs was especially memorable. Most prided themselves on being physically strong, muscular men. Clearly, some of them looked at me as a *haole* (Caucasian) weakling! Most of them were conservative Christians. Several had apparently decided that, as a non-Christian, I could not be a legitimate religious counselor; and they made it obvious that they disliked me and had little respect for me or for my work at the facility. As it happened, several of these guards were assigned to an area called "Special Holding," a place where some of the most violent inmates were housed in solitary confinement for 23 hours of the day in a six-foot by eight-foot cell with only a cement bed and a toilet. One of these inmates seemed also quite mentally disturbed. Before the ACOs would even open the door to his cell, they would first reach through a small opening in the door to handcuff and chain him. He was never without handcuffs and leg shackles when with a guard. When this inmate requested a religious counselor, I was asked if I would be willing to meet with him. Of course, I agreed.

When I arrived for our first meeting, the guards told me that they were going to handcuff and shackle this inmate (as usual) before they would allow me to enter his cell. I had a deep feeling in my heart. Ramji said to me, "You have to go in there with the faith that your compassion for him is what is going to protect you." Based on this, I was adamant that I did not want him to be handcuffed. "How can I treat him as a human being if he's chained?" I insisted. Reluctantly, the guards agreed, called inside the cell, told the inmate to move to the back of the cell, then almost pushed me inside and locked the door behind me! I think the inmate was shocked to see that I was willing to meet with him in this way. I continued to see him in the same way, in his cell and in other confined areas of the facility, for six years. Although many in the prison feared him, when he was with me, the violence and frightening intensity of his demeanor did not manifest. When the guards saw how I was able to work with this inmate, and what I was able to accomplish with him, some of them begrudgingly began to respect me. A few even became friendly with me. They began to see that physical might was not the only way to handle difficult inmates.

Lessons Learned

At some point around 2011, my work and life schedule made it too difficult to serve regularly as a counselor. I do, however, remain "on call." I have been deeply transformed by the almost two decades that I spent serving in this very real, very intense context of spiritual caregiving. I learned much from it, in three main areas. First, I have been transformed as a teacher. Working with inmates helped me to better appreciate the importance of presence, as well as empathic and active listening. I learned to meet people where they are and communicate concepts in a way that is relevant to them. At the same time, I learned the necessity of challenging students to grow emotionally as well as academically.

Second, my experience with prison chaplaincy has helped me to grow as a father. It has helped me to better understand my own children and to make active parenting more of a focus in my life and spiritual practice. I had observed that the majority of prisoners had three things in common: they never completed high school; they were raised by a single parent (usually a mother or grandmother); and drugs were an integral part of their lives. I realized that if we, as a society, can change any of these three elements in the lives of such individuals while they are still young, we can vastly improve the chances for them to avoid a life of crime and incarceration. The time I spent counseling inmates confirmed, for me, the necessity of cultivating a one-on-one relationship with my own children. I am fortunate that I have a close relationship with my daughter, son, and wife. We try to make each other a priority. I have seen that too many of my friends who are parents seem too busy with their careers and making money to spend enough time with their families. My time working in the prison gave me a different perspective.

Finally, serving as a spiritual caregiver in prison has helped me to make sense of my own upbringing and its role in my personal spiritual journey. From time to time, as I would reflect back on my life, I would think, "Why did I do all those things I did and live the life I did? Why did I not end up in prison like the inmates I was counseling?" Working with inmates gave me an answer to those questions. On occasion, I would first meet with an inmate who would look at me with skepticism, wondering how some Caucasian guy would know anything about his life. When this was the case, I would then tell him a bit about my own childhood in a South Central Los Angeles ghetto: in a gang by the age of seven; my best friend shot when I was ten; my involvement in illegal drugs; periods of homelessness; sometimes stealing to eat, and so on. Once inmates learned that my background was similar to theirs, most would change the way they looked at me; most would actually start to listen to what I had to say to them. *I began to sense that Ramji had me go through that so I could one day understand and talk to and help these people.* I could speak to inmates from a place of understanding. I could hear them and feel what they were going through. I could also get a sense of what they needed to hear, all these coming from both my upbringing as well as my monastic training. Just as these had helped me to be able to recognize and deal with my own issues, and to go within and pull them out by their roots, so it helped me to hear and feel the inmates and their problems as well.

My prior experiences gave me a context in which to reach inmates, but also a context in which to understand my own life. This confirms what I learned in my Hindu training, what my teachers emphasized so strongly: everything has a purpose in God's plan. My experiences in the prison convinced me that the role of a Hindu chaplain in the system is not just for Hindus. We have a chance to provide all people with an alternative understanding to their lives and perhaps contribute something that is missing from the western paradigm. I strongly believe our Hindu teachings are not simply meant to use to help other Hindus. They are there to serve all humanity.

Hinduism and Coaching in the Corporate Realm

Rasanath Das

"I have thought about jumping off the Brooklyn Bridge several times this week, Rasanath!" As always, this was a one-to-one session. The voice sounded exasperated, and yet very matter-of-fact. Her statement was not an exaggeration. It sent chills down my spine and I tried hard to mask my alarm bells, yet at the same time convey my genuine understanding of her situation.

She had joined this start-up a year ago as a member of the leadership team that had successfully raised Series A funding from top-tier venture capital firms in the US. She had a great success record behind her and everyone on the team was excited that she had come onboard. Neither one of us envisioned the situation she would be in a year from then. Yet, here we were, as she faced extreme pressure at work and stared at the prospect of being without a job, plus having to support two kids as a single mother. She had just gone through a painful divorce.

***

My work as a leadership coach brings me face-to-face with untold human suffering like the above-mentioned, in places that would, from the outside, look privileged and enviable. Mother Teresa once said (and I paraphrase), "I see more suffering in the eyes of people who live on Fifth Avenue than I do on the streets of Kolkata." As a coach, I work with individuals and groups on the leadership level across various organizations to help identify behaviors resulting from insecure egos that inevitably affect the fabric of trust and create unnecessary suffering for everyone within the organization—including themselves. A major part of my work, then, is to provide a framework and a language that helps to rebuild trust in interactions and communication by helping leaders understand, take responsibility, and manage their egos. No sweat!

I first became emotionally conscious of human suffering at work during my career as an investment banker on Wall Street from 2006 to 2008. I had wanted to work on Wall Street since I was 13 years old! When I finally landed my coveted job, I felt that things would be easier from that point on. What I experienced, instead, was extreme stress coming from relentless competition, politicking, and perpetual dissatisfaction in pursuit of success. I witnessed my own unhealthy ego tendencies, and played into my leaders' unhealthy ego tendencies, adding several cents of suffering to that environment. I exaggerated my successes that put others down visibly; I spoke loudly in meetings from a fear of being overshadowed by my colleagues; and I felt a deep sense of relief and secret joy that, when 60 percent of my class was laid off during those two years, I survived!

Paradoxically, and fortunately for me, a spiritual calling was living side-by-side all the ambitions. This calling had introduced me to the Bhagavad-Gita, from which I drew a lot of inspiration and insight. Over the course of my study of the Gita, I had made close friends with several monks from the Bhakti tradition of Hinduism, who lived in a monastery on the Lower East Side of Manhattan. When I started working on Wall Street, my desire to continue my spiritual pursuits impelled me to make the monastery my home. I slept on the floor, practiced two hours of meditation a day, and lived by the principles of monastic life, while simultaneously working on Wall Street.

The last straw that broke the banker's back was when I was staffed to work on a high-profile financial deal for *Playboy*. My spiritual pursuits gave me the eyes to recognize the shallowness of my successful image and the unconscious suffering it was creating for me and everyone around. It was intolerable. I realized that I had lost my essential self to my ego and had to do a lot of self-work to reclaim that. I quit my job and joined the monastery as a full-time monk.

At the monastery, I lived with 20 other monks from seven different countries and from very diverse upbringings. I was also in charge of the monastery's finances and operations—and these functions tested my ego to its limits! The very problems I encountered at work with the ego existed in the monastery as well. Surprise, surprise! I found my ego repeatedly justifying its hidden agendas and I also saw the same in my environment. The main difference here was that we had all come to the monastery, in some way or form, to work towards a higher level of consciousness. It took several honest conversations with two of my close monastic brothers and a lot of introspection to develop clarity and own my "stuff". With every breakthrough, I was also able to experience a greater sense of freedom and gratitude for how God was deliberately shaping my life.

It was also within the walls of the monastery that my work in leadership development as a coach and facilitator began. It started with facilitating workshops on the Bhagavad-Gita with one of my closest monastic brothers. We combined the timeless wisdom of the Gita, our God-given gifts in communication and life experiences, and pop-culture to make the teachings relevant and experiential for a New York audience that was busy, skeptical, yet seeking. These workshops grew organically. Within four years, we found ourselves being invited to facilitate personal development workshops for various organizations.

Being on the workshop-facilitation circuit was something that we had not anticipated, but we were quite excited—even if we were also somewhat intimidated by the new venue. The workplace, filled with so many Type-A personalities, is many times seen as a means to earn money and success, but rarely seen as a place of self-discovery, transformation, and actualization. We had an innocent, perhaps even naive, yet sincere desire to change this.

Three of the Gita's many tenets became the basis of our workshops in organizations:

1. Our inherent psycho-physical nature (*dharma*) is intimately tied to our ego; so, understanding our ego is key to be aligned with our life's purpose and our relationships.

2. The ego is strongly dependent on external validation and consequently becomes very attached to it. When the validation does not come as expected, the attachment and the resulting controlling behavior leads to unspoken suffering for ourselves and others.

3. When we understand and engage the gifts of our ego and learn to take relentless responsibility for its insecurities and not act on them, we can grow to develop a healthy ego that acts with character, integrity, and humility.

Every time we conducted our workshops, we were pleasantly surprised at how the work environment transformed into a crucible of honest conversations and personal transformation, even if only for the duration of the workshop. The experience for leaders and employees alike was an undeniable impression of what a healthy work culture could be like—if everyone could simply attempt to live according to the aforementioned tenets of the Gita.

We were further invited to engage in one-to-one and group coaching of leaders—in order to help individuals maintain the momentum of the inner work from the workshops. We had found our way to an incredible and fulfilling opportunity to strive to reduce the suffering and stress in corporate America, and through that also positively affect the personal lives of so many individuals—directly and indirectly. We formalized our work as a leadership-development company called Upbuild—which means "uplifting human consciousness."

Workplaces are critical environments for nurturing our identity, our sense of purpose, and our personal growth. On an average, people spend about 63 percent of their time at work—the largest portion of their wakeful life. Needless to say, the work environment has far-reaching effects on the physical, emotional, and spiritual life of an individual. Our existing corporate culture puts such a heavy price on a stereotyped notion of performance, productivity, and success that it consciously and unconsciously squeezes out our humanity. To function as a leader in such an environment is even harder, because the unspoken tenet is to toughen up, be aggressive, and race ahead. The unsustainable pressure and pace inevitably creates regular blowups and rash decisions that hurt the very fabric of relationships in the company and cause frequent existential crises for both the leaders and the people that they lead. And there is no language and no space for them to share what they are going through!

One of my coaching relationships was with a middle-aged chief executive officer (CEO) of an exchange-traded fund that had become one of the fastest growing financial services firms in the country. They had been the subject of several stories in *The Wall Street Journal*, had won numerous awards, and had attracted an extremely talented pool of employees who had come exclusively from Ivy League universities. Toward the end of our first meeting, the CEO confessed to me that he no longer wanted to run the company. Upon further inquiry, it became expressly clear that he was on the verge of emotional burnout. His relationship with his co-founder had become so toxic that he dreaded going into the office every day. When we first met, he had already decided to leave the company, but was so deeply conflicted about the decision. After all, this company was his baby! He had built all of this from nothing. Yet he now hated even thinking about it. In addition, all of this emotional stress was affecting his family life.

As he was sharing his situation, he was also evidently uncomfortable with his vulnerability. He was asking for help—but was doing so in such veiled terms that he left me wondering if our conversation was creating even more agony for him! Fortunately, I knew from prior experience that the best thing to do was to listen attentively, to ask questions in a curious yet encouraging manner, but not to compromise on uncovering the underlying causes of stress. Situations like this are so sensitive that any indications of sympathy or a tone of advice can make the person shut down. I personally have the tendency to want to "fix" problems. However, I have had to learn that the best thing I can bring to any problem is my full listening presence. Full presence is exhausting, but it gives permission for the other person to gradually explore everything fully and accept his/her vulnerability. Only then can any constructive help can be provided.

Attentive listening is *the* primary conduit through which someone's personal discovery and healing can be facilitated. This is so beautifully demonstrated in the beginning of the Bhagavad-Gita, when Arjuna, the protagonist, is expressing his painful despair to his dear friend, Krishna. Arjuna is an archer of incomparable competence. He is a powerful leader and is just about to fight a big battle for the sake of establishing justice and morality. And yet, he has discovered that the very people who were opposing him were members of his own family—people for whom he had deep respect and affection, but who had chosen to oppose him for very complex political reasons. And for an entire chapter, Arjuna expresses his agony; Krishna, who embodies the divine, simply listens to him with full attention. Only when invited to speak does Krishna speak—and speaks such penetrating wisdom that Arjuna is finally relieved of his agony.

In another situation, I worked with a young CEO of a recently funded start-up in Silicon Valley. He was in a very tricky situation. He had started his own business after very successful stints with two well known and highly respected corporations. His new software product company had a lot of initial success. However, about a year into my counseling relationship, his business suffered several breakdowns. He was facing tremendous pressure from his clients and investors alike. At around the same time, his much-loved mother, who lived in India, fell critically ill.

His identity as an icon of a Silicon Valley success was putting tremendous pressure on him. When he went into work, he felt like he was letting his mother down and was being absolutely selfish. Each day, when he spoke to his parents by phone, he felt pressure to be with them in India. He began to resent them for coming in the way of his dream. This severe vicious cycle of guilt was feeding itself every day.

For two months straight, I found our sessions to be very emotionally volatile. His situation was so fragile that I also became a source of frustration for him. He would lash out at me. He wanted a solution; but his inner conflict was breaking him apart and he had to hold someone responsible for it. It was a powerful lesson in recognizing my own helplessness in this situation. I found myself wanting not to engage with him any more. In addition, my personal biases on family matters also made me think he was not doing what was "right" for his family.

With some much-needed help from the monastic brother who was also my co-founder at Upbuild, I found strength in the principle of simply fully showing up for our sessions, of simply listening patiently without feeling the need to be my client's problem-fixer. At every session, I also had to remind myself of how deep his suffering was and how lonely going through an experience such as his could be. This helped me tap into much needed compassion. While sincerely praying for his wellbeing, I could recognize that I had to simply let God lead the way for both of us. It was also a lesson in my own personal surrender to simply be an instrument in the hands of the divine (rather than to attempt to play God in people's lives)—something I can frequently do. Smells of ego?

The experience was mystical! In every session from that point onward, the step-by-step solution just emerged. My client decided to go home to India for a while. He found the strength to work on his business's problems while simultaneously being physically present to his family at a point when his parents clearly needed him. He was by his mother's bedside when she passed away. Simultaneously, his team in Silicon Valley found remarkable ways to fix their product issues and the company found itself being pursued by potential acquirers for a very sizeable amount. It was a moving experience that brought substantial growth in both of us. While the start-up business that brought us together has now been acquired by a larger corporation, I have continued the coaching relationship with this client, facilitating his exploration of numerous other areas of personal growth.

***

"Let us figure this out step-by-step," I told her, even as the echo of her suicide exclamation continued to send chills down my spine! It is completely uncertain how the complexities in this client's life will clear up. My only resolve is to walk with her through the messes—while praying constantly, deep down, with all my sincerity, that God shows both of us the way.

I am constantly being pushed to strive to live by the tenets I profess. It is hard to help others grow if I am not endeavoring to grow myself. My personal experiences—both in investment banking and in the monastery—help me understand that I am in no way better than anyone I am trying to help. Sure enough, I am very grateful to have had experiences that provide me with a language to understand and communicate with the individuals I work with. However, I am reminded daily that the best thing I can ever do is to act as a mirror for the other person, with a sincere intention to facilitate discovery, to create practical action steps for growth, and—most importantly—to generate a mindset that enables unlocking (rather than coming in the way of) an individual's full potential.

Part Three

CARE AT CROSSROADS

Nurturing Knowledge

The Importance of Hindu Academics as Spiritual Caregivers

Murali Balaji[1]

In the 1960s, the Black Studies movement paved the way for an established presence on the study of African American life—and its global roots—in colleges and universities across the US. Beyond just the creation of departments and programs devoted to African American and Africana studies, the movement helped to create space for faculty of color in almost exclusively white environments.[2] As Gordon and Gordon note, African American studies also challenged hegemonic thinking on identity, disrupting the way many white academics cultivated ecosystems of knowledge creation (and dissemination) that often left people of color out.[3] The social isolation and alienation many students of color felt at non-minority serving institutions—and still do today—was considered a factor in higher dropout rates and a graduation disparity between minority students and their white counterparts.[4] While the move to curate spaces for students of color through the creation of academic departments has had its detractors, it has led to marginally higher representation of minority faculty members. Today, the majority of research institutions have dedicated African American/Africana studies departments, as well as other ethnic studies (Chicano/Latino/Latinx, Asian American,

---

1 The author wishes to thank Dr. Asha Shipman, the Director of Hindu Life and Hindu chaplain at Yale University, for her feedback and input.
2 F. Rojas (2006) "Social movement tactics, organizational change and the spread of African-American studies." *Social Forces* 84, 4, 2147–2166.
3 L.R. Gordon and J.A. Gordon (2006) *Not Only the Master's Tools: African American Studies in Theory and Practice*. St. Paul, MN: Paradigm.
4 C.M. Loo and G. Rolison (1986) "Alienation of ethnic minority students at a predominantly White university." *The Journal of Higher Education* 57, 1, 58–77.

and Native American) departments that have highlighted institutional responses to underrepresented communities. At the very least, such efforts have been a tacit acknowledgment by universities that they must have faculty who are representative of their student bodies.

In recent years, religious studies has undergone similar transformations, pushed in part by misunderstandings and animosity towards some minority religious groups, such as Muslims. Islamic Studies departments have become important bastions of knowledge creation to rebut anti-Muslim sentiment and have led to more Muslim American scholars gaining prominence. As Maira and Shihade argue, these growing fields of study help "to challenge the ever-expanding borders of an imperial project that operates through direct as well as proxy wars, neo-colonial occupation, and client states."[5] Additionally, the incubation of Muslim/Islamic studies and the hiring of Muslim American scholars has helped to better integrate Muslim American students traumatized by social ostracism and surveillance since 9/11/2001.

This is why no conversation about Hindu spiritual care can take place without one of the most glaring needs in academic spaces: Hindu scholars, particularly those who are attuned to the alienation and struggles of identity formation many Hindu American students face. As Hindu Americans of different backgrounds—particularly economically disadvantaged first-generation Hindus—matriculate into college, the need for a robust and empathetic Hindu American academic space is more important than ever. Hindu American academics, especially those who are in religious studies departments, can play a pivotal role as knowledge creators and spiritual caregivers. In this chapter, I make the case that the emergence of Hindu American scholars as spiritual caregivers is just as important in curating and sustaining empathetic spaces for Hindu spaces as chaplains.

The Other Comes to Campus: The Hindu American College Experience

To be sure, self-identifying Hindus in academia are not in significantly short supply. However, many Hindus—including academic advisers for Hindu student organizations—are often in non-humanities fields. As a result, the intellectual spaces for Hindus where Hinduism is actually

---

5   S. Maira and M. Shihade (2006) "Meeting Asian/Arab American studies: Thinking race, empire, and Zionism in the US." *Journal of Asian American Studies* 9, 2, 117–140.

studied continues to be dominated—and framed—by non-Hindus. As I have noted elsewhere, the field of Hinduism in academia has been "long dominated by two—sometimes opposing—frameworks: Orientalism, which fueled much of contemporary Indology, and Marxism, which was one of the ideological drivers of South Asian studies in the United States, Canada, and the United Kingdom."[6] Beneath the seemingly innocuous growth of Indology, however, was a clear condescension towards Hinduism as a lived tradition. Adluri and Bagchee, for example, note that much of contemporary Indology—which Hinduism is often studied under—is rooted in racist origins.[7]

Indology, which has significantly influenced what is now known as South Asia studies, has largely been cultivated, shaped, and dominated by white non-Hindu academics. This has problematized the extent to which attempting to research lived traditions can conflict with the sentiments of communities. Adluri and Bagchee have noted that racism towards Hindus (and in general, Indians) is often justified by non-Hindu academics under the guise of anti-majoritarianism.[8] This is frequently why Indology's inherent Orientalist problem is compounded by Marxist scholars who uphold those constructs in order to mainstream anti-Hindu sentiment in academic spaces. Nicholson, for example, notes that postcolonial and Marxist perspectives often depict Hinduism as a fabricated religion used to justify social norms in Indian society or used to localize Victorian orthodoxies.[9] As such, Hinduism is frequently presented as backwards, and Hindus who seek to speak in defense of the religion are often labeled as Hindu nationalists or Hindu fundamentalists. Moreover, the presentation of Hinduism is often framed from the lens of post-partition South Asian geopolitics, rather than the global diffusion and evolution of the religion and its diasporic communities. As such, Hindu Americans of diverse backgrounds, including those whose ancestry is from the West Indies, Africa, Southeast Asia, and other non-South Asian regions, are even further marginalized.

When the needs of Hindu American students are viewed with skepticism and suspicion, it can present a significant problem—sometimes

---

6   M. Balaji (2017) "Introduction: Digital Paths to the Divine? New Media, Hinduism, and the Transformation of Dharmic Discourse and Practice" In M. Balaji (ed.) *Digital Hinduism*. Lanham, MD: Lexington Books, p.xvi.
7   See V. Adluri and J. Bagchee (2014) *The Nay Science: A History of German Indology*. Oxford: Oxford University Press, p.427.
8   Adluri and Bagchee (2014).
9   A.J. Nicholson (2010) *Unifying Hinduism*. New York: Columbia University Press.

insurmountable—to nurturing a stable and welcoming space. That's because when academic institutions lack those who are being studied, they can lack empathy and further marginalize the subjects. As Jeffery D. Long notes:

> Indeed, it could be argued that the academia itself is not free from its own forms of privilege and marginalization... Hindus have rightly perceived an absence of empathy in representations of Hindu traditions in academic writing—particularly in school textbooks—when compared with representations of Judaism, Christianity, Islam, and Buddhism... In addition to the prevailing scholarship of today, there is a need for new scholarly approaches, including the perspectives of those who seek transformational readings of texts, as noted above.[10]

Long is one of the few scholars in the academy who has been able to balance the sentiments of being both the one studying and the one being studied. He is a white American Hindu who has written extensively on the need for creating a better understanding of Hindu theology in order to comprehensively explain Hinduism. This is a call echoed by other academics like Anantanand Rambachan and Rita Sherma, who are both theologians and practicing Hindus.[11] The absence of Hindu theology, they note, has provided Hindus—particularly Hindu Americans—very few structural defenses against academic deconstructions. I would add that Hindu American students are ill-equipped to reconcile the traditions they may have grown up with and the Otherness through which Hinduism is framed in largely Judeo-Christian academic contexts.

Non-Hindu scholars who have taken critical approaches to Hinduism and the Hindu American community argue that academic freedom is sacrosanct. There's no questioning that. However, there is much to be said about suffocating the personal spiritual journeys of Hindu American students, particularly those whose cultural and religious experiences are more and more likely to differ significantly from their parents. As the Hindu American Foundation (HAF) found in its two bullying reports in 2016 and 2018, respectively, at least one in four Hindu students report being bullied for their religious beliefs during their K–12 experiences.[12]

---

10 J.D. Long (2014) "Pick a side, we're at war!" *Los Angeles Review of Books*, September 4. https://lareviewofbooks.org/article/pick-side-war, accessed on March 12, 2018. Excerpted by permission of LARB.
11 See A. Rambachan (2015) *A Hindu Theology of Liberation*. Albany, NY: SUNY Press; and R. Sherma (2019) *Hinduism and the Divine: Foundations of Hindu Theology*. New York: IB Tauris.
12 See https://hafsite.org/resources/classroom-subjected, accessed on July 19, 2019.

That feeling of social isolation and alienation can be further compounded when they reach college and find learning environments that they perceive to be hostile to their religion. This reifies and reaffirms negative perceptions of Hinduism, and in some instances, can cause Hindu American students to devalue their religious beliefs. In an updated interpretation of Fanon's notion of internal inferiorization,[13] Hardiman *et al.* (2010) note that socialization in an "oppressive environment" that leads to a "hurtful and limiting" definition of a minority group leads directly to behavior by that group that demonstrates the devaluation imposed upon it by the dominant group.[14] This has played out on some campuses where students who were raised in Hindu households join South Asian activist organizations and engage in open hostility towards many Hindu student organizations, whom they accuse of being aligned with right-wing Hindu causes.[15] For example, an attempt to form a Hindu studies faculty position at the University of California-Irvine in 2016 was scuttled by protests led by graduate students and faculty members of Indian descent.[16] Despite private complaints about the way the issue was covered, many prominent Hindu American academics did not publicly try to counter the protests. As such, Hindu American academics may be exacerbating some of these tensions by not playing a more active role in supporting Hindu students.

Another challenge is indifference. Overall, the Hindu American community has yet to experience or define a collective trauma to mobilize more investments into academic space. The experiences of trauma shared by Caribbean Hindus, Fijian Hindus, and Bhutanese Hindus have not necessarily been integrated into the larger Hindu American narrative. While the legacy of anti-Semitism and the ongoing ostracization following 9/11 have moved the Jewish and Muslim communities to act in higher education, Hindus have not felt the same collective urgency to support sustainable spiritual care in academia. In fact, as Rambachan notes, today's young Hindus may have little sense that the Hindu tradition bears

---

13 F. Fanon (1963) *The Wretched of the Earth.* New York: Grove.
14 See R. Hardiman, B.W. Jackson, and P. Griffin (2010) "Conceptual foundations." In M. Adams, W. J. Blumenfeld, R. Castaneda, H.W. Hackman, M.L. Peters, and X. Zuniga (eds) *Readings for Diversity and Social Justice,* 2nd ed. Abingdon: Routledge, pp.31–32.
15 B. Mathew and V. Prashad (2000) "The protean forms of Yankee Hindutva." *Ethnic and Racial Studies 23,* 3, 516–534.
16 E. Redden (2016) "Return to Sender." *Inside Higher Education,* February 22. Retrieved from www.insidehighered.com/news/2016/02/22/uc-irvine-moves-reject-endowed-chair-gifts-donor-strong-opinions-about-study, accessed on March 12, 2018.

in any significant way on their professional success, choice of a spouse, or political sensibilities. "They will not see what religion contributes to the pursuit of their primary life goals or even understand themselves as having religious needs. The choice, as I see it for a new generation of Hindus in the US, is not between the Hindu tradition or another religion; it is between being Hindu or being non-religious."[17] Given this reality, plus the fact that America's social landscape is changing, and that college campuses are increasingly polarized in how religions are studied *and* practiced, the growth of Hindu American academicians is vital to the continued maturation of the Hindu American community.

Creating an Ecosystem: How Some Universities Are Responding

Hindu Americans may not necessarily find academic spaces friendly, but that's not to say that progress is not being made. For starters, more Hindu Americans on college campuses are learning important lessons in coalition-building. Additionally, the formation of Hindu councils at some colleges and universities is bringing faculty, staff, and students together in new ways. For example, Asha Shipman, the Director of Hindu Life and Hindu chaplain at Yale University, recently formed the Hindu Life Council at Yale. The council serves as a think-tank regarding contemporary religious, social, global, and intellectual issues that affect the Yale Hindu community. Their goal is "to create a vibrant, nurturing, inclusive and discerning experience for Hindus at Yale." As Shipman explains, Christian churches have had such councils for many years and they have been instrumental in monitoring community dynamics and needs, thereby augmenting the spiritual care-giving role of a chaplain.

Other institutions are also beginning to embrace an inclusion of Hindu theology into their religious studies offerings. As Long observes, theological teachings can be a referee of sorts between the way scholars interpret a religion and the way devotees practice it. He calls for a day when academia will provide space for "constructive Hindu thought" and greater development of Hindu theology as a discipline, such that Hindu texts may be taken seriously on their own terms—as has long been the case for Christian thought and Christian texts.[18] Indeed, Rita Sherma has helped to advance that story by building a Hindu studies program at

---

17 Rambachan (2015).
18 Long (2014).

the Graduate Theological Union in Berkeley, California, while Jeffery D. Long (Elizabethtown College), Anantanand Rambachan (St. Olaf), Graham Schweig (Christopher Newport University), and Ramdas Lamb (University of Hawai'i-Manoa) have helped to curate sustainable spaces for Hindu theology at their institutions. All of the scholars mentioned, however, are middle-aged and/or nearing retirement, making the need for younger Hindu American academicians all the more critical. Younger scholars, particularly those whose upbringing makes them empathetic to cultural issues faced by many American-born Hindus, would be better equipped to navigate through some of the pitfalls of campus identity politics while serving as critical liaisons between Hindu American students and other learning communities. Some academics, often housed in South Asian studies departments and programs, have become agents of change from within, advising Hindu student organizations and/or bringing to campus speakers equipped to discuss the vibrancy of Hinduism to diverse audiences. As one prominent American-born Hindu academic (who is also a department chair) told me, Hindu academics sometimes have to de-code what Hindu students want, given that many of the latter might not yet know what they want and need.

What Comes Next

Similar to what is happening with Hindu chaplains, a centralization of efforts among Hindu American academics to better coordinate and share best practices would be helpful. This might be easier said than done, given that Hinduism itself is highly decentralized, and college campuses might have some Hindu traditions more prominently represented than others. The Hindu American Foundation established an academic advisory council to try to coordinate campus efforts, but the council has largely fizzled out due to varying levels of commitment from council members. The Dharma Academy of North America (DANAM), co-founded by Rita Sherma and Ardash Deepak, has been critical in creating an academic support system for the study of Hinduism. As DANAM grows, it could become an incubator for a new generation of Hindu American academicians to connect their scholarship with their student populations on campus.

However the role of Hindu American scholars evolves, it is likely to shape the Hindu American experience for decades to come. As Long presciently observes, we have reached a critical juncture in the way academia engages with the Hindu American community.[19] Ignoring the needs of Hindu Americans and downplaying the importance of creating sustainably safe spaces would do irreparable harm to both academic institutions and the Hindu American learners who make up an increasing percentage of their student bodies. On the other hand, engaging with the community, and nurturing a critical mass of Hindu knowledge creators in the academy, is a recipe for creating and sustaining a healthy ecosystem of spiritual care, cultural competency, and empathy—all of which are needed now more than ever in the realm of higher education.

---

19 Long (2014).

Vocational Counseling
A Hindu Approach

Pulin Sanghvi

"What do you want to be when you grow up?" Many of us remember this question from our childhood. We recall the sense of anticipation attached to the vibrant possibilities of adulthood. In answering this question, some children take inspiration from film or television: "I want to be an astronaut" or "I want to be a movie star." My own son, on many occasions, has talked about his aspiration to become an NBA basketball player. However, he has not yet absorbed the reality that his father, the tallest in his family, may still not be quite as tall as the shortest of NBA stars. Other children think of role models in their own lives—teachers or nurses or police officers or fire fighters. In each case, the child is thinking of a role in society that they aspire to. If they remain true to that early dream, they will eventually begin to think about the path on which they will need to journey in order to reach that goal.

There is a related and equally important question that we only rarely think to ask children: "*Who* do you want to be when you grow up?" If we think to ask this question more often, we might get different types of responses. A young person might answer, "I want to be a kind and generous person who gives freely of her time to mentor and inspire others to make a difference in the world." In modern society, we have become better at helping young people figure out *what* they want to become. Relative to previous generations, fewer of our young people feel bound by the destiny of their families. We have opened up more paths to social mobility. The daughter of a farmer can become a doctor, and the son of a doctor can become a farmer. We encourage members of society to pick an aspirational role, to get education or training in that role, and eventually to apprentice in that role. The focus remains on the role. The journey of the individual is to grow to earn a place in the role.

At the same time, particularly among the current generation of university students, the *what* questions are no longer sufficient. This generation feels a hunger to find meaning in their careers; and, relative to previous generations, they expect to find it without delay. I know this well, as a program on building meaningful careers—which I created and implemented at Princeton and Stanford—has drawn thousands of student-participants in recent years. However, more broadly, society has not yet created the infrastructure to teach purpose. For example, few of our high schools, trade schools, colleges, and universities embrace purpose as a framing theme of how they educate young people. Instead, they focus on the more tangible *what* questions – on preparation of students to become doctors, lawyers, engineers, or mechanics.

How can a society teach meaning and purpose? The topics of meaning and purpose are deeply personal, and ambiguous by their very nature. Religion and faith have provided support on questions of meaning and purpose for thousands of years. The questions of *why* we are here and *what* we are meant to do are at the base of virtually every belief system in the world.

Like almost all religions in the world, the religions founded in ancient India—Buddhism, Hinduism, Jainism, and Sikhism—are based on beliefs, traditions, rituals, community, and shared cultural experiences that create tangible frameworks for navigating life. A young woman in Mumbai saying a short prayer to Ganesha with her family before an important job interview would share a great deal in common with her Christian friend in the US going through a similar ritual with his loved ones. But Indian religions are unique in the way that they turn the lens of faith inwards rather than outwards.

Buddhism, Hinduism, Jainism, and Sikhism are each anchored in the concept of *nirvana,* liberation from the cycle of birth and death. *Nirvana* means something different in each of these faiths. For example, in Buddhism, *nirvana* involves the realization of *anatman,* or non-self and emptiness, while in Hinduism, *nirvana* involves the attainment of knowledge of *ātman,* or *true self.* But in all four of the Indian faiths, *nirvana* is anchored in the individual rather than a higher power. Liberation comes not from salvation by a higher power, but instead by the deeply personal journey to still the mind and conquer desire.

On questions of purpose in the context of meaningful work, the Indian faiths offer an important perspective. Because the faiths themselves are founded on a framework of personal growth, they foster a shift in focus from the work back to the individual. However, each of these religions does this uniquely. For example, in offering rich frameworks and insight on the question of meaningful work, a concept that Hinduism shares with Buddhism is the idea of *anitya*: the impermanence of both physical and mental events. In Buddhism, impermanence reinforces the personal journey towards emptiness, and suggests that the release of attachment is a necessary condition for liberation to occur. Hinduism, on the other hand, asserts that there is *nitya* (permanence) in *ātman*, and therefore does not teach shedding of attachment to the extent Buddhism does. In particular, a significant implication of the Hindu worldview is that understanding the self has value, and in fact can be a vital step towards liberation.

These philosophical concepts have powerful and tangible implications to a framework for purpose and meaningful work. First, regardless of one's personal beliefs, the concept of *ātman* gives us a way to reframe the way an individual can approach understanding themselves. In Hindu spirituality, *ātman* refers to one's true self, the soul, the part of oneself that is eternal and unborn, the essence of the person that remains constant regardless of the influences of the world. While *ātman* has a nuanced meaning that varies within the different schools of Hinduism and Jainism, it points the way to an idea related to our work-life identity: our *work-life self*. The notion of *work-life self* is an artificial, rather than spiritual, construct. Nevertheless, it has value. Its core conceit is that each of us has an essence of our professional identity that represents our best selves in a work-life context. Our work-life self reflects the intersection of our values, our interests, our strengths, and our beliefs. This essence may evolve over the course of our lives as we grow, but its core will remain stable, as it is based in parts of ourselves, like our values, that also remain stable over time.

Let's bring the idea of a work-life self to life with an example. Imagine a young woman with a creative spirit. She is passionate and eloquent and able to harness words into narratives that inspire emotion in a reader. Her essence, her best self, is firmly anchored in creativity and language. At her best, she might become a novelist that wins the Pulitzer Prize. In the real world, circumstances and day-to-day pressures pull her out of alignment with her work-life self. When she is young, she worries that her interest in writing is unrealistic, and worries that she may not be able to pay the bills with what she will earn. As she graduates college at the age of 20, she decides to become a banker with the intention of saving enough money to eventually return to her writing. As a banker, she is out of alignment with her work-life self. She is earning enough money to pay the bills, but she spends her day mired in analysis when her heart dreams of writing poems. She is good enough at banking to remain successful within her firm, but her greatness never emerges during this phase of her life.

At the age of 30, this woman pauses and reflects. She has spent a decade working hard at a job that never inspired her. As a result, she was fighting resistance within herself every day at work. Finally, she decides to leave her job in order to begin writing. Her opportunity to re-align with her work-life self returns, but now new pressures create further distractions. She begins to worry about the path to becoming published—and worries again about paying the bills. At times, she doubts whether she is good enough to write a great novel. Then, a change in her personal life creates great personal stress, leaving her with writer's block. She is unable to write her book.

In this example, the pressures and doubts the young woman is facing are very real. But at the same time, Hinduism teaches us that each of her circumstances and pressures, in a sense, have become an illusion, distracting her from perceiving her work-life self. At the core, she is still who she has always been—a creative spirit with the potential to become a truly great novelist. But she still has not written her book. A career as a novelist remains distant—a potential state, as in quantum physics—that has not yet been realized.

This framing offers us two powerful insights in thinking about our careers. First, it suggests that the right focus for the individual is on the self rather than the results. The young woman may worry about the challenge of writing, or the journey to get published, or the pressure to earn enough from the book to pay the bills. But if she can just find the path to write the book that her best self is capable of, there is a good chance that all of those worries may take care of themselves. More broadly, this framing suggests that the real risk in each of our careers is losing too much time being out of alignment with our work-life self. The young woman has had understandable reasons at each juncture not to begin writing her book; but with each passing day, she is missing her underlying potential as a novelist who can move the world.

The novelist example is based on the conceit that the young woman has perfect knowledge and somehow fully recognizes her work-life self, but simply is distracted by the pressures of life from being in alignment with it. However, for most of us, even at an advanced stage of our careers, understanding our core remains the greatest challenge. Many of us remain beholden to paths we began when we were younger. We never were given the space or support to find our work-life self, so we took leaps of faith that we could figure it out later. But as we made progressive commitments to the paths we started, we found it more and more difficult to deviate from those paths. This suggests that one of the important positive changes that our society could make would be to engage more young people in the process of self-exploration from an early age. Self-knowledge becomes the cornerstone of the journey towards spending more of one's career in harmony with one's work-life self.

What is the path to self-knowledge? Hinduism introduces the concept of *pramāṇa*: multiple paths to knowledge. Across the various schools of Hindu thought, it is said there are six paths to true knowledge, of which three are often considered most reliable. The first is *pratyaska*, the perception that comes from direct experience. This is one of the most valued and reliable paths to self-knowledge, because our experiences create such powerful conditions for mental and emotional reactions that we can learn from. When we experience things directly, our reactions give us a wealth of information. My colleagues who are university professors often speak about a deep passion for their areas of research, and aversion to other areas of research that they have tried in the past. They speak of joy when they are with students or boredom when they are involved in departmental administration. These strong reactions to their experiences give them information that will be invaluable to their future choices. We often view experiences that provoke negative reactions as having been mistakes or failures. However, in the context of *pratyaska*, even negative experiences can be deeply influential in understanding the self. My students frequently speak about their negative experiences as giving them greater confidence to make choices and close doors that they decide are dead-ends.

In the real world, we constantly make decisions based upon indirect data (*anumana*) and testimony from others (*aptavakya*). Those sources of data are valuable and often more readily available than direct experience. They help us to narrow the universe of possibilities to a manageable number, and help us to make decisions on a timely basis. According to

Hindu thought, the important concept here is that the decisions we make, and the results of those decisions, are impermanent. We often focus on the decisions in front of us as having lasting consequences. If we make a good choice, our lives will work out better, and if we make a poor choice, then the mistake will haunt us. Yet, in the Hindu framework, both the choices we make and their consequences will be impermanent. In the long run, they will not matter. The true challenge in front of us is gain enough self-knowledge to keep moving closer to our core, and to give our careers as much time as possible to be in alignment with our work-life self.

Hinduism thus gives us a powerful framework for resilience in the face of adversity and challenge. If we can reframe risk-taking, challenges, and failure as some of the richest opportunities for self-knowledge, we can keep greater emotional distance from our failures and maintain a focus on growth and progress, rather than becoming stuck in a moment that we no longer have influence over. More than that, the concept of work-life self gives us a powerful basis for faith. If we believe that our work-life self lies under the surface, we realize that our strength does not lie in our titles, our educational degrees, or our work accomplishments. Instead, our strength lies in our true self, the core of our underlying potential, waiting to be released. This reframes our experiences, positive or negative, as learning opportunities, not as events of lasting consequence. We must retain some sense of consequence, for it is a sense of consequence (along with our core values) that helps us to steer clear of some choices that can cause harm, to ourselves or to others.

However, those of us who have spent time coaching and mentoring others recognize that few careers have unfolded without significant setbacks, challenges, or failures. It is rare that a choice made in good faith leads to consequences that one cannot recover from. The defining characteristic of great careers is not the avoidance of mistakes, but rather the resilience to bounce back from those mistakes. Hinduism offers a powerful framework for exploring purpose and meaningful work at a personal level. It suggests that each of us has a core—what I describe as a work-life self—that is waiting to be discovered. This core may take on new dimensions as we progress through life, but as it is based in fundamental parts of ourselves like our values, it remains a stable core. Our challenge is to find alignment with our core, become aware of the impermanent pressures and circumstances that distract us, and maintain a focus on the self rather than the outcomes. In Hindu thought, we can gain knowledge of ourselves through direct experience, indirect experience, and insights from others. The journey towards self-knowledge is a life-long commitment, but in Hindu thought, represents part of the age-old journey towards enlightenment. It is a journey worth taking.

Hindu Spiritual Care of LGBTQ People

Raja Gopal Bhattar

Inclusive spiritual and religious care is critical for many Hindu Lesbian Gay Bisexual Transgender and Queer (LGBTQ) people, or "Quindus" (Queer Hindus). Whether students are international students coming to the US for the first time or domestic students who are first- or second-generation Hindu American, spirituality and religion may play an important role in their identity exploration process. Chaplaincy grounded in understanding the intersection of these and other identities can foster a welcoming environment and contribute to a person's holistic wellbeing and healing. It can demystify how spirituality and faith are often important for supporting one's identity exploration, while also addressing structural heteronormativity, homophobia, biphobia, and transphobia within spiritual spaces. This chapter provides strategies based on my professional and spiritual work to support LGBTQ-inclusive care to individuals exploring Hindu LGBTQ identities.

Queerness and Hinduism

Hinduism as a religious philosophy thrives because of its pluralistic perspectives and inclusive nature. As one of the oldest religions in the world, I find Hinduism also to be one of the most inclusive at scriptural and practical levels. In addition to *Stri* (female) and *Purusha* (male) gender identity, Hindu Vedic scriptures identify the existence of *Tritiya Prakruti* (third-gender) as an important form of creation. Similarly, many mythologies exist of transgressing gender as a form of showing love for the Divine and Vishnu descending in various genders as a path to rescuing his devotees. Same-gender love is also openly expressed in ancient Hindu temples of Konark and Khajuraho and scriptures such as the Kama Sutra. Many saints and sages practicing *bhakti yoga* (unconditional devotion) often provide images of longing for Krishna as one awaits a lover.

In spite of such a rich history, much of the current practices of Hinduism seem devoid of any space for sexual and gender diversity beyond heteronormative ideals. In my career, I have often worked with Hindu students or desi/South-Asian religious traditions who perceive their sexual and/or gender identity as antithetical to or in conflict with their cultural and religious traditions. Having grown up in a Hindu temple within a long lineage of Hindu *pujaris* and *pandits*, I am very familiar with this perceived conflict. Yet, as part of my coming out and self-discovery process, I came across many mythologies and references to queerness within various Hindu texts. More importantly, coming from a Vaishnava family with Sri Krishna as our main family deity, I found solace in the Bhagavad-Gita, one of our spiritual texts. Though many people are familiar with this text, I remember being personally impacted by one particular stanza in my own journey:

> One's own duty (*swadharma*), though it may be done imperfectly and deemed worthless, is better than someone else's duty performed perfectly. Destruction in performing one's own duty is better than performing someone else's duty, which is dangerous. (BG 3.35)[1]

In other words, being true to oneself and nature is more important than fitting into someone else's reality. For me, this meant that accepting and being open about my sexuality and gender identity was not only important to me but also prescribed by my own religious tradition. This piece of scripture has often been a pillar of my work with students navigating their Hindu Queer identities.

Approaches to LGBTQ-Inclusive Hindu Spiritual Care

I met a young woman I'll call "Avani" when she entered campus as a first-year student. Her story, which she has given me permission to tell, helps to illustrate effective approaches to LBGTQ-inclusive Hindu spiritual care. Avani was pretty shy at first; but soon I saw her get involved

---

1 *śreyān svadharmo viguṇaḥ paradharmāt svanuṣṭhitāt svadharme nidhanaṃ śreyaḥ paradharmo bhayāvahaḥ.*

in campus-wide LGBTQ visibility and education work. One day, after a planning meeting, I learned more about her and her family. We shared favorite spots for finding vegetarian food on campus; we discussed her latest crush. I discovered that, not only did Avani identify as Hindu, her family originates from Karnataka, where my family is from; we speak the same regional language, Kannada. So, I tried to infuse Kannada in our conversations as I helped Avani see a bridge between her religious and sexual identities. I was familiar with the patriarchical nature of her family and how that influences her sense of agency and decision-making processes. I even sent her my graduate school thesis which focused on how my strong Hindu foundation has been critical to my career choice and appreciation of my sexuality.

Avani spoke about her fear of coming out to her family, especially as a young Indian woman in the US. She acknowledged her fear of being disowned by them. Not knowing how to talk about her own sexuality with her parents in the Kannada language caused some frustration. Although her parents spoke English, she felt that only by speaking to them in their native language could they understand all of her message. Avani noted that coming out in English would just reaffirm for her parents that LGBTQ identity was an "American thing" and antithetical to her Indian and Hindu identities. Further, she worried that coming out might mean she would lose not only her parents, but also her close connection with her younger sibling.

Over the next two years, Avani and I had many conversations. I shared my story of growing up in a temple, and how coming out didn't go so well for me; so I had come to realize that I had to make a conscious choice to build a strong, chosen family to support me. Finding other Hindu LGBTQ people has not only affirmed my identities and experiences but has given me a network of support that has held me when I have struggled to navigate these two aspects of my identity. To help her find community and to become aware of the many possible models of queer Desis on campus and in the greater community, I invited Avani to several gatherings at my house, including Deepavali/Diwali and vegetarian Thanksgiving. Deepavali is an important time for Hindus to gather in community and celebrate. That can be hard when our biological families don't acknowledge us. Further, in the US, it is difficult for many Hindus—especially college students—to go home during a period in the school year when midterms abound. More importantly for me, Deepavali at my house is not just for Hindus. I invite Muslims, Christians, Agnostics,

Atheists, and Buddhists to join me in offering *puja* and prayers to Hindu gods such as Sri Lakshmi and Sri Ganesha.

Thanksgiving is another time for chosen family. We share vegan food and stories of how we come together to celebrate community, while also challenging the colonialist and racist history of the holiday. Every time Avani would attend, I made sure to connect her with Hindu people who identified as LGBTQ, with conscious heterosexual allies, or with queer women of color—specifically queer Hindu women of color. Providing role models of practicing Hindus who were able to talk in Kannada and be accepting of queerness—regardless of their sexuality—was a powerful experience.

Finally, Avani had wanted me to meet her parents and share some of my own experiences in Kannada—so that they could know that people who identify as Hindu, queer, and Kannadigas exist in the world. Avani and I developed a plan for her conversation with her parents and ways to build her own safety network throughout their visit. I came to campus on the weekend to sit with Avani and her family in the LGBT Center for a few hours, talking, having tea, and answering questions. I talked in Kannada, sharing my journey of embracing my queerness and sharing about my deep religious roots in Hinduism, in an attempt to expand her parents' perspectives. I'm not sure how helpful it was for Avani's parents, but I could tell just being witness to this conversation was affirming of her identities and comfort. Although Avani finished her undergraduate studies several years ago, she has remained in touch with me. She has let me know that she continues to work with her parents as she lives her authentic life as an open queer woman. Avani recently created a beautiful piece of needlework that incorporated the Hindu symbol *Oṁ* embedded in the middle of a rainbow of colors. Seeing this piece reminded me of why our own visibility, even in our imperfection, is critical in enhancing young people's lives.

The approach I took with Avani has worked well with many of the students who have come by the LGBT Center. I have noticed that some of the shy ones are more talkative, more willing to share about their identity, when I wear *kurtas* (traditional long tunics) to work.

Sometimes, my offer to buy a student coffee so we can sit and talk more frankly has paved the way for a conversation that gets to the heart of what that student actually needs in practical terms. For example, a student may long to come out as transgender, but is genuinely fearful of losing family financial support that is crucial for continuing at the university.

In such cases, I stress that it is not important to come out to everyone at once; that one can do so in stages, yet still feel some level of authenticity; and that the most important person to come out to is oneself. I also offer students my support in accessing university services so that they can find community and transition at their own speed. Students are sometimes reluctant to make use of those services, but I continue to remind them of their availability.

Because I have been one of the co-facilitators of a statewide transgender youth leadership retreat, I have been in a unique position to make our university's transgender students aware of this opportunity to connect with others who are navigating their gender journey. I also made sure to mention community organizations supporting LGBTQ South Asians. As a genderqueer person myself, I often talk about how I understand queerness within a Hindu spiritual context and share my own journey of integrating it into that milieu.

I can equip Hindu community members with Hindu scriptures, mythologies, and strategies for expanding understanding of Hinduism's history of inclusive sexual and gender representations—and this can be very helpful when there is opportunity to work directly with the family of one of our LGBTQ students.

Strategies and Tips

Avani's story highlights the need for more conversations during which we can identify the intricate blend of sexuality, gender identity, and Hinduism in our students' lives. To increase the likelihood of such conversations, I practice a variety of strategies:

- I identify openly as Hindu and LGBTQ at Hindu Student Association gatherings, in LGBTQ student spaces, and when speaking with other spiritual leaders on campus.

- I discuss openly the impact of India's caste system in the US, specifically the benefits of being Hindu on campus and how people from other categories are not acknowledged or even erased in various contexts.

- I openly wear Hindu symbols, like an *Oṁ* pendant and kumkum on my forehead, on a daily basis.

- I display Hindu LGBTQ symbols such as a rainbow *Oṁ* symbol or an image of Sri Ardhanareeshwara (Shiva and Parvathi, joined as one, blending masculine and feminine energy) prominently in my office.
- I provide regular opportunities for Hindu LGBTQ students to meet for check-ins and trust-building.
- I bring in speakers who can highlight the intersection of Hindu and LGBTQ experiences.
- I share community resources widely.
- I display Hindu LGBTQ-themed books prominently in my office.
- I have built strong relationships with—and have served as a consultant for—campus colleagues who oversee student organizations such as Hindu student associations, Indian student associations, and LGBTQ student organizations.
- When I attend campus events, I wear my kurta and rainbow nametag.
- I use social media to talk about the intersection of Hindu and Queer identities and to help build network that enables students to see all the queer brown people across the world.

These strategies have proven their usefulness at my university. I hope others will implement them.

The Food-Centric Chaplain
Vaishali Gupta Chandrashekar

I served as the Hindu Chaplain at Wellesley College, Babson College, and Brandeis University from 2011 to 2016. However, I was not academically trained to be a chaplain. In fact, I studied Architecture in India and had a fulfilling and rewarding career as an architect for ten years before moving to the US. After that, I enjoyed being exclusively a mom for a few years, and nurturing my two young kids. Being a mom was a life-changing and perspective-shifting experience for me. I found myself consciously focusing on the health and happiness of my family much more than I ever had before. This conscious lifestyle was triggered by the fact that my son was dealing with a series of health issues. I was interested in helping him heal in a natural way, by focusing on his diet and lifestyle. Since I had always loved to cook, I already was making all meals for my family, but now I wanted to learn more about health, nutrition, and the connection to everyday life. So, to better equip myself as a primary caregiver and nurturer of my family, I decided to study further. I gained a deeper understanding in the area of health and nutrition and I trained to become a certified holistic health counselor from the Institute of Integrative Nutrition.

It was at this time and frame of mind when, by sheer coincidence, I met Professor Neelima Shukla-Bhatt, who herself was a former Hindu chaplain and a Professor of South Asian studies at Wellesley College. I excitedly told her about my current interest and study in health and wellness. I also told her about how I grew up in a unique environment in Mumbai, India, where I was exposed to the depth of the Indian culture and diverse Hindu practices from a very young age. I mentioned my personal struggles and learnings from adapting to a completely different environment in the US. She suggested that because of my background, experience, and training as a health counselor, I should consider applying for the currently open position of Hindu chaplain at Wellesley College. Honestly speaking, this really freaked me out. I was completely intimidated by the prospect of applying for a position that I had never heard of or had any prior understanding of. At the same time, I was intrigued by the opportunity to offer spiritual care to the students and the college community. I knew from personal experience and from my study as a health counselor that spiritual health would contribute greatly to the overall health of the student community and this would be a greatly meaningful experience for me. So, I decided to interview for this position. This role, as I found out soon after I started to work, was exactly as I had imagined—it was about connecting, nurturing, nourishing, and listening. As I reflect back, I can wholeheartedly say that the one thing that was central to my service as a Hindu chaplain in all three institutions was my love for cooking and feeding.

Now, I am no longer a chaplain and am devoting myself full time to teaching cooking and health coaching; this is still an expression of spiritual care for me, and it feels like an extension of my work at the colleges.

Key Ingredient: Food

It did not take very long for me to realize that the way to a campus's heart is through its stomach. I vividly remember my first *pūjā* (prayer service) with the students at Wellesley College; I was so nervous! The students were shy and quiet; but when they found out that I had brought yummy *prasad* (traditional Indian sweets that are offered after the prayer service) to distribute, it was as if a connection was formed and the ice had been broken. There was happy chatter and energy all around. This very soon became the norm. Many bonds were developed during weekly *pūjā* over delicious *prasad*. As a part of spiritual enrichment, we started reading and discussing the Bhagavad-Gita (Holy Hindu Scripture) after *pūjā* every week. Initially, this did not feel very relaxing, and the students came with notebooks and took notes just like they would do in a class. I felt that their energy was low; they looked tired. This defeated the purpose. My intention really was to make this Sunday gathering much more relaxed but also an energizing and fulfilling experience. I wanted the students to be able to be authentic, true to themselves, relaxed, comfortable, and let their stress melt away. I thought, perhaps feeding them would do the trick! Soon, I found myself cooking for the students. I made some simple homemade food and offered it before the Gita discussion sessions. The students loved it. They would all help lay out the food and then sit and enjoy their meal. Suddenly, there was energy and chatter in the room. I could see the students destress and relax. Our discussion after that was more energizing and engaging and they spoke openly and freely. Sometimes, they would bring their friends along (mainly to eat lunch) who probably would otherwise never have visited. Food was the main attraction but once they were well fed, they would connect and engage with each other, breathe, and relax to take a break from their stressful academic life. I could feel a certain heaviness lifting from their lives.

Apart from *pūjā* and the Gita discussion group, I—along with the Hindu student group at all three campuses—would host college-wide celebrations for the important Hindu holidays of Diwali and Holi. These were very popular and attended by hundreds of students. That the celebrations were always accompanied by a traditional Indian dinner that we would get from local Indian restaurants was a big draw for everyone. The student volunteers worked hard all afternoon to decorate the place and put on performances and make it truly celebratory. I always made sure that I organized an intimate, special, homemade lunch for them before all the setting up began. I wanted to make them feel appreciated and energized for all the work they were about to do. I do think that I can say that it was these gestures that had a big impact on my relationship with them.

Hospitality and feeding people have been such an important part of my culture that I cannot imagine trying to build a relationship of trust with anybody and not cooking for them or sharing a meal with them. To me, it is an expression of caregiving and a great foundation for a strong relationship.

As a Hindu chaplain, I understood that a big part of my job would be to provide spiritual care and counseling to the Hindu students. There were many students who identified as being Hindu and were raised on Hindu values, but who did not have a religious practice and/or chose not to come for the regular *pūjā* and Gita discussion sessions. It was important for me to create space for these students in my chaplaincy. Traditionally, there is no concept of a "chaplain" in Hinduism and many Hindus including me have grown up seeking wisdom and comfort from friends, family and others who we had some sort of prior trustworthy relationship with. So I knew it would be awkward/difficult for the students to seek me out when they were in crisis or when they needed care just because I was their chaplain. I also knew that there would be no one who would refuse an invitation to a lunch or a dinner! One thing about students whether Hindu or not is that they are always starved of good food. So, my offer of a casual meet up over lunch or dinner at a place which had warm fresh food would never be met with resistance. Wholesome food is like a big warm hug; no one can resist it. I was let in on problems relating to academics, boyfriends, parents, roommates, and a variety of other issues and I found that this was a perfect and safe way to reach out to those who seemed reluctant to come to my regular spiritual and religious offerings.

Working with Jain Students

As well as working with the Hindu students, I also worked with Jain students at all three colleges. My mother and grandmother both were raised Jain and I was quite familiar with the Jain practices. A big part of following Jainism is following a very strict Jain diet which is based on extreme non-violence. As well as being vegetarian, it also prohibits all root vegetables—like potatoes, onions, carrots, sweet potatoes, garlic, ginger, and lots of other stuff. Most of the time, the students found it extremely hard to adhere to this on the meal plan. They either suffered and ate a very unbalanced diet, which left them undernourished and not adequately prepared to deal with the rigors of college life, or tried to explain their diet to the college administration and dining-services staff and see if they could get wholesome, nutritious food while practicing their religion. Many times, while listening to the Jain students, I noticed that this issue caused a lot of stress in their daily lives. Even talking to somebody who could understand where they were coming from seemed to relieve a lot of it. My training in nutrition, combined with my love for food and cooking, gave me sufficient knowhow to help these students. I could talk to the chefs who made the college food. I could suggest slight changes in recipes, processes, and labeling which would then make meals conducive for consumption by anyone following a Jain diet. I taught cooking classes in the main campus kitchens for all the chefs at Wellesley and at Babson—educating them, and also practically showing them, how to make it possible to serve palatable, nutritious, balanced food no matter what dietary restrictions people had. I feel that pastoral care does not have to be limited in any way. Every aspect of body, mind, and spirit are connected. When you nourish any one of these, the others automatically thrive.

Making Connections with Other Chaplaincies and Campus Organizations

I was so lucky to be a part of the Multifaith Chaplaincy at Wellesley College, Babson College, and Brandeis University. Each of us chaplains looked for opportunities to connect with students from all faith communities, not just the ones from our own faith. I was very excited when one of the Unitarian-Universalist (UU) students reached out to me and invited me to teach a cooking class to the students from her "slow cooking" club. She told me that the UU Chaplain had mentioned that I love to cook and that I teach cooking classes in my spare time. Of course, I jumped at the opportunity to work with this amazing group of students from diverse cultures and backgrounds, for whom love for good food was a common thread that connected them. We made delicious traditional Indian slow-cooked food—the kind that you will only get at Indian homes and not Indian restaurants. The students were engaged and delighted. They shared stories from their childhood, their cultures, issues that mattered to them in this warm and safe environment. I enjoyed listening to them and there was an instant bond formed while cooking and eating together.

From this experience I learned that so much of being a chaplain is about listening without judgment in a safe space. I also learned that it is so much better for me to go to a place where the students hang out doing their stuff than for them to come to my office to meet me. This was far less intimidating for them.

After this positive experience, I reached out to other student groups on campus to create opportunity for association. A group called SCOOP focused on sustainability. It even managed a fruit and vegetable garden close to the campus, selling its produce to whoever wanted it. That time, at Wellesley College, there was another group of students who were a part of the Multifaith Council (MFC) which existed to promote discussion and dialogue between different religious organizations on campus. I and the associate Dean of Office of Religious and Spiritual Life at that time, Kelly Stone, were the staff facilitators for that group and were always looking for bonding activities for the students of the MFC. We invited all students who were interested to visit the garden grown by students of SCOOP and we harvested amazing produce from there and took it to the kitchen in one of the Residence Halls and made fresh salads, salsas, and other good stuff. It was absolutely magical! I found this a great way to bond with a great many students and to talk to them and form a comfortable and natural relationship with them. These were the students who stopped and chatted with me when I was walking around the campus, who came to all the Hindu holiday celebrations that I hosted, who invited me to the events that they hosted.

I was so encouraged by the response that my cooking and feeding was generating that I, supported by the Office of Religious and Spiritual life at Wellesley, decided to offer monthly healthy cooking sessions for the students. I called it "The Art of Nourishing." I publicized this as a cooking class; but once I started hosting, it became so much more. It was absolutely the place where the students could come and relax after their regular classes, cook together, talk about nutrition, and eat some amazing food together. I learned that, for the students, college life was about constant depletion and nourishment. They were getting depleted by the academic and other kinds of demands on them; they were getting nourished by what they were learning and by the friendships, inspiration, and resources that the college had to offer. So, I would create menus that would help them replenish what they had lost during their rigorous academic engagement. I would involve them in chopping, kneading, sprinkling, composing—all the beautiful aspects of cooking that are so therapeutic and rejuvenating. This was my authentic way of caring for them and they responded with their beautiful warm smiles, amazing thank you emails, and coming back for the class every time it was offered.

Chaplains were constantly asked by the college to offer study break programs that helped reduce stress during the week before exams. Often, I saw that the students would gather at the MFC kitchen and bake cookies or make some other stuff. I know that cooking can be a huge stress reliever so I offered small creative cooking workshops where we made Indian tea and street food. We used our hands to chop, mix, stir, sprinkle, taste, and all our senses were engaged and stimulated while we created delicious food. I could see the students visibly relax and loosen up. They would text their friends and invite them to join and soon it would be a party and I always felt they went from there happy and destressed and replenished.

Caring for Colleagues

With my immediate colleagues in the Religious Life team—and also with other staff members of the colleges I served—I adopted (not very consciously) the approach of leading with food. At Wellesley, we nine chaplains had a weekly team meeting where all the chaplains and the Dean of Religious and Spiritual Life gathered, connected, and discussed the affairs of the office. Each of us nine chaplains had the opportunity every week to open the team meeting with an activity or a discussion that they connected with. I usually opened the meeting with some food related discussion. I once passed around a platter of ingredients such as spices, herbs, and other aromatics and asked my fellow team members to smell them and talk about their experience: what they identified with and what they felt uncomfortable with—and why. I always loved getting to know people through their relationship with food.

I would also cook and bring something special to eat during our team meetings if it was a Hindu holiday or some special occasion such as welcoming a new team member. It was my way of sharing my culture which is quite often about making people feel cared for and special by offering them home-cooked food. All my colleagues knew I loved to cook. Some would often collaborate with me to offer creative programs to the students. I collaborated with the Jewish chaplain to teach a kosher Indian cooking class to the students associated with Hillel. We had rich discussions about kashrut! I have been able to carry all that learning to the Indian Kosher cooking classes I still teach.

At another instance, the Muslim chaplain, Amira, reached out to me when she wanted to learn to prepare some healthy, simple, homemade food. I loved the opportunity to be able to go to her house and help her with this. We chatted and learnt so much about each other. We still happen to be friends and keep in touch even though I am not at Wellesley any more.

I always feel a warm and fuzzy feeling whenever I cook a meal for somebody. When Victor Kazanjian, Dean of Religious and Spiritual life, was about to depart from Wellesley after many years of service, the chaplains asked me to prepare his farewell dinner. I was delighted and grateful! By cooking this meal, I was able to show my care and appreciation for him and my amazing colleagues.

As I look back, food has always been a very big part of my life and it was also a very big part of my chaplaincy. In fact, it has been at the heart of all the different roles I have assumed over the years—including chaplaincy, as I have explained. The love for cooking and feeding is the gift that I have received from God and I strive to share this gift with others. This is the main reason why, when my husband's change of job necessitated a move to New Jersey—and with it, the necessity for me to leave my job as the Hindu chaplain at Wellesley, Babson, and Brandeis—I decided to devote myself to teaching cooking full time. This continues to be a truly joyful experience for me. It is my sincere hope that along with teaching recipes and skills, I can continue to help people to look at cooking as an expression of love and care, to see feeding and nourishing others as a means of building strong bonds of trust and friendship.

Spiritually Counseling a Couple Prior to a Wedding

A Hindu Approach

Amrutur V. Srinivasan

The most common perception of spiritual care is that it is the type of counseling one needs when a traumatic and gut-wrenching event such as, for example, the death of a loved one, a serious illness, or a serious accident occurs that affects a whole family. The need for spiritual care arises as such a tragic development leads to fundamental questions about life, its meaning, grief, and a host of confusing thoughts that require a comforting analysis and interpretation. This involves a family elder or a priest who may offer a broad perspective of such events in the life of everyone in order to console and comfort. The objective is to offer guidance, a sort of hope in an otherwise hopeless situation, so the family may restore faith and continue with the pursuit of their lives even as they grieve.

But what about events which are entirely joyful and serve as highlights in an individual's life? In the Hindu tradition, naming a baby, the first haircut, *gurukulam* (the ancient practice when a child left the household to live with a guru at his ashram where the student studied the Vedas), the thread ceremony, and of course the wedding, are all celebrated with prayers, music, rituals, blessings, and sumptuous feasting. Why does one need spiritual care in such cases? The Vedas and the Grihya Sutras elaborate on the rituals while the Upanishads emphasize the need to look deeper. The epics teach the consequences of violating right conduct. A Hindu ritual priest can play a chaplain-like role by providing the participants with a broader and deeper perspective to the celebrations and spelling out the spiritual and practical implications of these events. Done well, a Hindu priest's skilled explanation and "translation" of the marriage ritual can itself be an act of spiritual care to the couple being wed. A Hindu wedding may be the most joyful, enjoyable, and exciting event that unites two families. The spiritual basis of this most significant step in the life of a loving couple is the subject matter of this chapter.

Centuries ago, civilized societies recognized and acknowledged the most basic instinct of all—the need for companionship—and founded an honorable institution known as marriage. Experience has shown that life is full of conflicts, questions, concerns, temptations, joys, sorrows, ups and downs, and Hindu ancestors set aside some guidelines to make sure that this institution is a permanent one capable of not only bringing happiness to two people but also providing a delicate balance so that the family enjoys the fullness of life within the framework of what is called *dharma*, the Hindu code of right conduct. *Dharma* serves as the very foundation of a spiritual caregiver's guidance to a couple. In fact this is built into the rituals, for example, when the priest chants a mantra at the moment the bride is to be given away and explains to the groom that his father-in-law-to-be first needs to know, and therefore asks, if the groom agrees to abide by the framework of *dharma* upon marrying his daughter. The ceremony proceeds only when the groom consents!

In their popular-press article entitled "Surprising key to the happiest couples," two psychologists conclude that "Romance talks about love, but it is friendship that puts love to the ultimate test." They continue, "If there is one prevailing wish that husbands and wives have for their marriage, it is to be close companions for life. While many men and women know that love is essential for such a lifelong bond, they often don't realize that love without close friendship is only a hormonal illusion. One cannot desire another person over the long haul without really being best friends with that person."[1] Modern psychologists may tout this as a newly discovered concept; but, in fact, a Hindu ancestor called Yudhishtira revealed this "secret" about 4,000 years ago. In the *Aranya Parva* of the Mahabharata (a great epic), one of the 120 questions the Yaksha (a forest spirit) asked Yudhishtira was: "Who is the friend of a householder?"[2]—to which the prince answered, "The friend of a householder is his spouse."[3] According to Hindus, therefore, the basis for marriage is friendship: friendship is

---

[1] C. Cowan and M. Kinder (1989) "Surprising key to the happiest couples." *Reader's Digest*, July.
[2] *kimsvin mitram grihesataha.*
[3] *bhāryā mitram grihesataha.*

the understanding, the promise, and the commitment that unites a man and a woman. There is absolutely no question about the role of a woman, her importance, her position in this equation that binds them together.

In the South Indian tradition, through the ceremony known as *māngalya dhāranam* the bond between the bride and the groom is forever confirmed and sealed by the tying of a golden necklace around the bride's neck by the groom. Ethically and morally, it is in that sacred moment that they become husband and wife. This is normally followed by a *homa* or fire ceremony in which Agni, the god of fire, the purifier of all, is invoked to serve as a witness to the wedding vows. Holding hands, and with fire as witness, the couple pledge their love to each other and thus initiate a new domestic hearth. Symbolic offerings are made into the fire in a gesture of gratitude and worship to the gods and symbolizing the offer of all their worldly possessions to God's grace. Initially, the couple goes around Agni four times pledging to adhere to the practice of what we call *chaturvidha phala purushārtha* (four aspects for fulfillment)—i.e., striving for the four aspects of life known as *dharma* (right conduct), *artha* (financial aspects), *kama* (aesthetic aspects) and *moksha* (liberation). Mutual wishes for prosperity, for children, and for a long, happy life together are given in a series of ceremonial offerings to the fire.

The concluding ceremony, common to all of India's regional traditions, is called *saptapadi* (seven steps). The couple hold hands as they take seven steps together around sacred fire, pledging to each other their eternal friendship. The *sakha* (friendship) element is important in Hindu weddings, as it signifies the nature of the promise and the commitment that bind a couple. The completion of the seventh step confirms a married status to the couple, according to Indian civil law.

Saptapadi has a single emphasis: spiritual upliftment of the couple as they live and grow together and have progeny. The very first verse, which is repeated before each of the seven steps, prays for progeny and long life.[4] Each step/vow then stipulates a quality desired to enhance life's experience. Most versions pray for nourishment (*isha*), strength (*urja*), traditional rites (*vrata*), love (*māyobhavā*), cattle (*pashu*), prosperity (*rāyasposha*), and sacred illumination (*hotra*). Here, "cattle" pertains to humans' responsibility to the animal and plant kingdom; "prosperity" includes more than wealth. What the couple declare after they have taken those seven steps is unquestionably the foundation for a successful

---

4   See A.V. Srinivasan (2010) *Hindu Wedding: The Guide*. Anderson, IN: White River Press, p.83.

marriage in the Hindu approach. Together they chant: "With these seven steps you have become my friend; may I deserve your friendship; may my friendship make me one with you; may your friendship make you one with me."[5]

The Hindu wedding ceremony is based on Vedic traditions and rituals originating in the Rig Veda, the earliest of the four ancient Sanskrit books of knowledge which form the basis of Hinduism. Conjugal union has always been considered an important religious celebration, defining the beginning of *grihastha ashram:* the householder stage of life.[6] The Vedic ideal of marriage, according to Abhinash Chandra Bose, "is that of perfect monogamy, the life-long companionship of two people. This practice must have been well established, as is evident from the fact that the Vedic Rishi (sage of the Vedic era), seeking comparisons for perfect duality for the Twin Deities, Ashvins, gives along with examples of two eyes, two lips, etc., that of a married couple."[7]

A serious study of the Vedas reveals how practical the findings of the ancient sages truly are. Vedic sages are positive in their acceptance of life and death, life's struggles and imperfections, positive in their acceptance of the ultimate values—of truth, goodness, and beauty. Vedic sages loved life as well as God and every wish of theirs for the good things of the earth took the form of an ardent prayer. Such prayers are blended into a Vedic wedding ceremony. Certain Vedic prayers are directed towards acquiring intellectual power, wisdom, efficiency, spiritual vigor, higher talent, etc. leading to the acquisition of *brahmateja* (the radiance of intellect). Certain other prayers are for strength, valor, spiritual power, conquering power, fearlessness, and other qualities of heroism known as *kshātraveerya* (physical prowess). The Vedas proclaim that the true goal of life is freedom and this freedom from attachment, freedom from our lower selves brings such joy that it is simply incomparable to the usual kinds of joy most recognize. Therefore, Hindus considered that fulfillment in life comes when one accomplishes the four aspects of life stated earlier.

The demands of *artha* and *kama* in the life of married people are in apparent conflict with the dictates of *dharma* and *moksha*. This in fact was a question on the subject asked of Yudhishtira by the Yaksha: *dharma,*

---

5   *sakhā sapta padi bhava; sakhyam te gameyam; sakhyam te mayoshah; sakhyam te mayoshtah.* Srinivasan (2010), p.84.
6   The traditional "four stages of life" are *Brahmacharya* (student), *Grihastha* (householder), *Vanaprastha* (retired), and *Sannyasa* (renunciate).
7   A.C. Bose (1970) *The Call of the Vedas.* New York: Bharatiya Vidya Bhavan, p.259.

artha, and *kama* conflict with each other; how can these contraries be reconciled?[8] How can a householder necessarily involved in the pursuit of good life seeking *artha* and *kama* in raising a family and serving a community not find himself in conflict with *dharma* and how can he strive for *moksha*? Notice that *artha* and *kama* are safely sandwiched between *dharma* and *moksha*. If salvation is to be your goal, the ancient Hindus said, then by all means participate fully in the affairs of society, raise a family, enjoy the good life in a responsible way, serve the community—all within the framework of *dharma*. Can a householder reconcile these contrary requirements? According to Yudhishtira, there is only one way and that is: when *dharma* and one's spouse are in harmony, then *dharma, artha,* and *kama* are reconciled.[9] Thus, in order to keep that delicate balance among the attributes of *artha* and *kama,* one must have a spouse who is *dharmic*. It is that protection coming from such a spouse, that torch light, that spirit of friendship and cooperation and sacrifice that gives a reasonable chance for a couple to succeed in meeting this challenge of conflicting attributes. A ritual priest who can help the couple preparing for marriage to understand this is certainly offering valuable spiritual care—just as a chaplain would.

And finally, as with other traditions, blessing takes place several times throughout the Hindu wedding ceremony. As each blessing is pronounced by the priest, the audience is asked to approve and declare: "it shall be so" by using a single Sanskrit word: *tathāstu*. At the pinnacle of this series of blessings, the groom is compared to Varuna (a king) and Brhaspati (a sage), thus is mandated to be steadfast; and the bride is compared to goddess Mahalakshmi with a mandate that her relationship with her husband be similar to that of Lakshmi with god Vishnu. Very high expectations indeed!

In order to drive home the rules, roles, responsibilities, ups and downs that are real in a married life, the spiritual caregiver might explain that each step in the ceremony conveys implicitly or explicitly an understanding between the couple. In becoming a life companion, the woman plays a unique and necessary role: she receives the burden of providing the umbrella of *dharma* so that the family she raises will be a *dharmic* one.

---

8   *Dharmashcārthasca kāmashca paraspara virodhinaha eshām nitya viruddhānam kathamekatra sangamaha.* A.V. Srinivasan (2002) *A Hindu Primer:Yaksha Prashn,* 2nd ed. East Glastonbury, CT: Periplus Line, p.61.

9   *Yadā dharmasca bhāryāca paraspara vashānugau tadā dharmārtha kāmānām trayānamapi sangamaha.*

That is why a wife, in a traditional Hindu household, is always called a *dharmapatni* (wife-in-*dharma*).

Many of us North American Hindus who spent our childhood in India had a support system that worked to mold our character silently, patiently, and naturally. We received our strength without the assistance of any organized effort, gradually, unconsciously, and unmistakably because of all the supporting components: parents, other relatives, festivals, social and religious gatherings, music, stories, temples, people in the community, schools, and teachers. The combination of that rich background and the education received both at home and abroad sustains the Hindu community now in the US. Since, typically, such a Hindu support system is not part of the social fabric into which North American Hindu children are born, there is need for trained professionals to be available and ready to guide when called for.

And it is indeed being called for! Over the past five decades, it has become clear to me that Hindu parents often lack basic knowledge of the religion's practices—although they very much relish the fact that their son or daughter wishes to respect their heritage. By contrast, when young people now approach me asking me to perform their wedding, I am touched by their desire to understand each of the several steps they will be taking during the ceremony and I am happy to oblige. I first make sure that *they* want a Hindu wedding and are not having one merely to please someone else. Most young people are concerned about the time it takes to complete the ceremony. I try to impress upon them the need to retain certain essential steps and that the time involved will depend upon how well they remember and perform what they have learned during the meetings with me. I emphasize the need for a good rehearsal to work out the logistics as well as to practice the ceremonial steps with all the principals attending.[10] I have tried to help families by developing a format and procedure based on the scriptures, with necessary variations to suit individual family traditions. Through this effort I have been able to convey to the families that the procedures prescribed by our ancestors are full of meaning and beauty as the scriptures charge the couple with responsibilities they inherit by virtue of the union. I am happy to report it has worked very well. The key, as we discovered, is the successful integration of discipline with joy!

---

10   See A.V. Srinivasan (2017) *Managing Your Hindu Wedding in North America: The Day Before and THE Day!: A Guide to Couples, their Families and Priest*. East Glastonbury, CT: Periplus Line.

Hindu weddings are complex. A priest or a chaplain counseling Hindu couples and performing Hindu weddings needs to have proper training, accreditation, and expertise. Those who do are then able to prepare a couple to enjoy their day in a meaningful and joyful manner. The resulting ceremony will be akin to "watching a symphony"—as one New Jersey groom's uncle described a wedding I officiated a few years ago. Hindu chaplains who will be called upon to counsel couples about their impending weddings, and then to conduct the ceremony, should have a thorough knowledge base that has been systematically developed through study of the Vedas, Upanishads, Epics, Grihya *Sūtras*, and Puranas. Undoubtedly, a knowledge of Sanskrit is essential—as translations of these scriptures into English vary a lot and may even be misleading. Conversely, Hindu ritual priests should consider enhancing their own counseling skills so that they will be ready and able to provide sensitive spiritual care as well as a well-executed ritual. The need is clearly there; the timing could not be more urgent. Such an effort would need the Hindu community's support. When it succeeds, it will secure the wellbeing of succeeding generations in the Hindu diaspora.

Hindu Approaches to Climate Trauma

Gopal D. Patel

"Please bring sand." This heartfelt request was from a young Hindu environmental activist from the Pacific Islands. She was in Rome, Italy, with more than 100 other young religious environmental leaders from across the world. This was the summer of 2015; three weeks earlier Pope Francis had released *Laudato Si'* (Praised Be), which outlined Catholic teachings on caring for Mother Earth.[1] It was also five months before the United Nations climate negotiations in Paris, France. The year 2015 was a pivotal one in global efforts to address climate change, and here was a young Hindu woman asking for sand to take back to the Pacific to stop the islands she and her friends call home drowning as sea levels rose. I sat and listened to her plea along with the other conference participants, some of whom were crying.

Four weeks later, I was in the Indian coastal city of Vishakapatnam, more commonly known as Vizag, in the Eastern state of Andhra Pradesh. I was with a group of environmental activists on a climate change pilgrimage of India. We were visiting Hindu religious sites in India that are vulnerable to effects of climate change, and also those which provide examples of significant efforts to combat climate change. A year earlier Vizag was hit by Cyclone Hudhud, a storm which caused more than $3 billion in damages and took 124 lives. We had come to see first-hand how residents were affected by the hurricane, and how they had coped in the aftermath. The sights and stories were heartbreaking. We saw the remains of homes completely washed away, heard stories of people

---

1 Pope Francis (2015) *Encyclical Letter* Laudato Si' *of the Holy Father Francis on Care for Our Common Home*. Rome: The Vatican, May 24.

struggling in the immediate aftermath for basic necessities, and met families who were still homeless and depending on charitable donations for survival.

Six years earlier, I had co-founded the Bhumi Project, a global Hindu environmental initiative based at the Oxford Centre for Hindu Studies that worked with international multifaith environmental organizations such as the Alliance of Religions and Conservation and GreenFaith. During those six years, the focus of our work had been to educate people about recycling, waste management, and mitigating the environmental impact of religious pilgrimages across India. Our work was well received and growing; we had conducted workshops with Hindu temples across India, pioneered tiger conservation work in India with religious leaders, and engaged more than 30,000 people across India on caring for the environment. I had even been invited to give a talk at the White House and had been honored for my work by Prince Philip at an intimate gathering at Buckingham Palace.

These two experiences in 2015, however, significantly changed the Bhumi Project's work and my personal engagement with environmental concerns. Climate change had not been an issue we had worked on. We had seen it as too big an issue, having no clear solutions, and difficult to explain to people. We also felt, naively, that climate change wasn't a concern for Hindus. Hearing these stories in Rome and Vizag made me realize how wrong we were. It became apparent that Hindus were already facing the effects of climate change. As I learned more about the science and global impacts of climate change, I began to realize—and worry—that every single person on the planet will be affected by it.

Subsequently, I began to think back to the training I had in pastoral care during my time as a students' chaplain at Imperial College London, and as a Hindu monk prior to that. I began connecting these two worlds and asking myself: how do we care for people who are suffering from climate change trauma?

The Impact of Climate Change on Health and Wellbeing

It is now accepted science that the global temperature of the planet is rising due to human activity—specifically, the burning of fossil fuels, which releases carbon dioxide into the atmosphere, thus trapping heat. The mass burning of fossil fuels started in the late 1800s, at the start of the industrial revolution. Since then, the global temperature of the planet has risen by about one degree centigrade. The 2015 Paris Climate Agreement aims to limit temperature rise by the end of this century by two degrees compared to pre-industrial levels. This two-degree target is an upper limit; they say a 1.5-degree rise is preferred. These numbers, seemingly small, have significant global implications. The slightest rise in global temperatures can have far-reaching consequences. As temperatures rise and natural eco-systems come under more pressure, a range of scenarios begin to play out. Chances of war and conflict increase, food prices rise, droughts become more common, and extreme weather becomes more frequent.

The effects of a warming planet have many direct and indirect effects on the health and wellbeing of individuals and communities. The physical health impacts can be considered easier to perceive and understand. These include malnutrition due to crop failings, ill-health due to waterborne diseases during flooding, and heat stroke from exposure to high temperatures. Less is known, however, about the physiological and mental health impacts of climate change. In recent years, however, there has been a growing body of research in this area.

In 2005, Hurricane Katrina hit the US coastal city of New Orleans. Some 1,800 people died as a result of the storm. A number of post-Katrina studies have examined the storm's mental health impact on New Orleans residents who survived it. One study of 392 low-income parents showed that "the prevalence of probable serious mental illness doubled, and nearly half of the respondents exhibited probable PTSD [post-traumatic stress disorder]."[2] Another study showed that suicide rates went up by 50 percent post-Katrina.[3]

In India, research has shown that since 1980 the rising suicides of farmers can be linked to rising temperatures and falling crop yields.[4] However, it is not just those who are directly impacted by extreme weather and climate change who suffer related trauma. Those who work in the climate change field report of "climate burnout." A notable example

---

2 See J. Rhodes and C. Chan (2010) "The impact of Hurricane Katrina on the mental and physical health of low-income parents in New Orleans." *American Journal of Orthopsychiatry* 80, 2, 237–247.
3 See R.C. Kessler *et al.* (2008) "Trends in mental illness and suicidality after Hurricane Katrina." *Molecular Psychiatry* 13, 4, 374–384.
4 See F.C. Sham (2017) "Why 60,000 Indian farmers committed suicide: Climate change the culprit." *Hong Kong Observatory Blog*, November 2. www.hko.gov.hk/blog/en/archives/00000211.htm, accessed on May 9, 2018.

is that of Camille Parmesan. In 2007, she was a co-recipient (with former US Vice-President Al Gore) of the Nobel Peace Prize for her work in authoring a seminal report on climate change: the Third Assessment Report of the Intergovernmental Panel on Climate Change (IPCC). Seven years later, however, she claimed to be "professionally depressed" because of the lack of support for her work in the US. She therefore decided to move to England, where public acceptance of climate change and government support is much higher.[5]

A 2017 report by the American Psychological Association and ecoAmerica examines the impacts of the trauma of climate change. In individuals, climate change trauma may lead to shock, compounded emotional stress, or even full-blown PTSD; to stress on physical health; to strains on social relationships; or to escalation of aggressive and violent behavior—thus to mental health emergencies. It may involve the loss of personally important places, to loss of autonomy and control, to loss of personal and occupational identity. It may manifest as helplessness, depression, fear, fatalism, resignation, and eco-anxiety. In communities, climate change trauma may lead to a decreased sense of cohesion, to disruption in a sense of continuity and belonging, to increased interpersonal aggression—such as domestic abuse and crime, or to intergroup aggression—such as political conflict and war.[6]

Hindu Solutions

Given the broad and far-reaching impact of climate change on the wellbeing of individuals and communities, what can we draw upon from Hindu religious practices, cultures, and traditions that may inform a Hindu model of care in an age of climate crises? I would like to offer three primary approaches that draw upon Hindu traditions: *sādhana*, *sevā*, and *sanga*.

Sādhana

Sādhana, or spiritual practice, is a regular activity intended to offer the practitioner a sense of grounding and connectedness to others, to

---

5   See M. Thomas (2014) "Climate depression is for real. Just ask a scientist." *Grist*, October 28. https://grist.org/climate-energy/climate-depression-is-for-real-just-ask-a-scientist, accessed May 9, 2018.
6   See S. Clayton, C.M. Manning, K. Krygsman, and M. Speiser (2017) *Mental Health and Our Changing Climate: Impacts, Implications, and Guidance*. Washington, DC: American Psychological Association and ecoAmerica, March.

the planet, and to God. Observant Hindus will often have a daily *sādhana* that connects them with their particular deity of worship, or to a particular goal toward which they are aspiring. For example, the *sādhana* for Siva devotees may be to offer daily worship to a Siva Lingum, whereas the *sādhana* of a devotee of Krishna may be to offer daily worship to a tulasi tree. Many Hindus also fast on certain days of the week for a variety of reasons, such practices are also considered *sādhana*.

Given that climate change can make people feel a sense of loss of identity or place, *sādhana* connected to the earth can offer a sense of grounding. For those who already have a spiritual practice, we should encourage them to continue with such practices. We also might explore whether any aspect of the client's *sādhana* currently contains, or could incorporate, an environmental component. For example, if the client is already chanting daily on beads made from rudraksha or tulsi, the spiritual caregiver might ask them to reflect and meditate on the materials the beads are made from. Rudraksha and tulsi both come from the earth, and by meditating on them daily, we become connected to the earth.

We may also introduce new practices. For example, many Hindus touch the earth before getting out of bed in the morning, in order to give thanks and ask for permission to walk upon Her. Other Hindus leave fruits and water outside for local animals and insects to enjoy; others symbolically offer water to the sun. There are myriad similar examples across Hindu traditions which connect the practitioner to the earth and natural world which can be used incorporated into a daily *sādhana*.

Sevā

Sevā, or sacred service, is the act of serving society and God with love and devotion. A principle found across Hindu traditions, *sevā* is considered an external manifestation of our consciousness. How we love and serve others reflects our love for God.

Due to the overwhelming nature of climate change, people can feel paralyzed—unable to imagine how they should act in order to help stop it. They may feel that their individual contributions to stopping climate change are insignificant compared to the large wholesale changes which are needed, such as the elimination of the fossil fuel industry. For Hindus living in western economically developed countries, there may be a level of guilt in knowing that climate change is largely due to the behavior of western countries, and that poorer countries such as India will face the effects more acutely.

It is therefore important to encourage *sevā* for the environment. Such *sevā* could be expressed through personal lifestyle choices, or through activism and advocacy. Regardless of the all-consuming nature of climate change, there always is something we can do individually to decrease our burden and impact on the planet. Employing *ahimsa* (non-violence) as central to this outlook, Hindus can be encouraged to consider what in their personal lives they can change. Can they reduce or eliminate meat and dairy from their diets—thereby no longer supporting the most environmentally damaging industry on the planet? Can they recycle more and use less single-use plastic? Perhaps they can consider taking fewer flights per year. These choices, although seemingly small, can be a source of empowerment and control to an individual in the midst of a seemingly uncontrollable situation. To further strengthen this work, there may be regional, national, or international environmental concerns to which Hindus may be drawn to help as individuals. Again, for Hindus living in the West, connecting with environmental issues in India can create a strong sense of purpose. There are a number of causes they could engage with: pollution of sacred rivers, planting of trees, water and sanitation issues, supporting farmers and rural communities.

Sanga

Sanga, the act of coming together in groups, is important in many Hindu traditions. These groups promote community cohesion, lead to strengthening of friendships, and offer opportunities to share challenges we may be facing in life. A *sanga* has no formal structure. They can be as simple as two people meeting for coffee, or a group of mothers coming together regularly to discuss the challenges of raising spiritually minded children in a major city.

It is important that those suffering from trauma due to climate change do not feel alone. Such individuals can draw much benefit from access to supportive social networks. Be they online or off-line in structure, these networks allow individuals to connect and share openly their concerns about climate change. Additionally, it is important for individuals to feel connected to their parents, mentors, or role models. Such connections allow individuals to reaffirm roots and provide a sense of grounding.

As spiritual caregivers we may consider holding regular eco-*sangas*. These can be semi-formal gatherings where people come together to discuss topics related to the environmental and climate change. In such gatherings it would be important to have someone designated to lead the conversation, to allow everyone to express their thoughts and feelings on the topic, and to close with some actionable items each person could implement in their lives and spiritual practices.

Additional Considerations

In 2015, Oxford-based Climate Outreach conducted the first-ever study to understand what language is appropriate when talking about climate change with Hindu audiences.[7] Part of a wider study with other faith traditions, the findings revealed stark differences in the ways Hindus think about the planet and the environment in comparison to other religious traditions. Awareness of this is helpful when talking with Hindus about climate change. *Journey*; *path*; *responsibility*: these were words Hindus strongly felt reflected their worldviews and understanding about climate change. "Climate justice," however, did not feature—despite being a common phrase in the climate movement; nor was language around "judgment" and "blame" felt to reflect Hindu sensibilities. These differences are important. For Hindus, language featuring terms such as judgment, justice, and blame do not feature prominently in religious teachings. Rather, concepts around responsibility and personal accountability are more common, and it is important to frame conversations on addressing climate change with these terms.

Additionally, we may want to consider drawing upon Hindu stories or teachings about the environment when helping those suffering from climate trauma. In the Bhagavata Purana alone there are a number of stories with an environmental message: the dialogue between *dharma* the bull and Mother Earth represented by a cow; the story of Lord Varaha saving the Earth; or of Lord Krishna subduing the Kaliya serpent in the Yamuna river. All of these stories can be interpreted from an ecological perspective, as can other stories from other Hindu epics such as the Mahabharata and Ramayana. By reinterpreting and reimagining these stories with an environmental lens, we can give them renewed meaning and significance in an age of climate crisis and for those suffering from climate trauma.

---

7   Climate Outreach (2016) "Guide: Faith and Climate Change—Talking with People of 5 Major Faiths." February 16. https://climateoutreach.org/resources/climate-change-faith, accessed on December 11, 2018.

The Challenge

Never before has the human family faced such a large existential threat to our wellbeing. In the coming decades, every single person on the planet will be either directly or indirectly affected by climate change. As spiritual caregivers, our role in this crisis is only slowly starting to emerge. The effects of climate trauma will be significant, and we will have important roles to play in caring for these people. Hindu traditions and practices have a lot to contribute to this field of work. In this chapter, I have offered some initial suggestions about how to frame and develop such work. As the climate crisis intensifies, this work will have to be expanded and all Hindu caregivers will need to be served in the causes and solutions to climate change.

Dealing with Trauma

Re-interpreting Hindu Narratives as Lessons for Healing

Shrestha Singh

I sit on the blue couch on the second floor of a colonial home-turned-office building on Massachusetts Avenue. All eyes of my therapy group are on me as my therapist places a large teddy bear in an empty Windsor chair directly across from me and says, "Here. This is your inner child: Little Shrestha. Are you open to talking to her?" I look at the faces of my fellow group-*therapees* (Is this a word? It should be. It sounds better than "patients," or "adults with childhood trauma," or "folks with a strange kind of PTSD"; less dramatic than "trauma survivors") hoping for commiseration, for a look that affirms that this is crazy, ridiculous. But then again, so are we.

"Sure," I sigh; "why not?"—shaking my head with embarrassment at the scene of a 27-year-old woman talking to a teddy bear and hoping it will free her from the grips of shame and anxiety embedded into her in childhood. In a few weeks, we will receive a tiny stuffed elephant that we carry around with us and take care of whenever we are triggered, re-parenting our inner children in a way we never got to be parented. In a month, we will go into the basement and scream about our caregivers and hit a red punching bag with a baseball bat. My therapist, fellow group-therapees, and I all have trucker mouths; luckily, the cussing is welcomed, even encouraged. We write letters to our parents detailing all the hurt they caused, all the ways they abandoned us or cut us down. We make family trees of dysfunctional relationships, that we put on our walls at home, so as to remind ourselves that this thing started before us, and if we work at it, it could end with us. The strangest part of it all is: it works. After years of trying different forms of therapy, I am starting to feel the grip of sadness loosen its hold on me. Not completely, but enough to feel more light-hearted than I have in years.

I am a Hindu college chaplain. I entered into this field both because I wanted to be like the mentors who had offered me the positive regard and attention I had craved from my own parents when I was a youngster and because I know from experience how hard it is to make your way as the kid of South Asian immigrants in America. So, I became the person I wished I had when I was younger: someone who "got it;" someone to whom a "young me" would have been able to talk to about life and culture and religion and expectations and dreams and family. For many of my students, Hinduism, like Judaism, is as cultural as it is religious. It permeates our ways of being, thinking, communicating, and interacting with one another. For many South Asian American students, then, it means that regardless of how they identify with their religious tradition, it is a part of the tapestry of their lives, a thread that runs through it, visible or not, conscious or unconscious. (This is not to assert that South Asian-ness is equivalent with Hindu-ness; but that a large number of the South Asian-identifying students that I work with were raised in Hindu households.)

I see my role as chaplain as a cultural as well as spiritual one—not only to help students with their explicitly spiritual concerns, but to help them link their everyday concerns and dilemmas to living a *whole* life, living a life that stems from that place of *brahman* (fullness) within them. Students who come to me share stories that are similar to my own. Stories about:

- parents who fought constantly
- a parent who regularly threatened to leave
- children who went searching for that parent in distress until they grew numb to it
- children who became go-betweens for their parents
- parents who treated their children as *their* caregivers, therapists, and confidantes—all while their kids yearned for the same support, but received little
- children who witnessed domestic abuse: oftentimes, fathers who hit mothers, and mothers who, in turn, hit their children

- children who got locked out of houses whenever they "disobeyed"
- children whose parents are in denial about their being gay, lesbian, queer, or transgender because, "what will people think of us?"
- children whose mothers emotionally blackmail them, who hack into their social media accounts and later accost them about what they've found
- parents who never learned the crucial skill of listening to their children even when they do not agree.

These are the young *desi* Americans who have taken a seat on the teal couch in my office, who have come in to talk about a meeting or a recommendation letter, but whose truths are clawing to get out. Those truths end up emerging sideways to someone who looks like them and sounds like them and who just might possibly get it.

Many of us do not consider these experiences a form of trauma. For a long time, I didn't either. They were just "the way *desi* families are." I saw the details of these stories as merely what goes along with being the first generation raised on American soil, part of the jarring experience and rupture that is migration. Trauma, I thought, was something that characterized survivors of sexual assault or veterans of war—not young people whose parents did not love them well enough. But when I read Bessel van der Kolk's landmark book on trauma, *The Body Keeps the Score*, his descriptions of reactions to traumatic events felt eerily familiar. I saw myself in his descriptions of patients he had worked with: "He felt emotionally distant from everybody, as though his heart were frozen and he was living behind a glass wall. That numbness extended to himself, as well… [He] tried to stay busy, working, drinking, and drugging—doing anything to avoid confronting his own demons."[1] I remembered the sweating hot flashes when my first boyfriend would embrace me, the string of toxic intimate relationships that followed, the anxiety and depression that had been my companions since I was ten years old. What if I too had something eerily similar to post-traumatic stress disorder?

It was in my late 20s that I learned that there was a kind of PTSD called C-PTSD, or "complex" trauma. Psychologist and trauma expert Christine Courtois describes this as "a type of trauma that occurs repeatedly and cumulatively, usually over a period of time and within specific

---

1 B. van der Kolk (2014) *The Body Keeps the Score: Brain, Mind, and Body in the Healing of Trauma*. London: Viking Penguin, p.14.

relationships and contexts."[2] These contexts can involve neglect, abuse, or abandonment by caregivers—both emotional and physical. A father who was emotionally unavailable and constantly at work could be a form of emotional abandonment, based on a child's experience of that father. A mother consistently dismissing her child's feelings of hurt and telling her that her experience is false could be a form of emotional abuse or manipulation if experienced that way. Over time, complex trauma can lead to a loss of a sense of safety, self-worth, and trust, and the tendency to recreate situations that mimic the original trauma. One may have trouble setting boundaries or being emotionally close to others, or constantly feel like those close to them are not to be trusted. One might repeatedly get into relationships with emotionally unavailable partners. One might seek out a partner who is abusive in the same way one of their parents was. One might become the abuser themselves. In all of these instances, the subconscious self is trying to recreate the situation that pained it in the hopes of finding long-overdue resolution.

The symptoms and stories that accompany such complex childhood traumatic experiences show up in my conversations with *desi* students often. My students sometimes ask me whether setting boundaries with their families or distancing themselves from toxic and controlling behaviors is "un-Hindu" of them. One student came to me and asked whether being queer was not "following her *dharma*" or her duty to her parents, who would not tolerate anything but heterosexuality. My answer to both of these students was a resounding "No!" but I realized that many other Hindus might not answer the same way. My students have often pointed a finger at Hindu culture as a force that has bolstered the unhealthy dynamics and messages in their lives. For better or for worse, our cultural prejudices and expectations become the lens through which we interpret religious texts and doctrines, and we fail to recognize how mutually implicated culture and faith are. By equating our cultural biases and prejudices to our religions' deepest values, we can keep ourselves shackled to ways of being that are not lifegiving. In fact, they can be death-dealing, spiritually, emotionally, and even physically.

The cultural lens of the immigrant generation may differ widely from their children's. Whatever those lenses are, they cloud our vision. They lead us to overlook those interpretations of our religious traditions that go against what we believe in and what is comfortable for us. When we look

---

2   C. Courtois (2004) "Complex trauma, complex reactions." *Psychotherapy: Theory, Research, Practice, Training 41*, 4, 412.

at the scriptures through the hermeneutics of trauma survivors, through the lens of the struggle to live fully while navigating multiple cultural identities, dealing with the expectations of family as well as facing societal racism, Islamophobia, and the pressure to assimilate, we will see things in the texts that our families did not see. These new understandings of our faith are just as legitimate as those of our parents' generation. I focus in this essay on these interpretations, positing that there are forces within Hinduism that can speak to the healing of trauma and to the creation of wellness. If we look for it, teachings and stories within Hinduism show us that undoing the toxic family dynamics that have saddled us with unhealthy patterns of being does not "go against one's culture and traditions." In fact, this work of healing has a basis within—and is actually in line with—Hindu traditions!

Sita's Boundary-Setting in the Ramayana

Desi families are often enmeshed. That is, their members—no matter what their age—live by a set of rules (spoken or unspoken). Therapist Chris Lewis gives examples of such rules:

- Don't talk to outsiders about what goes on in our family. That is our business and our business only.

- What Mom and Dad [or Mom and Mom, or Dad and Dad] say/believe/think/feel about you is what is right—never mind that you are 45 years old and have been on your own for 27 years.

- It's okay for you to be a little bit different from us in some ways, but there is a line that you can't cross in this family and still be accepted (maybe you can't be a Democrat, or a gay person, or marry outside of our race).

- The cost of being different is to be cut off. We cannot accept differences that challenge our rigid sense of who this family is.

- Even as adults, you will conform to the wishes of "the family" instead of making your own mind up about how, where, and with whom you wish to live your life.[3]

---

3   C. Lewis, (2013) "The enmeshed family and how to 'unmesh'." Blog post on Maria Droste Counseling Center website, July 8. www.mariadroste.org/2013/07/the-enmeshed-family-what-it-is-and-how-to-unmesh, accessed on April 25, 2019.

These rules may sound familiar to children of immigrants. "Stand up to my parents or elders? Insist on personal space? Speak my truth? These are not what 'good Hindu kids' do! Is it not written that you must 'Treat your mother like a god. Treat your father like a god' (Taittiriyaka Upanishad 1.11.2)?" Trauma survivors often struggle with setting boundaries. We take on others' problems as our own, have a hard time saying "no" out of fear of displeasing others, and give in to others' demands—only to boil with resentment and anger later.

Yet we see this very behavior of boundary-setting celebrated in the Hindu epic the Ramayana, as the storytellers share with us the consequences of boundaries being trespassed. The Ramayana tells the story of Rama, the prince of Kosala, and his wife Sita and brother Lakshmana, who are exiled to the forest for 14 years. When Sita is kidnapped by the demon King Ravana, Rama and a ragtag army wage war on Ravana in order to get her back. The Ramayana is often understood as a handbook on the duties of relationships, portraying the ideal son, husband, brother, and wife. Rama, Lakshmana, and Sita, therefore, are supposed to be epitomes of righteousness. Yet even the righteous, following their *dharmic* paths, set boundaries and assert their bodily autonomy.

Two moments in particular come to mind. During their exile in the forest, Rama is lured away from their hut by a demon in the guise of a deer. When he has been away for too long, Sita begins to worry. She tells her brother-in-law Lakshmana to go in search of Rama. Lakshmana hesitates. Would it be safe to leave Sita there alone? He decides to draw a line in the sand around the hut, famously known as the Lakshmana Rekha: the line that cannot be crossed. If crossed by anyone other than Sita, Lakshmana, or Rama, the boundary will burn the trespasser to ashes. While Lakshmana is away, the demon king Ravana appears in the guise of a beggar and asks Sita for alms. When Sita explains that she cannot cross the line in the sand but that she can throw food to him, Ravana shames her for setting and maintaining such a boundary. He effectively accuses her of caring more for her own safety than his needs and asserts that it is dishonorable to throw alms to a beggar. He must be treated with respect, he argues, and have alms placed squarely in his palms. Sita feels guilty, manipulated by Ravana. She breaks her own rule, prioritizing another's needs over her own need for safety and space, and Ravana instantly kidnaps her. If only, we readers wish, if only she had maintained the line! If only she had not crossed it or allowed another to convince her to let it down; if only she had not allowed another to manipulate and shame her into fulfilling his desires!

What if the Lakshmana Rekha is an example of what happens when we fail to stick to what we know we need? What if it is a metaphor for those occasions on which we allow our boundaries to be crossed, or cross them ourselves, in order to please others? When our mothers' need to know where we are at all times makes us feel as though we are suffocating, might we draw a Lakshmana Rekha around that need? Even though it may make us uncomfortable to do so, can we draw the boundary and refuse to budge? Or, do we allow our mothers' pleading and fearfulness take control? Do we allow it to cross the boundary we have set—even if it damages our own wellbeing?

We see this once more when, yet again, a man tries to get Sita to fulfill his wishes rather than her own. While Sita is in captivity in Ravana's palace, Ravana visits her often, trying to convince her to give up her loyalty to her husband and to be his consort instead. He tells her that she will be the queen of all the women in his harem if she chooses to be with him. Enraged, Sita places a blade of grass between the two of them, a physical symbol of the line he cannot cross. With a blade as her barrier, she tells him that she will not tolerate being violated, nor will she acquiesce to his wishes. Remember that the Ramayana is a handbook for righteousness; many scholars have attested to Sita's righteousness in maintaining chastity during her captivity. Here is another interpretation, however: not only is Sita *dharmic* as a wife, she is *dharmic* as someone subject to another's authority! It can be *dharmic* not to acquiesce to another person's wishes; it can be *dharmic* to protect one's bodily autonomy; it can be *dharmic* to speak truth to power and authority. We can set and keep boundaries, and that is okay.

What Trauma Does and What Healing Might Look Like

Hindu mythology seems to be rife with stories of trauma. Many Hindus are familiar with the epic story of the Mahabharata, which tells the tale of the royal Kaurava and Pandava brothers' struggle for the throne of Hastinapura. In a key scene of the epic, the eldest Pandava brother Yudhishthira, intoxicated by a high-stakes game of dice, gambles away his kingdom, his brothers, himself, and even his own wife, the legendary and tough Draupadi. Gloating, the Kaurava brothers call Draupadi into the room from her own quarters, where she—menstruating—has separated herself from the men of the palace. When she presents herself, Duryodhana cruelly pulls at her clothes, attempting to disrobe her in front of the court—a clear form of sexual assault. The Lord Krishna intervenes so that her robes become never-ending. Eventually, Duryodhana stops, exhausted from pulling on the endless yards of cloth. Draupadi, however, is humiliated and furious; she vows that she will not rest until she has washed her hair in Duryodhana's blood. One of the key reasons that the brothers end up at war is Draupadi's need for vengeance. Woundedness breeds anger and disconnection, which in turn cause more woundedness—and Draupadi is indeed wounded. The pain of the harassment and shame understandably cause her to push for vengeance and violence on the part of her husband. Trauma does its work here, creating greater anger and disconnection.

Duryodhana, the eldest of the Kaurava brothers, is another example of the workings of trauma. We learn in the epic that his need to breed destruction on his own family comes from his feeling unloved and neglected as a child, having lived constantly in master-warrior Arjuna's shadow. The listener senses that he feels a gaping hole inside of himself, a deep seated anger and resentment. Perhaps vanquishing Arjuna and the Pandavas and those who remind him of his own pain will vanquish the resentment once and for all, he must believe. He chooses to destroy rather than pay attention to the wounded child within himself. Rather than empathizing and choosing to give space to his own hurt, he reacts. The wounded parts of him are running the show. And with both Draupadi and Duryodhana, we see that such woundedness, when left to fester, can only lead to more broken relationships, an atmosphere of disdain and distrust, and the desire to destroy—the effects of traumatic events.

What would it look like to heal from all this pain? In the Upanishads, there is a dialogue between the teacher, Varuna, and his son, Bhrgu. Bhrgu wants to learn about the nature of *brahman* from his father; and as he learns, he compares *brahman* to food, to mind, to perception. Each time Bhrgu shares a new understanding on *brahman*, his father pushes him to explore a bit further. Finally, he returns to his father and shares that "Fullness [is] *brahman*. From fullness all beings are born; by fullness they live after birth, and into fullness they return" (Taittiriya Upanishad 3.6.1). In *A Hindu Theology of Liberation*, Anantanand Rambachan says of this verse: "This important text suggests powerfully that we must think of creation as expressing the limitlessness of the infinite, an overflow of divine fullness and a celebration of what the infinite is."[4] *Brahman*—the

---

4   A. Rambachan (2015) *A Hindu Theology of Liberation: Not-Two Is Not One*. Albany, NY: SUNY Press, pp.68–69.

divine—that life force that undergirds the universe, then, is fullness—a fullness and completeness that already resides in each and every one of us, in all creation. Our work as humans is to recognize that fullness within ourselves and one another and to allow our actions to stem from that place. Healing childhood and intergenerational trauma, to me, is about recognizing that fullness. It is about seeing ourselves as imbued with *brahman*, learning to value the self and celebrate our creation, not in a self-indulgent and narcissistic manner, but in a manner that brings forth more life, for ourselves, for others, for the world. By doing so we get at ways of living and being that give and sustain life, or that are in line with *dharma*, the root of which is the Sanskrit syllable *dhr*, meaning that which sustains.

Becoming the Ones We Have Yearned For

One last story: after the terrible ordeal in which Ravana sexually harasses her, Sita is rescued by Rama, but then sent again to live in the forest when her chastity is questioned. She returns to Ayodhya one day with her two grown sons, sons of Rama, born in the forest, and is questioned again about her chastity. Exhausted and heartbroken by having to constantly prove her integrity, Sita chooses to go back to her mother, Mother Earth, who cracks open the earth beneath Sita's feet and welcomes Sita with open arms, no questions asked. She does not tell Sita, "Beta, you should stay with your husband and children," or "Are you sure you did not have sex with Ravana?" Instead, Mother Earth is the epitome of unconditional love. No matter her scars or wounds, Sita is cared for and loved by her mother. Mother Earth is who we are called to be—the good parent, the loving adult who many of us have longed for and not found in our own families. Our task is to become her ourselves, so we can do the work that Sita must do when she disappears into the Earth. She will share her pains as her mother sits by her, smoothing her hair and listening with love and care, asking her what she needs, and doing her best to help her recognize her own fullness—the fullness of the divine that resides within her—and to live from that place once more.

Interpretations of Hindu teachings and stories have real effects on our lives—they can teach us that womanhood equals obedience or that defiance is *dharmic*. They can teach us that asserting our needs is unrighteous or that refusing ill-treatment is a mark of faithfulness. The interpretations, the lens through which we read Hindu stories, can make us or break us. I want for them to make us—to challenge and empower us to do the difficult work of restorative healing. The toxicity can be undone, and the religious backing for it is profound.

Heal on, family, heal on.

Bibliography

Books

Adams, M., Blumenfeld, W.J., Castaneda, R., Hackman, H.W., Peters, L.M., and Zuniga, X. (eds) (2010) *Readings for Diversity and Social Justice*, 2nd ed. Abingdon: Routledge.

Adluri, V. and Bagchee, J. (2014) *The Nay Science: A History of German Indology*. Oxford: Oxford University Press.

Balaji, M. (ed.) (2017) *Digital Hinduism*. Lanham, MD: Lexington Books.

Basu, B.D. (trans.) (1934) *The Vedanta-Sutras of Badarayana with the Commentary of Baladeva*. Allahabad, India: L.M. Basu, Panini Office.

Beckerlegge, G. (2006) *Swami Vivekananda's Legacy of Service; A Study of the Ramakrishna Math and Mission*. New Delhi: Oxford University Press.

Swami, B. (2012) *Śrīmadbhagavadgītā Svāminārāyaṇabhāṣyam*. Shahibaug, Amdavad, India: Swaminarayan Aksharpith.

Bhaktivedanta Swami Prabhupada, A.C. (trans.) (1987) *Śrīmad-Bhāgavatam*. Alachua, FL: The Bhaktivedanta Book Trust International.

Bhaktivedanta Swami, A.C. (1970) *The Krishna Book*. Alachua, FL: The Bhaktivedanta Book Trust.

Bhanu Swami, H.H. (trans.) (2004) *Sarartha Darsini : Tenth Canto Commentaries on Srimad Bhagavatam*. Mathura, India: Mahanidhi Swami.

Dasa, B. (2006) *Unveiling His Lotus Feet, a Detailed Overview of Srimad Bhagavatam, Cantos One–Four*. Vrindavan, India: Vrindavana Institute for Higher Education.

Bose, A.C. (1970) *The Call of the Vedas*. New York: Bharatiya Vidya Bhavan.

Bottome, P. (1939) *Alfred Adler: Apostle of Freedom*. New York: Faber and Faber.

Brereton, J. and Jamison, S. (2014) *The R̥gveda*. Oxford: Oxford University Press.

Bryant, E.F. (2009) *The Yoga Sūtras of Patañjali: A New Edition, Translation, and Commentary with Insights from the Traditional Commentators*. New York: North Point Press.

Clayton, S., Manning, C., Krygsman, K., and Speiser, M. (2017) *Mental Health and Our Changing Climate: Impacts, Implications, and Guidance*. Washington, DC: American Psychological Association and ecoAmerica.

Coburn, T.B. (1991) *Encountering the Goddess: A Translation of the Devi-Mahaymta and a Study of Its Interpretation*. Albany, NY: State University of New York Press.

Easwaran, E. (trans.) (2007) *The Upanishads*, 2nd ed. Berkeley, CA: Nilgiri Press.

Fanon, F. (1963) *The Wretched of the Earth.* New York: Grove.
Flood, G. (1996) *An Introduction to Hinduism.* Cambridge: Cambridge University Press.
Flueckiger, J.B. (2015) *Everyday Hinduism.* Oxford: Wiley Blackwell.
Forster-Smith, L.A. (ed.) (2013) *College and University Chaplaincy in the 21st Century: A Multifaith Look at the Practice of Ministry on Campuses across America.* Woodstock, VT: SkyLight Paths Publishing.
Galanti, G.-A. (2004) *Caring for Patients from Different Cultures,* 3rd ed. Philadelphia, PA: University of Pennsylvania Press.
Gambhirananda, S. (1957) *History of the Ramakrishna Math and Mission.* Mayavati, India: Advaita Ashrama.
Geertz, C. (1966) "Religion as a Cultural System." In M. Banton (ed.) *Anthropological Approaches to the Study of Religion.* London: Tavistock Publications.
Giles, C.A. and Miller, W.B. (2013) *The Arts of Contemplative Care: Pioneering Voices in Buddhist Chaplaincy and Pastoral Work.* Boston, MA: Wisdom Publications.
Gordon, L.R. and Gordon, J.A. (2006) *Not Only the Master's Tools: African American Studies in Theory and Practice.* St. Paul, MN: Paradigm.
Queensland Government (2011) *Health Care Providers' Handbook on Hindu Patients.* Brisbane, Queensland, Australia: Queensland Government.
Herman, A.L. (1976) *The Problem of Evil and Indian Thought.* Delhi: Motilal Banarsidass.
Jain, A.R. (2014) *Selling Yoga: From Counterculture to Pop Culture.* Oxford: Oxford University Press.
James, W. (1890) *The Principles of Psychology.* New York: Henry Holt.
JTPBJ (trans. and ed.) (1915) *The Complete Works of Swami Vivekananda,* 2nd ed. Mayavati, India: Gauranga Press.
Kübler-Ross, E. and Kessler, D.A. (2005) *On Grief and Grieving: Finding the Meaning of Grief Through the Five Stages of Loss.* New York: Scribner Publications.
Kumar, P. (ed.) (2006) *Natyasastra of Bharatamuni: Text with commentary of Abhinavabharati and English translation.* Delhi: New Bharatiya Book Corporation.
Lartey, E.Y. (2003) *In Living Color: An Intercultural Approach to Pastoral Care and Counseling,* 2nd ed. Philadelphia, PA: Jessica Kingsley Publishers.
McDermott, R.F. (2008) "Evil, Motherhood, and the Hindu Goddess Kālī." In D.M. Eckel and B.L. Herling (eds) *Deliver Us from Evil.* New York: Continuum.
McDermott, R.F. (2011) *Revelry, Rivalry, and Longing for the Goddesses of Bengal: The Fortunes of Hindu Festivals.* New York: Columbia University Press.
McDermott, R.F. (2001) *Singing to the Goddess: Poems to Kālī and Umā from Bengal.* New York: Oxford University Press.
Menen, A. (1970) *The Space within the Heart.* New York: McGraw-Hill.
Monier-Williams, M. (1899) *A Sanskrit-English Dictionary.* Oxford: Clarendon Press.
Mukhopādhyāy, H. (ed.) *Ramayaṇ Kṛttibās Biracita.* Kolkata, India: Sāhitya Samsad.
Nicholson, A.J. (2010) *Unifying Hinduism.* New York: Columbia University Press.
Nikhilananada, S. (trans.) (1949, 1952, 1956, 1959) *The Upanishads with Commentary.* New York: Ramakrishna-Vivekananda Center.

Nikhilananda, S. (ed.) (1953) *Vivekananda: The Yogas and Other Works*. New York: Ramakrishna-Vivekananda Center of New York.
Nikhilananda, S. (trans.) (1977) *The Gospel of Ramakrishna*. New York: Ramakrishna Vedanta Center.
O'Flaherty, W. (1980) *The Origins of Evil in Hindu Mythology*. Berkeley, CA: University of California Press.
Olivelle, P. (2005) *Manu's Code of Law: A Critical Edition and Translation of the Mānava-Dharmaśāstra*. Oxford: Oxford University Press.
Paramtattvadas, S. (2017) *An Introduction to Swaminarayan Hindu Theology*. Cambridge: Cambridge University Press.
Pearson, A.M. (1996) *"Because it Gives Me Peace of Mind": Ritual Fasts in the Religious Lives of Hindu Women*. Albany, NY: State University of New York Press.
Pope Francis (2015) *Encyclical Letter* Laudato Si' *of the Holy Father Francis on Care for Our Common Home*. Rome: The Vatican, May 24.
Radhanath, S. (2015) *The Journey Within: Exploring the Path of Bhakti*. San Rafael, CA: Mandala Publishing.
Rambachan, A. (2015) *A Hindu Theology of Liberation*. Albany, NY: State University of New York Press.
Rambachan, A. (2006) *The Advaita Worldview: God, World and Humanity*. Albany, NY: State University of New York Press..
Rangacharya, A. (1996) *The Natyasastra: English Translation with Critical Notes*. New Delhi: Munshiram Mnoharlal Publishers.
Roberts, S.B. (ed.) (2012) *Professional Spiritual and Pastoral Care: A Practical Clergy and Chaplain's Handbook*. Woodstock, VT: SkyLight Paths Publishing.
Saradananda, S. (1952) *Sri Ramakrishna: The Great Master*, trans. Swami Jagadananda. Mylapore, India: Sri Ramakrishna Math.
Saraswati, S.D. (trans.) (2011) *Bhagavadgita*. Chennai, India: Arsha Vidya Research and Publication Trust.
Schipani, D.S. (ed.) (2013) *Multifaith Views in Spiritual Care*. Kitchchener, Ontario: Pandora Press.
Shastri, B. (trans.) (1991) *Kālikā Purāṇa*. Delhi: Nag Publishers.
Sherma, R.D. (2019) *Hinduism and the Divine: Foundations of Hindu Theology*. New York: IB Tauris.
Srinivasan, A.V. (2002) *A Hindu Primer: Yaksha Prashna*, 2nd ed. East Glastonbury, CT: Periplus Line.
Srinivasan, A.V. (2010) *Hindu Wedding: The Guide*. Anderson, IN: White River Press.
Srinivasan, A.V. (2017) *Managing Your Hindu Wedding in North America: The Day Before and THE Day!: A Guide to Couples, Their Families and Priest*. East Glastonbury, CT: Periplus Line.
Srinivasan, A.V. (2014) *Yaksha Prashna*. East Glastonbury, CT: Periplus Line.
Sutton, N., Chander, V., and Das, S.R. (2017) *Hindu Chaplaincy*. Oxford, UK: Oxford Centre for Hindu Studies.
Swift, C., Cobb, M., and Todd, A. (2015) *A Handbook of Chaplaincy Studies: Understanding Spiritual Care in Public Places*. Farnham, Surrey: Ashgate.
Thakur, B. (1998) *Jaiva Dharma*. Mathura, India: Gaudiya Vedanta Publications.

BAPS Sadhus (trans.) (2001) *The Vachanāmrut*. Shahibaug, Amdavad, India: Swaminarayan Aksharpith.
Tyagananda, S. (2014) *Walking the Walk*. Kolkata: Advaita Ashrama.
Valpey, K.R. (2009) "The *Bhagavatapurana* as a *Mahabharata* Reflection." In P. Koskikallio and M. Jezic (eds) *Parallels and Comparisons: Proceedings of the Fourth Dubrovnik International Conference on the Sanskrit Epics and Puranas, September 2005*. Zagreb: Croatian Academy of Sciences and Arts.
Van der Kolk, B. (2014) *The Body Keeps the Score: Brain, Mind, and Body in the Healing of Trauma*. New York: Viking Penguin.
Vato, S. (trans.) (2006) *Sadhu Amrutvijaydas*. Shahibaug, Amdavad, India: Swaminarayan Aksharpith.
Vivekananda, S. (1979) *Complete Works*, Vol. 1. Kolkata: Advaita Ashrama.
Wilkins, W.J. (2003) *Hindu Mythology*. New Delhi: D.K. Printworld.

Print Journals

Aho, K. (2013) "Depression and embodiment: Phenomenological reflections on motility, affectivity, and transcendence." *Medicine, Healthcare, and Philosophy 16*, 4, 751–755.
Alcorta, C.S. and Sosis, R. (2005) "Ritual emotion and sacred symbols." *Human Nature 16*, 4, 323–359.
Chander, V. (2013) "A Room with a View: Accommodating Hindu religious practice on a college campus." *The Journal of College and Character*, May.
Clooney, F.X. (1989) "Evil, divine omnipotence, and human freedom: Vedanta's theology of karma." *The Journal of Religion 69*, 4.
Courtois, C. (2004) "Complex trauma, complex reactions." *Psychotherapy: Theory, Research, Practice, Training 41*, 4, 182–191.
Germer, C.K. and Neff, K.D. (2013) "Self-compassion in clinical practice." *Journal of Clinical Psychology 69*, 8, 856–867.
Hall, C.W., Row, K.A., Wuensch, K.L., and Godley, K.R. (2013) "The role of self-compassion in physical and psychological well-being." *Journal of Psychology 147*, 4, 311–323.
Kessler, R.C. *et al.* (2008) "Trends in mental illness and suicidality after Hurricane Katrina." *Molecular Psychiatry 13*, 4, 374–384.
Levin, J. (2017) "'For They Knew Not What It Was': Rethinking the tacit narrative history of religion and health research." *Journal of Religion and Health 56*, 28–46.
Loo, C.M. and Rolison, G. (1986) "Alienation of ethnic minority students at a predominantly White university." *The Journal of Higher Education 57*, 1, 58–77.
López, L. and Dyck, A.J. (2009) "Educating physicians for moral excellence in the twenty-first century." *Journal of Religious Ethics 37*, 4.
Maira, S. and Shihade, M. (2006) "Meeting Asian/Arab American studies: Thinking race, empire, and Zionism in the US." *Journal of Asian American Studies 9*, 2, 117–140.

Mathew, B. and Prashad, V. (2000) "The protean forms of Yankee Hindutva." *Ethnic and Racial Studies 23*, 3, 516–534.

Mazumdar, S. and Mazumdar, S. (2004) "Religion and place attachment: A study of sacred spaces." *Journal of Environmental Psychology 24*, 385–397.

Ramakrishnan, P. (2015) "Theory and practice of chaplain's spiritual care process: A psychiatrist's experiences of chaplaincy and conceptualizing trans-personal model of mindfulness." *Indian Journal of Psychiatry 57*, 1, 21–29.

Ramakrishnan, P. (2015) "'You are here: Locating 'spirituality' on the map of the current medical world." *Current Opinion in Psychiatry 28*, 5, 393–401.

Ratcliffe, M. (2013) "The phenomenology of depression and the nature of empathy." *Medicine, Health Care and Philosophy 17*, 269–280.

Rhodes, J. and Chan, C. (2010) "The impact of Hurricane Katrina on the mental and physical health of low-income parents in New Orleans." *American Journal of Orthopsychiatry 80*, 2, 237–247.

Rojas, F. (2006) "Social movement tactics, organizational change and the spread of African-American studies." *Social Forces 84*, 4, 2147–2166.

Shear, M.K., Ghesquiere, A,. and Glickman, K. (2013) "Bereavement and complicated grief." *Current Psychiatry Report 15*, 11, 406.

Van Sant, J.E. and Patterson, B.J. (2013) "Getting in and getting out whole: nurse-patient connections in the psychiatric setting." *Issues in Mental Health Nursing 34*, 1, 36–45.

Woods-Giscombé, C.L. and Black, A.R. (2010) "Mind-body interventions to reduce risk for health disparities related to stress and strength among African American women: The potential of mindfulness-based stress reduction, loving-kindness, and the NTU therapeutic framework." *Complementary Health Practice Review 15*, 3, 115–131.

Online Resources

Brand, R. (2003) "Jewish trojans—oxymoron no more." *Jewish Journal*, August 21. http://jewishjournal.com/culture/lifestyle/education/8271, accessed on April 24, 2019.

Bruni, F. (2017) "The real campus scourge." *New York Times online*, September 2. www.nytimes.com/2017/09/02/opinion/sunday/college-freshman-mental-health.html, accessed on July 30, 2018.

Chakraborty, A. (2018) "Forum to counsel terminally ill patients." *Sunday Times of India*. August 12. https://timesofindia.indiatimes.com/city/kolkata/forum-to-counsel-terminally-ill-patients/articleshow/65371624.cms. Accessed August 4, 2019.

Chaudhary, R. (2012, updated 2017) "For Air Force academy cadets, faith traditions spark innovation." *Huffpost*, October 17, 2012, updated December 6, 2017. www.huffingtonpost.com/ravi-chaudhary/for-air-force-academy-cadets-faith-traditions-spark-innovation_b_1965800.html, accessed on April 24, 2019.

Climate Outreach (2016) "Guide: Faith and climate change—talking with people of 5 major faiths." February 16. https://climateoutreach.org/resources/climate-change-faith, accessed on November 12, 2018.

Dutt, E. (2016) "Remembering our patriots." *Desi Talk* website, July 8. http://epaper.desitalk.com/2016_07_08/files/assets/basic-html/page12.html, accessed on July 2, 2019.

Ganeri, J. (n.d.) "The tree of knowledge is not an apple or an oak but a banyan." *Aeon.com*. https://aeon.co/ideas/the-tree-of-knowledge-is-not-an-apple-or-an-oak-but-a-banyan, accessed on September 23, 2018.

Lakshman, N. (2014) "Interview: 'Gita my basis for counselling Hindus in the military.'" *The Hindu*, November 17. www.thehindu.com/opinion/interview/gita-my-basis-for-counselling-hindus-in-us-military/article6605265.ece, accessed on July 26, 2018.

Lawrence, D.J. (2018) "A new proposal: Three levels of chaplaincy and pastoral expertise." *College of Pastoral Supervision and Psychotherapy*, February 1. www.cpsp.org/pastoralreportarticles/5713636, accessed on April 25, 2019.

Lewis, C. (2013) "The enmeshed family and how to 'unmesh'." Blog post on Maria Droste Counseling Center website, July 8. www.mariadroste.org/2013/07/the-enmeshed-family-what-it-is-and-how-to-unmesh, accessed on April 25, 2019.

Long, J.D. (2014) "Pick a side, we're at war!" *Los Angeles Review of Books*, September 4. https://lareviewofbooks.org/article/pick-side-war/#, accessed on April 25, 2019.

Mahayogananda, S. (2009) "The science of worship." Vedanta Center of Greater Washington DC published lectures, May 24. www.vedantadc.org/the-science-of-worship-swami-mahayogananda, accessed on April 25, 2019.

Melwani, L. (2016) "She was the US Army's first Hindu chaplain." *Lassi with Lavinia* blog, November 11. www.lassiwithlavina.com/features/people/meet-the-us-armys-first-hindu-chaplain/html, accessed on April 25, 2019.

Metropolitan Chicago Healthcare Council (2002) "*Guidelines for Health Care Providers Interacting with Patients of the Hindu Religion and Their Families.*" www.advocatehealth.com/assets/documents/faith/cghindu.pdf, accessed on April 25, 2019.

Murray, R. (2009) "Army Chaplains Corps: Serving 'God and Country' for 234 years with 25,000 chaplains." *US Army* website blog, July 9. www.army.mil/article/24086/army_chaplains_corps_serving_god_and_country_for_234_years_with_25000_chaplains, accessed on April 25, 2019.

Novotney, A. (2014) "Students under pressure." *Monitor on Psychology*, online magazine of the American Psychological Association 45, 8 36. www.apa.org/monitor/2014/09/cover-pressure, accessed on July 2, 2019.

Powell, R.C. (2011) "Report from India: A pastoral care department that runs its own hospital." On College of Pastoral Supervision and Psychotherapy blog, July 18. www.cpsp.org/pastoralreportarticles/3778981, accessed on April 25, 2019.

Rambachan, A. (2015) "The future of Hinduism in America's changing religious landscape." *Huffington Post*, May 26. www.huffingtonpost.com/anantanand-rambachan/the-future-of-hinduism-in-americas-changing-religious-landscape_b_7348140.html, accessed on April 25, 2019.

Ramakrishnamacharyulu, K.V. and Geervani, P. (general editors and supervising translators) (n.d.) *Valmiki Ramayana*. www.valmiki.iitk.ac.in, accessed on April 25, 2019.

Redden, E. (2016) "Return to sender." *Inside Higher Education*, February 22. www.insidehighered.com/news/2016/02/22/uc-irvine-moves-reject-endowed-chair-gifts-donor-strong-opinions-about-study, accessed on April 25, 2019.

Sarvaananda, S. (2009) "The Hindu chaplain: Our faith's tolerant beliefs and powerful practices enable us to minster effectively to all in need." *Hinduism Today*, July/August/September. www.hinduismtoday.com/modules/sartsection/category.php?categoryid=386, accessed on April 25, 2019.

Sarvaananda, S. (2016) "What is real life? What is real death?" *Integral Yoga Magazine*, Winter. http://integralyogamagazine.org/winter-2016-integral-yoga-magazine, accessed on April 25, 2019.

Sarvaananda, S. (2016) "Yogic preparation for death." *Integral Yoga Magazine*, Winter. http://integralyogamagazine.org/winter-2016-integral-yoga-magazine, accessed on April 25, 2019.

Seltzer, R (2017) "Racial gap among senior administrators widens." *Inside Higher Ed*, March 2. www.insidehighered.com/news/2017/03/02/racial-gap-among-senior-administrators-widens, accessed on April 25, 2019.

Sham, F.C. (2017) "Why 60,000 Indian farmers committed suicide: Climate change the culprit." On *Hong Kong Observatory Blog*, November 2. www.hko.gov.hk/blog/en/archives/00000211.htm, accessed on May 9, 2018.

Sherma, R. (2013) "A new kind of dharma leadership: the necessity of a Hindu American chaplaincy." *The Interfaith Observer Journal*, September. https://interfaith-observer.squarespace.com/journal-articles/2013/9/6/the-necessity-of-a-hindu-american-chaplaincy.html, accessed on April 25, 2019.

Shipman, A. (2017) "Hindu chaplaincy." *Convergence on Campus*, October 4. www.convergenceoncampus.org/2017/10/04/hindu-chaplaincy-asha-shipman, accessed on April 25, 2019.

Silverman, A.H. (2017) "At the University of Southern California, a humanist chaplain takes the lead." *The Humanist*, September 5. www.thehumanist.com/features/interviews/university-southern-california-humanist-chaplain-takes-lead, accessed on April 25, 2019.

Srinivasan, R. (n.d., prior to July 2009) "My battle within: The identity crisis of a Hindu soldier in the US Army." *Hindu American Foundation* blog. www.hafsite.org/media/pr/rajiv-srinivasan, accessed on April 25, 2019.

Thomas, M. (2014) "Climate depression is for real. Just ask a scientist." *Grist*, October 28. Accessed on September 5, 2018.

USC Communications (n.d.) "The era of the founders." www.about.usc.edu/history/founders, accessed on April 25, 2019.

Xia, R. (2017) "Most college head chaplains are Christian. At USC, a Hindu leads the way." *LA Now, Los Angeles Times*, April 3 www.latimes.com/local/lanow/la-me-usc-chaplain-20170403-story.html, accessed on April 25, 2019.

Contributors

Murali Balaji, PhD
Principal, Maruthi Educational Consulting

Lecturer, Annenberg School for Communication, University of Pennsylvania

Raja Gopal Bhattar
Consultant and author

formerly, Assistant Vice Provost and Executive Director of the Center for Identity + Inclusion, University of Chicago

Joseph Ghanashyam Caruso
Hindu Palliative Care Chaplain, New York Presbyterian Hospital

Co-founder of InSpirit—an end-of-life care initiative providing support, education, and spiritual care to the dying and those caring for them

Vineet Chander, JD
Coordinator of Hindu Life and Hindu Chaplain, Princeton University

Veera and Sam S. Jain Scholar of Vedanta Studies, New York University

Co-author, *Hindu Chaplaincy* (2017)

Vaishali Gupta Chandrashekar

Creative Cooking Coach; Health and Wellness Coach

formerly, Hindu Chaplain at Wellesley College, Brandeis University, and Babson College

Christopher Key Chapple, PhD

Doshi Professor of Indic and Comparative Theology; Director, Master of Arts in Yoga Studies Program, Loyola Marymount University

Author, *Karma and Creativity* (1986); *Nonviolence to Animals, Earth, and Self in Asian Traditions* (1993)

Gopal K. Gupta, DPhil

Associate Professor of Religious Studies, University of Evansville

Author, *Maya in the Bhagavata Purana: Human Suffering and Divine Play* (forthcoming, 2020)

Varun Khanna, PhD

Visiting Assistant Professor of Classics (Sanskrit), Swarthmore College

Ramdas Lamb, PhD

Professor of Religion, University of Hawai'i at Mānoa

formerly, State of Hawai'i prison system spiritual caregiver

Author, *Rapt in the Name: The Ramnamis, Ramnam, and Untouchable Religion in Central India* (2002)

Jeffery D. Long, PhD

Professor of Religion and Asian Studies, Elizabethtown College

Author, *A Vision for Hinduism: Beyond Hindu Nationalism* (2007); *The Historical Dictionary of Hinduism* (2011)

Rachel Fell McDermott, MDiv; PhD

Professor of Asian and Middle Eastern Cultures, Barnard College

Author, *Singing to the Goddess: Poems to Kālī and Umā from Bengal* (2001)

Shamā Mehtā, MA in Patoral Ministry, BCC

Board-Certified Chaplain, Beaumont Health, Michigan

Lucinda Mosher, ThD

Faculty Associate in Interfaith Studies, Hartford Seminary

President, NeighborFaith Consultancy

Author, *Personhood, Illness, and Death in America's Multifaith Neighborhoods: A Practical Guide* (2018)

Ramakrishnan Parameshwaran, MD, MDiv, ACPE-Clinical Chaplain

PhD Candidate, Graduate Theological Union, University of California (Berkeley)

Chaplain Fellow, Stanford Health Care

Gopal D. Patel

Director, *The Bhumi Project*—a global Hindu response to climate change

Advisor, United Nations Task Force on Religion and Development

formerly, Students' Chaplain, Imperial College, London

Viraj Patel, MA

PhD Student, The University of Chicago Divinity School

Anantanand Rambachan, PhD
Professor of Religion, St. Olaf College

Author, *Essays in Hindu Theology* (2019); *The Advaita Worldview: God, World, and Humanity* (2006)

Rasanath Das, MBA
Co-founder, Upbuild—an educational social enterprise aimed at maximizing the human potential by creating environments that inspire genuine purpose and authentic connection

Shaunaka Rishi Das
Director, Oxford Centre for Hindu Studies

Hindu Chaplain, University of Oxford

Co-author, *Hindu Chaplaincy* (2017)

Pulin Sanghvi, MBA
Motivational speaker; member, National Board of Directors for *Positive Coaching Alliance*

formerly, inaugural Executive Director of Career Services, Princeton University

formerly, Assistant Dean and Director of the Career Management Center, Stanford Graduate School of Business

Swami Sarvaananda, PhD, BCC
Dean, School of Divinity, Hindu University of America

Bramachari V. Sharan, PhD
Director for Dharmic Life and Hindu Spiritual Advisor

Adjunct Professor of Linguistics, Asian Studies, Theology and Religious Studies, Georgetown University

Madhu Vedak Sharma, MSW, PhD

Hindu Chaplain, Duke University

Hindu Campus Minister, University of North Carolina

Author, *Dharmic Advisor: A Modern Way* (2016)

Tahil Sharma

Volunteer Hindu Religious Director, University of Southern California

Hindu-Sikh Interfaith Minister-in-Residence, Episcopal Diocese of Los Angeles

Faith Outreach Manager, Brave New Films

Rita D. Sherma, PhD

Director and Associate Professor of Dharma Studies, Mira and Ajay Shingal Center for Dharma Studies; Core Doctoral Faculty, Graduate Theological Union (Berkeley, California)

Author, *Hinduism and the Divine: Foundations of Hindu Theology* (2019); *Vivekananda: His Life, Legacy, & Liberative Ethics* (2019)

Asha Shipman, PhD

Director of Hindu Life and Hindu Chaplain, Yale University

Shrestha Singh, MDiv

Spiritual Director in private practice (Chicago), http://shresthasingh.com

formerly, Chaplain to Students of Dharmic Traditions, Brandeis University; School Minister, Brooks School (Andover, Massachusetts); Hindu Chaplain, Wellesley College

Amrutur V. Srinivasan, PhD

Lecturer on Hinduism

Officiant for Hindu Weddings and other ceremonies

Author, *The Vedic Wedding: Origins, Tradition and Practice* (2007); *Hinduism for Dummies* (2011)

Subject Index

Abhinavagupta 101
academics 21, 223–4, 229–30
　creating an ecosystem 228–9
　Hindu American college experience 224–8
Adler, Alfred 56
Advaita Vedanta 19, 33, 142
　problem with Advaitic interpretation 33
　theology of diversity 43–5
　theology of optimism 45–7
　theology of reverence 41–3
　tradition of Advaita Vedanta 39–40
affection 57–8
African American studies 223
ahimsa 55, 57, 68, 197, 266
Air Force Academy Chapel 196
Akhilananda, Swami 159–60
Alliance of Religions and Conservation 262
American *dharma* 19, 27
　evolving Hindu *dharma* in America 27, 30
　what is a trained chaplain? 29
American Psychological Association 264
Arjuna 35, 37, 47, 53–4, 57–8, 61, 64–5, 153, 154, 197–8, 217
　self and body 86–9
Association of Professional Chaplains (APC) 15, 20, 29, 133, 140
　Board Certification 134–8
　Board Certification for Hindu and Buddhist applicants 135–6
atma 40, 45, 83, 86
Atmavidyananda, Swami 191
Aurobindo, Sri 33
Australia 117
avidyā 40, 45

Babson College 245, 248, 249, 251
Badarayana 106
Baladeva 108
Balaji, Murali 21
BAPS Shri Swaminarayan Mandir, Bartlett, Illinois 83
Berkeley Center for Religion, Peace and World Affairs 171
Best, Mildred 137
Bhadresh, Swami 85
Bhagavad-Gita 19, 39, 40, 41, 42–3, 46–7, 64–5, 72–3, 117, 123, 146, 150, 154, 155, 214–17, 240
　karma-yoga 78
　military service 197–200
　self and body 86–9
Bhagavata Purana 20, 50, 72, 267
　problem of evil in the Bhagavata Purana 109–12
Bhagwan, Swaminarayan 85
Bhakti *see* Vaishnava Bhakti
Bharatamuni 100–1
Bhattar, Raja Gopal 21–2
Bhumi Project 22, 262
Bible 120
Black Studies 223
Board Certification 134–5, 140
　Hindu and Buddhist applicants 135–6
　uphill work 136–8
Board of Chaplaincy Certification Incorporated 20
body art 182–3
boundary-setting 273–5
Brahma-Sutra 39, 40
brahman 33–6, 40–1, 44, 45, 270, 276–7
Brandeis University 245, 249, 251

293

breathing exercises 69
Buddha 64, 65, 69
Buddhism 15, 16, 17, 27, 61, 62, 67, 232
Buddhists 28, 29, 70, 159–60, 200
  Certified Buddhist Chaplain qualification 135–6
bullying 226

Cakravartin, Viśvanātha 109
Canada 15
caregiving 42–5
  Krishna Bhakti and care 49–52
  optimism 45–7
Caruso, Joseph Ghanashyam 20
Chaitanya, Sri 57
Chander, Vineet 19, 123
Chandrashekar, Vaishali Gupta 22
chaplaincy 15–22
  case for Hindu chaplaincy 37–8, 147
  what is a trained chaplain? 29
  what is Hindu chaplaincy? 31–3
  yoga and the intent of chaplaincy 68–70
  yoga chaplaincy 63–6
  yoga therapy and chaplaincy 67–8
Chapple, Christopher Key 19
childhood trauma 269–70
  cultural pressures 272–3
  family relationships 270–2, 273–4
Childs, Ozro W. 185
Chinmaya Mission 188, 194
Chinmayananda, Swami 33
choice 53–4
Christianity 15–16, 17–18, 158, 174, 185, 228
Christians 28, 29, 70, 79, 122, 140, 146, 196
  being Hindu, counseling Christians 207–9
  Orthodox Christians 149–51
Christopher Newport University 229
clarity 73–5
climate change 22, 261–2, 268
  addressing Hindu audiences 267
  Hindu solutions 264–7
  impact of climate change on health and wellbeing 262–4
Climate Outreach 267
Clinical Pastoral Education (CPE) 134–5, 138–9

College and University Professional Association for Human Resources 186
compassion 41–2, 104, 154
  Rama in the Forest 93–7, 98, 99, 101–2, 103
Connecticut Ashram 133–5, 137–40
cooking and chaplaincy 22, 245–6
  caring for colleagues 250–2
  key ingredient: food 246–8
  making connections with other chaplaincies and campus organizations 249–50
  working with Jain students 248
corporate chaplaincy 21, 213–19
counseling 202–4
Covenant House, New York City 68
cultural pressures 272–3
Cyclone Hudhud 261–2

darshana 49, 130
Das, Rasanath 21
Das, Shaunaka Rishi 19
death 64–5, 142–3, 144
  Katha Upanishad 127–8
Deepak, Ardash 229
Department of Defense 194, 200
depression 98, 103
Deshika, Sri Vedanta 175
detachment 37, 38, 46–7
Devi 119
Devi, Sarada (Holy Mother) 161
Dharm, Pratima 117, 194–5
dharma 22, 50–1, 105, 142, 197–9
  military service 197–200
  reconciling *dharma* and *moksha* 256–7
Dharma Academy of North America (DANAM) 229
diacritics 22–3
diversity 43–5
  University of Southern California, Los Angeles 185–92
Downey, John G. 185
dying 64–5
  end-of-life care 20, 149–56

ego 214–15
Elizabethtown College 229
emotional healing 22

Subject Index

empathy 98–100, 152–3
end-of-life care 20, 149–50
   Hinduism 150–6
equality 53
ethnic studies 223–4
evil 106–12

family relationships 270–2, 273–4
fossil fuels 262–3
Fred Lenz Foundation 68
Freud, Sigmund 102

Gandhi, Indira 63
Gandhi, Mahatma 56, 62–3, 68, 124–5, 197, 207
Georgetown University 21, 167, 171–2
global warming 262–3
God 41–2, 44–5, 142, 159
   connecting to divinity 77–80
   problem of evil in the Vedanta-sutra 106–8 (diacritics italics)
   surrender to God 154–5
Goddess 115–18
   Shakta theology as a response to the problem of suffering 118–22
Gomez-Brake, Vanessa 186–7
Gore, Al 264
Graduate Theological Union, Berkeley, California 228–9
Greenfaith 262
grief 19–20, 93, 140, 253
   emotional aesthetics 100–2
   end-of-life care 153–4
   Rama in the Forest 93–7
   Valmiki Ramayana's contribution towards Hindu chaplaincy 102–4
   Western paradigms of healing, empathy and projection 97–100
Grihya Sutras 253, 259
Gupta, Gopal K. 20
Gurdieff, C.I. 53
gurus 83–4, 116, 140
   distinction between spiritual teachers and lay priests 163–5, 167–8
   guru as pastoral caregiver 90

Haines, Dick 137
harm 55

Harvard University 115, 159–64
healing 98–100
healthcare 20
Hellman, Isaias W. 185
Hindu-American chaplaincy *see* American *dharma*
Hindu American Foundation (HAF) 226, 229
Hindu chaplaincy 31–3, 157–9, 164–5
   case for Hindu chaplaincy 37–8, 147
   Hindu chaplaincy in the US 168–70
   Hindu priests and gurus 163–5, 167–8
   Ramayana on Hindu chaplains 170–2, 175–6
   Swami Tyagananda at Harvard and MIT 159–65
   Vashishtha and the nature of Hindu chaplaincy in higher education 173–5
Hindu Student Organization, USC 187–92
Hinduism 15, 17, 18, 19–22, 174, 232
   distinction between spiritual teachers and lay priests 163–5, 167–8
   end-of-life care 150–6
   Hindu temples 178–9
   Hindu theological anthropology 84–9
   sādhana 264–5
   sanga 266–7
   sevā 29, 42, 158–9, 265–6
Hindus 70, 72, 200
   do Hindus need chaplains? 27–9
   raising awareness in Hindu spaces 139–40
hospice chaplaincy 138–9
hospital chaplaincy 20, 141–7
Humanists 186–7, 200
humility 57
Hurricane Katrina 263

Indology 225
Integral Yoga 115, 133–4
interfaith work 30, 134, 136, 138–40, 147
   Georgetown University 169, 172, 175
   University of Southern California, Los Angeles 190–1
Intergovernmental Panel on Climate Change (IPCC) 264
International Association of Yoga Therapists 67

International Society for Krishna
Consciousness (ISKCON) 187–8
intersectionality 21–2
investment banking 214, 219
Isha Upanishad 20, 40, 41, 124–7, 142
Islam 174
Islamic studies 224
Īśvara-praṇidhāna 77–80
Iyengar, B. K. S. 70

Jainism 61, 62, 64, 67, 70, 197, 200, 232
dietary restrictions 248
Jesuits 21, 167, 171–2, 175
Jews 28, 29, 79, 140, 200, 227, 251
Judaism 15, 27, 174

Kar, Minati 121–2
karma 36–7, 142–3
karma yoga 78, 158–9
prison chaplaincy 204–5
problem of suffering 107–10
Katha Upanishad 20, 61, 127–30
Kazanjian, Victor 251
Kessler, David A. 99
Khanna, Varun 19
King, Martin Luther, Jr. 68, 138
Kinsley, David 121
Koul, Neha 189–90, 191
Krishna 19, 35, 37, 47, 53–5, 57–8, 61,
64–5, 117, 153, 154, 155, 197–8, 217
Krishna Bhakti and care 49–52
problem of suffering 110–14
self and body 86–9
kriyā-yoga 71–3
Kübler-Ross, Elisabeth 93, 97–8, 99
Kuvalyanada, Swami 63

Laemmle, Susan 186
Lamb, Ramdas 21, 229
languages 145–6
leadership coaching 213–14, 215
workshops 215–16
Lee-King Day 138
LGBTQ 21–2, 239
approaches to LGBTQ-inclusive Hindu
spiritual care 240–3

queerness and Hinduism 239–40
strategies and tips 243–4
Linquist, Ted 135, 136
listening 141–2, 152, 217
Long, Jeffery D. 20–1, 229
loss 19–20, 93, 140, 253
climate change 264
emotional aesthetics 100–2
end-of-life care 153–4
Rama in the Forest 93–7
Western paradigms of healing, empathy
and projection 97–100
Loyola Marymount University (LMU) 19,
67–8

Mahabharata 55, 72, 105–6, 197–8, 254,
267, 275–6
Maharaj, Mahant Swami 83, 90
Maharaj, Pramukh Swami 83
Maharshi, Ramana 33
Mandela, Nelson 68
Marx, Groucho 56
Marxism 225
Massachusetts Institute of Technology
(MIT) 159–64
Mauni Baba 122
McDermott, Rachel Fell 20
mehendi 182–3
Mehtā, Shamā 20
military chaplaincy 117, 193–4
military chaplains in the US 194–6
what care might non-Hindu chaplains
offer? 196–200
Misra, Vascapati 108
Modi, Narendra 63
moksha 35–8, 40, 84, 85, 142
reconciling *dharma* and *moksha* 256–7
monks 21, 115, 201, 204, 214–15, 219
Ramakrishna Order 158–9, 162–5
Mother Teresa 213
Mrtyu Mrtyunjay, Kolkata 116
Murray, Joan 137
Muslims 28, 29, 79, 145, 159–60, 175, 196,
200, 224, 227, 251

Native Americans 29, 202
Natyashastra 100

New Orleans, US 263
nivṛtti dharma 33–8
non-violence 68, 196–9
North America 15, 22
nuptial counseling 22, 257–9

optimism 45–7
Orientalism 225
Oxford Centre for Hindu Studies 262

Pagans 29
Paramahansa, Sri Ramakrishna 21, 33, 42, 44–5, 119–20, 157, 158
Paramananda, Swami 160
Parameshwaran, Ramakrishnan 19–20
Parliament of World Religions, Chicago 1893 45, 46, 63
Parmesan, Camille 263–4
pastoral care 15–17, 84, 90–1
  guru as pastoral caregiver 90
  Krishna's pastoral care 87–9
  kriyā-yoga as a framework for pastoral care 71–3
Patañjali Yoga Sutras 19, 62, 69, 71, 80–1
Īśvara-praṇidhāna 77–80
  kriya-yoga as a framework for pastoral care 71–3
  svādhyāya 75–7
  tapas 73–5
Patel, Gopal D. 22
Patel, Viraj 19
Payne, Larry 67
Philip, Prince 262
Playboy 214
post traumatic stress disorder (PTSD) 22, 65–6, 263, 264
  C-PTSD (complex trauma) 271–2
pravṛtti dharma 34, 38
  nature of *pravṛtti dharma* 35–7
pre-nuptial counseling 22, 257–9
presence 16–17, 152
Princeton University 19, 21, 71, 232
prison chaplaincy 21, 201–4
  being Hindu, counseling Christians 207–9
  lessons learned 209–11
  tools and methods 204–7

projection 98–100
punarjanma 84–5

Quindus (Queer Hindus) 239
  approaches to LGBTQ-inclusive Hindu spiritual care 240–3
  queerness and Hinduism 239–40

Radhakrishnan, Sarvepalli 33
Ramakrishna (Sri Ramakrishna Paramahansa) 21, 33, 42, 44–5, 119–20, 157, 158, 161
  Mission 42, 159, 187
  Order 158–60, 162–4
  Vedanta Center 115
  Vedanta Society 159–60, 161, 164, 187
Ramayana 72, 106, 121, 175–6, 197, 267
  Rama in the Forest 93–7
  Sita and Mother Earth 277
  Sita's boundary-setting in the Ramayana 273–5
  Vashishtha 170–5
Rambachan, Anantanand 19, 226, 227–8, 276, 229
rape 65
rasa theory 93, 104 (italics)
  emotional aesthetics 100–2
  Rama in the Forest 93–7
  Western paradigms of healing, empathy and projection 97–100
Ray, Satyajit 119
reverence 41–3
roles in society 231–2
  religious interpretations 232–3
  self-knowledge 235–7
  work-life self 233–5
Rumi, Jalaluddin 152

sacred space 21, 177–8, 181–3, 188–9
  emotional responses 179–80
  Hindu temples 178–9
  mental and physical health 180–1
sādhana 264–5
Sampraday, Swaminarayan 85
sanga 266–7
Sanghvi, Pulan 21

Sarvaananda, Swami 20, 115, 117, 133, 140
  education 133-4
  qualifying as Board-Certified Chaplain 134-8
  work after qualification 138-40
Sarvagatananda, Swami 160
Satchidananda, Swami 20, 115, 133
Schweig, Graham 229
self 40, 45, 83
  self and body 86-9
  true self 128
self-compassion 19-20, 104
  Rama in the Forest 93-7, 99
self-doubt 66
self-esteem 143-4
self-knowledge 235-7
Sen, Ramprased 120-1
service 28-9, 37, 42, 154, 158-9
sevā 29, 42, 158-9, 265-6
Shakta 20, 115-18
  Shakta theology as a response to the problem of suffering 118-22
Shankara 40, 43-4
Sharan, Brahmachari V. 21, 115
Sharma, Madju Vedak 20
Sherma, Rita 19, 228-9
Shipman, Asha 21, 223, 228
Shukla-Batt, Neelima 245-6
Sikhism 190-1, 200, 232
Singh, Shrestha 22
Sivananda, Swami 70
Sivapalan, Eesen 189-90
Soni, Varun 186-8, 192
spiritual care 15, 16
  Isha Upanishad 124-7
Springfield College, Massachusetts 133
Śrīdhara Svami 109
Srinivasan, Amrutur V. 22
St Francis de Sales 175
St. Olaf College 229
Stone, Kelly 249
stress 66
  stress and climate change 263-4
study 75-7
suffering 20, 105-6, 112-14, 115-18, 142, 154
  problem of evil in the Bhagavata Purana 109-12

problem of evil in the *Vedanta-sūtra* 106-8
Shakta theology as a response to the problem of suffering 118-22
svādhyāya 75-7

Tagare, Ganesh 105
tapas 73-5 (italics)
teaching by example 56
Teilhard de Chardin, Pierre 53
theoretical foundations for spiritual care 19, 31, 38
  Advaita Vedanta 33-5
  case for Hindu chaplaincy 37-8
  nature of *pravṛtti dharma* 35-7
  what is Hindu chaplaincy? 31-3
trauma 22, 65-6
  becoming the ones we have yearned for 277-8
  childhood trauma 269-73
  Sita's boundary-setting in the Ramayana 273-5
  what trauma does and what healing might look like 275-7
Tyagananda, Swami 21, 41-2, 115, 157
  Swami Tyagananda at Harvard and MIT 159-65

UK 15, 22
university chaplaincy 20-1, 159-65, 245-52
University of Connecticut 133
University of Hawai'i-Manoa 229
University of Southern California (USC) 21, 185-92
  Hindu Prayer Space 188-9
University of Virginia 115, 134
Upanishads 20, 39-40, 44, 72, 107, 123-4, 130, 142, 187, 276-7
  Isha Upanishad 20, 40, 41, 124-7, 142
  Katha Upanishad 127-30
  weddings 253, 259
  yoga 61, 67, 69
Upbuild 216, 218
US 15, 16, 22
  Hindu chaplaincy in the US 168-70
  introduction of yoga 63
  see American *dharma*

Vaishnava 20
Vaishnava Bhakti 19, 49, 58–9
    acharya (teaching by example) 56
    ahimsa (without harm) 55
    amanitva (humility) 57
    applied theology of Vaishnava care 52–8
    iccha (choice) 53–4
    Krishna Bhakti and care 49–52
    priti (affection) 57–8
    sama darshana (equal vision) 53
Valmiki Ramayana 19, 93–9, 102–3, 170
Vashishtha 170–5
Vedanta 157–63
Vedanta Kesari, The 160
Vedanta-sūtra 106–8, 123
Vedas 39–40, 43–4, 61, 124
    weddings 253, 256, 259
Venice Family Clinic 67
violence 65, 196–9
    climate change 264
Vishakapatnam (Vizag), India 262–2
Vivekananda, Swami 21, 33, 42, 45, 63, 119, 158–61, 164–5, 182, 187
vocational counselling 21, 231–7
Vyasa 106

Wall Street Journal, The 216
Washington, George 194

weddings 22, 253–4
    ceremonies 255–6, 257
    dharma and *moksha* 256–7
    marriage and friendship 254–5
    pre-nuptial counseling 257–9
Wellesley College 245–6, 248–51
Widney, Robert Maclay 185
work-life self 233–5
workplace 213–14
    leadership coaching 215–16
    personal identity 216–18

Yale University 21, 188, 228
    Hindu Prayer Room 177–83
yoga 19, 61–3, 70
    death and dying 64–5
    harassment, rape and killing 65–6
    Integral Yoga 115, 133–4
    kriyā-yoga as a framework for pastoral care 71–3
    stress and self-doubt 66
    yoga and the intent of chaplaincy 68–70
    yoga chaplaincy 63–6
    yoga therapy and chaplaincy 67–8
Yoga Alliance 67
Yogananda, Paramahansa 63

Author Index

Adams, M. 227
Adluri, V. 225
Aho, K. 98
Alcorta, C.S. 180

Bagchee, J. 225
Balaji, M. 225
BAPS Sadhus 86
Basu, B.D. 107, 108
Bhaktivedanta Swami, A.C. 50, 51
Black, A.R. 99
Blumenfeld, W.J. 227
Bose, A.C. 256
Bottome, P. 56
Brereton, J. 170
Bruni, F. 181
Bryant, E.F. 72, 73, 74, 75, 76, 78, 80

Castaneda, R. 227
Chakraborty, A. 116
Chan, C. 263
Chander, V. 168–9, 172, 193
Chaudhary, R. 195
Clayton, S. 264
Climate Outreach 267
Clooney, F.X. 108
Coburn, T.B. 119, 121
Courtois, C. 271–2

Das, R. 21, 213
Das, S.R. 193
Dasa, B. 109
Dutt, E. 193
Dyck, A.J. 98

Easwaran, E. 124, 130

Fanon, F. 227
Flood, G. 167
Flueckiger, J.B. 158
Forster-Smith, L.A. 17, 18

Gambhirananda, S. 158
Ganeri, J. 32
Geertz, C. 180
Geervani, P. 94
Germer, C.K. 99
Ghesquiere, A. 99
Giles, C.A. 16, 17
Glickman, K. 99
Godley, K.R. 99
Gordon, J.A. 223
Gordon, L.R. 223

Hackman, H.W. 227
Hall, C.W. 99
Herman, A.L. 106

Jain, A.R. 81
James, W. 103
Jamison, S. 170

Kessler, D.A. 99
Kessler, R.C. 263
Krygsman, K. 264
Kübler-Ross, E. 99
Kumar, P. 100

Lakshman, N. 117
Lartey, E.Y. 15–16
Lawrence, D.J. 116
Levin, J. 180
Lewis, C. 273
Long, J.D. 226
Loo, C.M. 223
López, L. 98

Mahayogananda, S. 180
Maira, S. 224
Manning, C. 264
Mathew, B. 227
Mazumdar, S. 179–80
McDermott, R.F. 115, 121
Melwani, L. 195
Menen, A. 178
Metropolitan Chicago Healthcare Council 116
Miller, W.B. 16
Monier-Williams, M. 170
Mukhopādhyāy, H. 121
Murray, R. 194

Neff, K.D. 99
Nicholson, A.J. 225
Nikhilananada, S. 44, 45, 46, 119, 128
Novotney, A. 181

O'Flaherty, W. *107–8*
Olivelle, P. 170

Paramtattvadas, S. 85, 86, 87, 88
Patterson, B.J. 99
Pearson, A.M. 120
Peters, L.M. 227
Pope Francis 261
Powell, R.C. 116
Prashad, V. 227

Queensland Government 117

Ramakrishnamacharyulu, K.V. 94
Ramakrishnan, P. 103
Rambachan, A. 19, 33, 226, 227–8, 276
Rangacharya, A. 101
Rasanath, Das 21, 213

Ratcliffe, M. 100, 103
Redden, E. 227
Rhodes, J. 263
Rishi Das S. 19, 193
Roberts, S.B. 15
Rojas, F. 223
Rolison, G. 223
Row, K.A. 99

Saradananda, S. 42
Saraswati, S.D. 47
Sarvaananda, S. 115, 117, 139
Schipani, D.S. 16, 18, 79
Seltzer, R. 186
Sham, F.C. 263
Shastri, B. 120
Shear, M.K. 99
Sherma, R.D. 27, 169, 226
Shihade, M. 224
Shipman, A. 188
Silverman, A.H. 187
Sosis, R. 180
Speiser, M. 264
Srinivasan, A.V. 178, 255, 256, 257, 258
Srinivasan, R. 196
Sutton, N. 193

Thakur, B. 51
Thomas, M. 264
Tyagananda, S. 42, 159, 160

USC Communications 185

Valpey, K.R. 113
Van der Kolk, B. 271
Van Sant, J.E. 99
Vato, S. 85
Vivekananda, S. 45, 46, 158–9, 182

Wilkins, W.J. 173
Woods-Giscombé, C.L. 99
Wuensch, K.L. 99

Xia, R. 186

Zuniga, X. 227